Saving the Reagan Presidency

Saving the Reagan Presidency

Trust Is the Coin of the Realm

DAVID M. ABSHIRE

Foreword by Richard E. Neustadt

Texas A&M University Press • College Station

The paper used in this book
meets the minimum requirements
of the American National Standard for Permanence
of Paper for Printed Library Materials, z39.48-1984.
Binding materials have been chosen for durability.

LIBRARY OF CONGRESS CATALOGING-IN-PUBLICATION DATA

Abshire, David M.
    Saving the Reagan presidency : trust is the coin of the
realm / David M. Abshire ; foreword by Richard E. Neustadt.—1st ed.
        p. cm.—(The presidency and leadership)
    Includes bibliographical references and index.
    ISBN 1-58544-466-9 (alk. paper)
        1. United States—Politics and government—1981–1989.
2. Reagan, Ronald.   3. Reagan, Ronald—Friends and associates.
4. Iran–Contra Affair, 1985–1990.   5. Political corruption—
United States.   6. Political ethics—United States.
I. Neustadt, Richard E.   II. Titles.   III. Series.
E876.A285   2005   2005002904

Contents

Foreword

As president of the United States, Ronald Reagan is likely to be well remembered by historians for at least two successes. One of those is tugging his country in a conservative direction. This he achieved initially by rhetoric and tax cuts, then by tolerating substantial federal deficits, which had the effect of limiting congressional appetites for costly social welfare measures. That cause-and-effect relationship Reagan discovered pragmatically. The discovery was not lost on his party and has been applied again, it seems, by his current successor, George W. Bush. The other thing historians are almost sure to recall is Reagan's set of measures in defense and diplomacy that contributed to the retrenchment and then collapse of the Soviet Union, hence to the end of the Cold War in 1989, after more than forty years. The Soviets' belief in American technological prowess (which Reagan brandished, without convincing much of his own side) seems to have been a key factor in causing Moscow to quit.

Reagan is likely to be remembered also for one extraordinary failure in the conduct of foreign relations, the so-called Iran-contra affair of 1985–1986. This caused a public uproar at the time, and, while it left few traces in diplomacy, its impact in America ensured that it has been extensively researched and discussed in both scholarly and popular publications.

Up to now, however, what has not been described or discussed in any depth is Reagan's remarkable recovery from that misadventure, filling the credibility gap that its discovery imposed upon him and thus freeing him to pursue with Soviet leaders, notably President Gorbachev, the détente facilitating their climb-down from the Cold War.

Reagan's recovery is no less important a piece of presidential history than was Iran-contra itself, so a detailed exposition of it has been troubling by its absence from the literature and also from our understanding of what presidents can do to help themselves conduct their office successfully. For Reagan succeeded precisely where

Lyndon Johnson, Richard Nixon, and Bill Clinton failed in repairing credibility gaps created by their own words and behavior.

This success, which all of their successors would do well to heed, has now been set forth in appropriate detail by the effective memoir I here introduce. Its author, David Abshire, was Reagan's chief executant, his temporary special counselor for the task of getting at the truth behind the scandalous affair and making it all public in good time. That was the key to recovery. Reagan plainly got the point, and Abshire, then U.S. ambassador to NATO, was brought back to Washington for the purpose. His assignment and its satisfactory performance contributed greatly to this third Reagan success.

Had this memoir been available to Clinton, perhaps he would have avoided lying to the American people, while withholding the truth from his wife, in the Monica Lewinsky affair. Had Abshire's account been published before aides put into the younger Bush's mouth unwarranted assertions about British intelligence on Saddam Hussein's supposed nuclear program, perhaps those aides would have known better than to take even so small a first step toward another credibility gap.

As Abshire's account makes plain, Reagan's recovering from Iran-contra rested on four interconnected pillars. One was Abshire's own position and performance as a temporary, senior White House aide with open access to the president, independent of a bristly, self-important chief of staff, Don Regan. Abshire also had superior status as a "member of the Cabinet" and assistants of his own selection.

Second was the creation of the "Tower Board," an independent commission of inquiry, high-level in its bipartisan membership and given a short deadline to sift the documentary and human testimony on what occurred and how and then report its findings both to the president and the public.

Third was Reagan's statement in advance, in the very act of launching these endeavors, that his sole wish was to "let it all hang out" and, to that end, he would not invoke executive privilege on either documents or evidence from anyone, himself included. To this he stuck, in sharp contrast with Nixon.

Fourth was Reagan's renewed reliance on the service of his own wife, Nancy, as a disinterested consultant on potential public consequences, for his personal, historical repute, of all actions attributed to him. To a president of Reagan's sort, who kept his mind on his own principles but often scanted daily details, his wife's interventions were invaluable. She read the papers carefully, kept up with friends all over Washington, and tracked details as they might impact on his future standing. But this she could do only when her sources kept her current. In the Iran-contra case, replete with secrecy, they could not do so until after public failure had erupted. Thereafter, however, throughout the president's recovery, she performed stoutly, as Abshire tells us, grateful for her collaboration.

In 1990, in the first and final edition of *Presidential Power,* I wrote speculatively about Nancy Reagan's service to her husband. I owe thanks to Ambassador Abshire for confirming my speculation. He strengthens my belief that any president who chooses to conduct his office somewhat in Reagan's way, habitually rising "above" details, needs someone equally disinterested to perform Nancy's function. Does our present president have such a person handy? Devoted enough? Informed enough? He may well have the need. The question is, has he found means to meet it? The same question can be asked of George W. Bush's successor.

Thirteen years ago, I also wrote speculatively on the crucial role in leading Reagan into Iran-contra played by the then director of Central Intelligence, William Casey. Some serious chroniclers of that affair had absolved Casey; I could not. Presuming Reagan would have wished for reassurance on the Iran initiative from a trusted senior source, which he could obtain from neither his secretary of state nor his secretary of defense—since for once they had agreed and both opposed the sale of arms to Iran—I reasoned there was no one else but Casey to make up the lack and further that he had serious motives to do so. The reasoning was strengthened in my eyes by Nancy Reagan's subsequent campaign to obtain Casey's resignation, even on his deathbed, about which Regan, after his own departure, would complain. Again, I have Abshire to thank for backing up my speculation with his own far more authoritative view.

David Abshire's accomplishment in helping Reagan rid himself of the incubus of Iran-contra is all the greater since the president, although sincere in his determination to let it all hang out and thus to discover the truth for himself, was almost unable to believe it once the Tower Report reached him. What stood in Reagan's way was his own conviction that to trade arms for hostages would be morally repugnant and his consequent reluctance to acknowledge to himself that he had acted so. By Abshire's account, he and Nancy between them, armed with the report, argued the president into seeing and accepting what he had been brought to do, in just those terms. That he ultimately did so is a tribute to the three of them.

Reading this authoritative account of Reagan's notable success in putting that scandal behind him raises a further question. Why have other presidents with equal need—like Nixon or even Clinton—failed so signally to do precisely that and thus, in Reagan's fashion, neutralize dangerous failure with remedial success? Abshire probes this question with respect to both those issues. The comparisons are telling. They seem to me to make this book required reading for all presidents and White House aides to come—especially the aides, who in their eagerness to serve might harm a future president as much as, in the course of Iran-contra, some of Reagan's aides harmed him.

Richard E. Neustadt
Harvard University

Wellfleet, Massachusetts
September, 2003

Acknowledgments

I want to express appreciation to Mary Lenn Dixon of Texas A&M University Press for her coordination of this book's publication and for taking great interest in my work. Thank you also to Stephanie George and Carol Hoke. For several reasons I am especially happy to have Texas A&M as a publisher. It is an honor to be part of a Presidential Series directed by James Pfiffner; I have deep admiration for the Bush Presidential Library at Texas A&M, now directed by Roman Popadiuk and where I have had the pleasure of cochairing two conferences; lastly, Texas A&M is where my father, James E. Abshire Sr., taught just before World War I while pursuing doctoral studies at Princeton University. He instilled my interest in history in the first place.

I am in debt to several scholars and journalists who have reviewed my various drafts, including Michael Beschloss, David Gergen, Fred Greenstein, James Pfiffner, and especially Lou Cannon for his detailed critiques. I am forever indebted to Richard Neustadt, who carefully read my manuscript and provided a detailed foreword, one of the last works he wrote before his death in 2003. I have both deep affection for Dick and unbound admiration for his works on the American presidency. Appreciation goes to my talented former White House colleagues, Razvigor ("Raz") Bazala, Charles Brower, Dennis Kloske, Alan Raul, and Peter Wallison. I offer special thanks to Rhett Dawson, Brent Scowcroft, and Clark McFadden for conversation with regard to their perspective of the Tower Board proceedings. I also thank Robert Strauss for sharing the story of his meeting with President Reagan.

Any thanks are inadequate for my former colleague at the State Department, Marshall Wright, for his incomparable advice and editorial help. I greatly appreciate the help of Brock Brower and Richard Whalen, two gifted writers. I owe special appreciation to Nancy Reagan for our meetings in 1999 and for her diary readings. I would also like to express gratitude to the archivists and director, Mark Burson, of the Reagan Presidential Library for their help with research and photographs.

I would like to express appreciation to the following helpful individuals who served with me at the Center for the Study of the Presidency and previously at the Center for Strategic and International Studies and who have in some way assisted me in this endeavor: Stan Burnett, Elise Callaghan, Jay Collins, Wesley Cross, Phyllis d'Hoop, Tiffany Fountain, Aaron Myers, Jeremy Goldberg, Mat Harrington, Michael Kearns, Andy Kelly, Tom Kirlin, Fred Ludtke, Mary Marik, Cora Mendoza, Joshua Naftalis, Jeff Olson, William Stokes, Adam Tarosky, Jeff Thomas, Elizabeth Whitmore, Lucas Whittmann, and, finally, my long-time advisor, Jon Vondracek.

I give special thanks to my beautiful wife, Carolyn Abshire, for her continuous support and love.

Saving the Reagan Presidency

Introduction

Crisis of the Reagan Presidency

On an ominous November 3, 1986, a Lebanese periodical, *Al-Shiraa*, announced that the United States had sold weapons to Iran. The story spread like wildfire in the American press; one shocking headline read, "Reagan Trades Arms for Hostages." After three days of deadly White House silence, the president denied it all. "We will never pay off terrorists because that only encourages more of it," he declared in his reassuring manner.

The president's statement did not agree with the facts, but a more detailed explanation is needed. In November, 1979, President Carter dealt with a dramatic hostage crisis when four hundred Iranian radicals, members of the Revolutionary Guard, broke into the walled grounds of the U.S. Embassy in Teheran and held fifty-two U.S. employees. Further amplifying the disaster, in April, 1980, Carter authorized a rescue attempt, but Marine Corps helicopters broke down, and eight U.S. Marines were killed. Secretary of State Cyrus Vance resigned in protest for not being fully consulted on the operation. For all practical purposes, Carter's presidency was destroyed. Reagan next assumed responsibility for ending the Iran hostage crisis. The whole thing was like a recurring nightmare.

Soon thereafter, as ambassador to NATO, I met Defense Secretary Cap Weinberger at the Brussels military airport as he arrived for our defense ministers' meeting. Once in his limousine, he buried his head in his hands and exclaimed to me, "Not again, not after Watergate!" The exposure of the Iran-contra affair was both sudden and earthshaking. Simply put, the survival of the presidency was threatened. Since 1963, the White House had been star crossed: the

Kennedy assassination, Lyndon Johnson and Vietnam, Richard Nixon and Watergate, and Jimmy Carter's hostage crisis in Iran. In contrast, Ronald Reagan, the first president to serve two terms since Dwight Eisenhower, finally restored the power and continuity of successful presidential leadership.

How did the Reagan disaster come about? With Reagan's inauguration in January, 1981, the fifty-two U.S. hostages in Teheran were released. In 1984, the Hezbollah, a Shiite movement in Lebanon closely connected with the Iranian Revolutionary Guard, seized three U.S. citizens. In 1985, the group abducted four more. One of the seven was the CIA station chief in Lebanon. The national security adviser at the time, Robert McFarlane, backed by the CIA chief, Bill Casey, induced the president to become involved in a highly secret arms-for-hostages deal. Iran needed arms in its war against Iraq, and the hostages held by the Hezbollah were the special bait. The secret U.S. scheme contradicted the much-publicized program called Operation Staunch—a high-postured effort led by Secretary of State George Shultz—to ensure that no allies gave any arms to Iran, a country publicly labeled as supporting terrorism.

In the ensuing days of late November, 1986, more revelations of arms sales to Iran shook the president's credibility. To the Congress and the press, it became increasingly clear that the Reagan administration had violated its no-concessions policy of withholding weapons from all nations that sponsored terrorism. It had also contradicted its own specific embargo on arms sales to Iran.[1]

Things soon got worse. The initial White House investigations were mishandled, and the national security adviser led Reagan into making a disastrous speech on November 13. His address was filled with inaccurate statements, such as his pronouncement that all the weapons and spare parts shipped to Iran "could easily fit into a single cargo plane." Actually, the first two shipments in August and September of 1985 totaled 504 tube-launched, wire-guided antitank missiles (TOWs). An uncharacteristically defensive Reagan declared that the "unprecedented speculation" and countless reports had been not only wrong but also "potentially dangerous to the hostages and destructive of the opportunity before us." The president assured the public that "our no-concessions policy remains in force."

After the speech, polls showed that only 14 percent of the public believed the president's story. Yet things could get much worse. At this very time, the National Security Council staff member, a very aggressive, freewheeling Lt. Col. Oliver North, a U.S. Marine, was still trying to trade more arms for hostages. On November 19, an even more confused Reagan conducted a prime-time press conference filled with more inaccuracies, including a monstrous one that the United States had not been involved with Israel as an intermediary in supplying weapons to Iran.

Attorney General Ed Meese was worried and started to investigate what Reagan's subordinates had actually done in the Iranian arms deals. Then, a second shoe dropped like a concrete block: The investigation turned up a telltale memo by Lt. Col. Oliver North. Operating directly out of the executive office of the president, North had inflated the price of arms going to Iran and illegally diverted the profits to the contras, the anti-Sandinista forces opposing the Marxist regime in the Central American country of Nicaragua. When Meese informed Reagan, the president was devastated, and the blood drained from his face.

In addition, the funding of Nicaraguan rebels—the contras or freedom fighters, as Reagan proudly proclaimed them—defied the Boland Amendment, which was a congressional restriction aimed at preventing such support. While the Boland Amendment had some ambiguities, a Reagan authorization of the diversion of funds clearly could have been a heinous offense. That would have constituted "theft of government property"—stealing and using funds for unauthorized purposes. The U.S. Constitution, Article 1, Section 9, states that "no money shall be drawn from the treasury, but in consequence of appropriations made by law." The Anti-Deficiency Act (31 USC 1517, 1519) makes it a felony to spend money without appropriation. If Reagan did know, he could also have been guilty of a cover-up and obstruction of justice. And if he were guilty of these, the acts would be grounds for impeachment.

A presidential crisis was afoot, and though a world away in Brussels at the time as ambassador to NATO, I would soon find myself drawn into an unfolding drama of trying to save the Reagan presidency. Just after Christmas, the president phoned me for help.

CHAPTER 1

A Philosophy of Government

Before plunging further into this study of a presidential crisis, the reader deserves a word about my background and why I came to write this memoir of presidential tragedy and eventual presidential triumph. I believe that explaining my previous experience in Washington may help the reader understand my particular approach to that national crisis.

I grew up loving history. It was in the late 1950s that I earned my doctorate in American history at Georgetown University; my studies had focused on the crises of U.S. presidents. I never guessed that three decades later I would be thrown into circumstances where the survival of an American presidency hung in the balance. Much less would I have guessed that I would meet alone a dozen times with an immensely important president who was under great stress. I was to know the Reagan presidency at its highest point, just after the triumphant 1985 Geneva Summit with Gorbachev. I knew it also at its lowest point, when a faltering president stood before the Tower Board, which was investigating the Iran-contra affair.

As for me, my forty-year career had been shaped by both the Cold War and a protracted executive-legislative struggle that had commenced long before my late-December, 1986, Cabinet appointment as special counselor to President Reagan. As a 1951 graduate of West Point and an infantry platoon leader and company commander in the Korean War, I experienced the consequences of President Truman's precedent-setting action on the Korean peninsula. Without congressional consultation, he decreed that U.S. troops be committed to war, thus beginning a series of undeclared wars in the last half of the twentieth century.

While instructing at the infantry school soon after the cease-fire—with promotion slow —I concluded there would be war no more and future action would be in Washington. So I left the service to retool myself, reveling in graduate studies in history at Georgetown University. In the autumn of 1958, as a newlywed in need of income to support a family, I, an east Tennessee Republican, landed a writing job at the Republican Congressional Campaign Committee. Moving from the Georgetown spires of academia to the trenches of partisan politics, I learned the literary art of mudslinging to destroy opposition candidates. My reward with the new Congress was a prize position on the then small staff of the minority leader, old-line Republican Charles Halleck.

Good fortune shone again on me when a dissatisfied band of younger members including John Rhodes, Gerry Ford, and Mel Laird, perhaps egged on by President Eisenhower to modernize the Republican Party, nearly overthrew Halleck. Representative Halleck was forced to activate the House Republican Party Committee, which had been mandated in the Congressional Reorganization Act of 1946.[1] Sporting my brand-new Ph.D., I was named as its first director.

Climbing out of the partisan trenches, I was now part of an attempt to streamline the governance of the house Republicans and, in certain cases, legislation. I learned this meant cooperation with approachable Democrats. Regular breakfast meetings at the Eisenhower White House further broadened my exposure in government.

There I was much taken by Ike's wise and suave congressional liaison, Bryce Harlow. This diminutive man—a model of civility, agile, courtly, and intuitive—was marvelous with the King's English. A colonel in the reserve forces, he was also an exemplar of country before partisanship, having served as chief of staff to a Georgia Democrat, Carl Vinson, the powerful House Armed Services Committee chair.

From Harlow, my newly found mentor, I learned the mantra "Trust is the coin of the realm." He would say this often, with an implied nod toward President Eisenhower. The Congress implicitly trusted five-star Ike. Harlow knew that the members of the Constitutional Convention had put similar trust in their future commander-in-chief, George Washington, when he presided over their deliberations. They crafted Article II of the Constitution with him in mind. When John Kennedy won the presidency, my White House breakfasts in Harlow's company ended. The creative Bill Baroody, president of the American

Enterprise Association (AEA), lured me to his organization to expand contact with younger members of Congress and to broaden AEA's studies beyond domestic issues.[2] Under mentor Baroody, I learned the art of think-tank leadership. After a year with his help, I was able to venture out on my own. With the approval of Georgetown University's president, I went to Adm. Arleigh Burke—the three-term, just-retired chief of naval operations, Pacific-war hero, and father of the Polaris submarine—and persuaded him to join me in founding a strategic studies center at my alma mater, later named the Center for Strategic and International Studies (CSIS). Burke and I shared a concern about the compartmentalization in both the executive and legislative branches and the difficulty of achieving a strategic, integrative approach to public-policy issues. Our nation's capital was too fragmented. If Burke had thought compartmentalization was bad then, he should see it now.

Until then, I had worked mostly with Republicans. But I knew from Harlow's mentoring and the study of American history, especially my dissertation, that politicians had to build coalitions to do truly important things. That dissertation was about the disputed Hayes-Tilden presidential election of 1876. State militias were mobilizing, and the election results were thrown into Congress. Open conflict was in part averted because a former Confederate colonel from Tennessee, Sen. David M. Key, crossed party lines and agreed to serve in the Cabinet of Pres. Rutherford B. Hayes, a Republican.[3] That act helped bring the crisis to an end. This was my greatest lesson in the national rewards of courageous coalition bipartisanship in times of crisis.

Perhaps our new think tank could help fill a growing strategic void in a bipartisan manner and produce a more unified strategic approach. Our effort had to overarch party lines to have lasting effectiveness. Rigorous adherence to this principle led to tremendous growth over the next four decades. In the 1980s, CSIS became a freestanding and independent Washington public-policy institution known around the world.

Less than a decade after the center's founding, Richard Nixon moved the Republicans back into the White House, and the brilliant Harvard professor Henry Kissinger emerged as his powerful national security advisor. No policy adviser was in closer touch with President Nixon but farther from the reach of Capitol Hill. As national security adviser in the office of the president, Kissinger was never required to testify before Congress.[4] This protected him personally but left the president's policies naked to bitter winds on the Hill. The antiwar movement was by then being led by some of the same Democrats who had sponsored our initial Vietnam troop commitment. These Democrats were contributing to a rapid loss of support for the president's strategic leadership. Furthermore, distrust between the White House and the State Department was acute. In short, none of the important players—the White House, the State Department, and the Congress—trusted one another.

As one effort to close the fissures, in the spring of 1970, Bryce Harlow recommended to Nixon that I be appointed assistant secretary of state for congressional relations. Historically, this was an extremely important position when held by George Kennan and, later, Dean Acheson. Harlow argued that Kissinger knew me well from participating in CSIS conferences, and this friendship would help the White House–State Department relationship. As for Congress, the often-whimsical former Rhodes scholar from Arkansas, William Fulbright, chaired the Senate Foreign Relations Committee. He was the author of the Gulf of Tonkin Resolution, which was the basis for President Johnson's escalation of U.S. involvement in Vietnam. Fulbright later contended that President Johnson had deceived him on the facts of the Tonkin affair that led to the resolution,[5] and he switched positions to become the leader of the antiwar movement in the Senate. Harlow argued that somebody new had to establish rapport with the committee because both Democrats and Republicans were increasingly uniting against a rather high-handed White House.

In April, 1970, I moved into the State Department. This was just before U.S. military forces swept into the Cambodian enclaves of the Communist aggressors. This dramatic move occurred without prior notification of any member of Congress. It was a brilliant example of how not to conduct congressional relations, of how to undermine public support, and of how to play into the opponents' hands in Hanoi. Even surprised Republican members broke party loyalty and spoke out angrily. Campuses were soon in an uproar—four young people were killed and others wounded by the panicked National Guard at Kent State—and demonstrators surrounded the State Department as I arrived at work in the mornings.

I questioned my wisdom in taking the job, especially when the patrician Dean Acheson summoned me to his house in Georgetown one rainy afternoon to tell me how he once ran things in my position as assistant secretary.[6] He believed in a strong presidency. This tall, eloquent, sardonic man then offered a rundown on the Senate Foreign Relations Committee, my "committee of jurisdiction," as he put it. He spared almost no one from criticism, especially its chair, Bill Fulbright, whom he labeled a dilettante.

Despite—or perhaps because of—Acheson's colorful warnings about the members of the Foreign Relations Committee, I learned by necessity the art of deep consultation and coalition building on Capitol Hill. Trying to practice civility, I found ways to approach both recalcitrant Republicans and disillusioned Democrats. I was helped by my earlier staff experiences on Capitol Hill and therefore by my recognition that Pennsylvania Avenue is a two-way street. I soon learned that an effective congressional liaison has to be a diplomat, a political scientist, and even, at times, a psychiatrist. A departmental liaison must learn to listen in order to understand the members of Congress, recognize their special interests, empathize with their genuine political obstacles, respect their principles, be secretly amused by their foibles, and above all earn their trust. The liaison must hope to introduce new facts or factors that can enable the members to move to higher ground or make compromises. Dean Acheson had told me from his experience, now invaluable, that changes could be made to a piece of legislation, even if minor, by gaining the support of a key member. Members must have political cover or credibility for a change in position. And, above all, the liaison must have some allies and advisors.[7]

A dramatic example of an indispensable, bipartisan ally came my way when an end-the-war amendment passed the Senate and appeared to be headed for passage in the House. One of the most erudite and influential liberal Democrats in the House was handsome, smart, and bookish Richard Bolling of Missouri. Bolling and I shared some common roots at the University of the South, on the mountain at Sewanee, Tennessee.[8]

I called on Bolling in his office and plaintively explained that Henry Kissinger would have to wrap up his negotiations in Paris if this end-the-war amendment passed. After further discussion and reflection, Bolling said he would move on the floor of the House to strike it. In pleased surprise, I asked whether he needed any assistance on his speech. "Nope," he said, "it's very simple. I'm very much against

Richard Nixon and everything he represents politically. I don't even like him personally. But I'll not vote to undercut our commander-in-chief at this critical time in the war and in the negotiations."

Several days later I watched from the gallery as the impeccable, liberal Bolling rose on the house floor, uttered those lines, and boldly moved to strike the amendment. He had credibility; by voice vote, he carried the House of Representatives.[9]

I experienced another equally dramatic case on the senate side. In the late 1960s and early 1970s, stories leaked about secret CIA funding of Radio Liberty and Radio Free Europe. A small group of senators moved to abruptly cut off the funding. The disabling amendment passed the Senate but not the House. In the ensuing conference, the anti-radio senate chair, Bill Fulbright, had a heated argument with the pro-radio house chair, Thomas Morgan. Finally, "Doc" Morgan (as this physician-representative was called) told me in exasperation that I would have to show him a mutually acceptable plan. He would not meet again over this issue with the disagreeable Fulbright. That was fine for him but not for the radios and me.

Funding for the radios was due to expire in ten days, and I was stunned to learn that Chairman Fulbright had left for an extended two-week Caribbean vacation. It seemed to me almost organized to be the funeral for Radio Free Europe and Radio Liberty. In desperation, I went to the Democratic majority leader, the tactician Mike Mansfield of Montana. "Senator, I know you're not for these radios. But I don't believe you think this is the way the Congress should operate. It's not the way to govern." During a long pause I tensely waited for his reply. "I'll tell the chief of staff of the Foreign Relations Committee to work up a plan with you to fund the radios for a year through the State Department while things are worked out." This was a major political victory because these radios played an important role in winning the battle of ideas in the Cold War by bringing truth beyond the Iron Curtain.[10]

I knew that executive-legislative conflicts had been endemic in the history of the republic. I even wrote a small book on that subject in which I described how George Washington had stomped out of the Senate in his first and last attempt at direct consultation.[11] I had studied the partisan-ridden impeachment proceeding by the radical Republicans against Andrew Johnson. I had seen firsthand how politicians can take one position when their party occupies the White

House and another when serving in Congress. Hubert Humphrey was a powerful Democrat who befriended me. He once summed up this phenomenon for me: "Dave, you must know from your history that where a man sits at a given time will determine where he stands."

I took a gregarious Hubert Humphrey into Secretary of State Bill Rogers's office after the former vice president had been reelected to the Senate. He had moved from the vice president's seat to his senate seat. Rogers congratulated him on being seated again on the Foreign Relations Committee. It was hardly Rogers's favorite body at that point.

Humphrey responded, "Bill, I don't think I'll make a very acceptable member up there. After having the responsibility as vice president, I'm not nearly irresponsible enough to be on that committee." Rogers laughed with Humphrey, but Acheson echoed loudly in my memory.

In 1973, in a valiant attempt to modify all the exasperation of executive-legislative turmoil, Congress established the blue-ribbon Commission for the Organization of Government for the Conduct of Foreign Policy. This was a constructive effort, chaired by famed former ambassador Robert Murphy. Senator Fulbright deserves some credit for initiating this commission. Its membership included luminaries such as Sen. Mike Mansfield and Vice Pres. Nelson Rockefeller.[12] I was also asked to serve. The purpose, once again, was to devise a better organizational structure and methods for the executive and legislative branches to handle foreign policy. With our constructive report, I think it would have been inconceivable to commission members that anything like the bizarre Iran-contra episode could ever happen. Ironically, Bill Casey, the future CIA director later criticized for the Iran-contra episode, was also on that commission.

Also in 1973, I had been asked to return to the Nixon administration, this time not to the State Department as before, but to the White House. By late April, 1973, Richard Nixon was sinking into the mire of Watergate. In desperation, he fired H. R. Haldeman and John Ehrlichman and asked Gen. Alexander Haig to be his new chief of staff.

I remember the day that I received Al Haig's call. I knew why he and Nixon wanted me: to help handle Watergate, to help head off an impeachment, and to help defend the president on Capitol Hill.

When I served as assistant secretary of state for congressional relations, Nixon had referred to me privately as his "field marshal" on Capitol Hill—a high-postured title that was quite the opposite of my behind-the-scenes role.[13]

The evening General Haig called, my wife, Carolyn, and I were at one of those grand Washington mansions, the Sulgrave Club, for dinner with her mother and stepfather, 1927 Annapolis graduate Adm. George "Andy" Anderson. The tall, silver-haired Anderson was the 1962 Cuban missile crisis Chief of Naval Operations (CNO) who tangled with Secretary of Defense Robert McNamara. Over drinks, I told Andy of the Haig call.

"You're accepting, of course."

"No, Andy," I replied.

"But you went to West Point," snapped the true-blue admiral. "When the commander in chief asks for you, you respond." That was his clear protocol.

"My problem is with the commander in chief. I don't believe he's telling the truth."

It seems quaint today, but the admiral said, "You don't think he would lie to the entire American people? Did you hear the president's speech?" Nixon had just given a national radio and television speech from the Oval Office. He said he was "appalled" and "shocked" when he first heard of the Watergate break-in and had repeatedly asked whether any member of his administration was involved. He claimed that he had been assured otherwise and that new information had come to him only now. "I was determined that we should get to the bottom of the matter and that the truth should be fully brought out—no matter who was involved."[14]

"Of course I heard the president's speech, but somehow I don't believe him," I replied sorrowfully. "I told Al Haig that I had just returned from government service to CSIS. I couldn't jump ship again so soon." As time would show, my intuition was all too right.

Eight years later, in 1983, I was asked to take leave from CSIS to assume the post of U.S. ambassador to NATO. Western Europe was in disarray as antiwar demonstrations proliferated and we were attempting to deploy medium-range missiles to counter the deliberate blackmail by the Soviets with SS-20s. At the time, Congress resented the Europeans' unwillingness to take up more of the financial burden through their defense budgets. This situation was enormously exacerbated by the lack of commonality among weapons, which was a major factor in inefficient defense investments. Yet again, all these problems had to be addressed at both ends of Pennsylvania Avenue. As NATO ambassador in the busy year of 1985, I had to spend weeks at a time on Capitol Hill and also make hundreds of phone calls to the capitol from Brussels. Although not official, I was as much the ambassador to Congress as ambassador to NATO.

Unlike many with whom I worked, especially those executive-branch lawyers schooled in Article II, Section 2 of the Constitution (about the powers of the commander in chief, making treaties, and appointing officials), I never viewed partnership with Congress as giving away executive prerogatives. Justice Robert Jackson said that the power of the sovereign is maximized when the president acts together with the Congress. Not only was this good constitutional law, it was also good strategy. As one who had read much military history at West Point and even before, I knew that unity of effort was the first principle of any successful strategy to build power and influence.[15]

Now we turn to the book at hand and the story of my role in early 1987 as special counselor to the president on the Iran-contra inquiry. This book carries forward the double-barreled story of both executive and legislative responsibility—and irresponsibility—as played out during the Iran-contra episode and the investigations. At its core, the crisis was an executive-legislative struggle over control of foreign policy. Mutual distrust and a confusion of constitutional functions shrouded the struggle. One-time Reagan speechwriter Landon Parvin commented to me that the Iran-contra affair was a morality play: "Forces of truth, naïveté, manipulation, and deceit were at work." If, as Bryce Harlow said, trust was the coin of the realm, then the coinage was certainly debased, and trust across party lines was destroyed. There was violation of the law and then cover-up justified on the ground that the other party in Congress was being irresponsible and their own cause was noble. By the end of 1986, the Reagan presidency was unwinding. The Iran-contra revelation raised questions about the president's judgment, credibility, and management style. The task that followed this tragedy was to restore that coin of the realm of trust for it to again become the basis of Reagan's leadership. This is the subject of what follows.

A West Point graduate, David Abshire (at right) served as an infantry platoon leader and company commander in the Korean War.

As the first staff director of the House Republican Policy Committee in 1960, Abshire briefs Vice President Nixon and Congressman Gerald Ford.

In 1973, the Commission on the Organization of the Government for the Conduct of Foreign Policy, chaired by Ambassador Robert Murphy, included Sen. Mike Mansfield, Bill Casey, Anne Armstrong, and Abshire.

The President's Foreign Intelligence Advisory Board meeting in 1982. From left to right: Paul Seabury, John S. Foster Jr., Adm. Thomas H. Moorer, Edward Bennett Williams, H. Ross Perot, Robert F. Six, Clare Boothe Luce, Leo Cherne, Anne Armstrong, Seymour Weiss, William Baker, David M. Abshire, Martin Anderson, W. Glenn Campbell, and Leon Jaworski.

After his swearing in as NATO ambassador in 1983, Abshire is congratulated by President Reagan and Vice President Bush in the Old Executive Office Building.

Abshire presents strategic arms negotiators to fellow NATO ambassadors at a meeting of the North Atlantic Council. From left to right: Ambassadors Maynard Glitman, John Tower, Max Kampelman, and Abshire.

NATO ambassador Abshire escorts the new NATO secretary general, Lord Peter Carrington, to meet with the president.

Dear Dave – I hope you know how welcome you are. Very Best Wishes & Regards. Ronald Reagan

On January 12, 1987, Abshire meets privately with President Reagan for the first time after Reagan's return from the hospital. Nancy Reagan ordered that the picture not be released to the press since the president looked so frail.

David Abshire presents his plan, "Beyond the Tower Board Report," to Reagan on February 4, 1987, while Regan listens.

Judge Charles Brower, Peter Wallison, and Abshire meet with President Reagan before the first Tower Board meeting.

On February 26, 1987, Abshire meets alone with the president immediately preceding the receipt of the Tower Board report in the Cabinet Room. Abshire stresses that this is the president's report and that it is important to fully accept its recommendations.

On February 26, 1987, at the Tower Board meeting, President Reagan listens to Chairman Tower's report. Senator Muskie sits at Reagan's left.

Abshire's staff meets with President Reagan to express their gratitude for the privilege of serving him. In response, Reagan jokes, "I'm the one to give the thanks. You didn't find me guilty!"

On March 28, 1988, Nancy Reagan, Abshire, and Brock Brower reminisce about White House experiences.

CHAPTER 2

Summons from the President

In the Watergate hearings, Sen. Howard Baker posed the central question, "What did the president know and when did he know it?" He was referring to President Nixon, but now his question applied to President Reagan.

The national security advisor, Vice Adm. John Poindexter, sat a few steps away from the Oval Office. The big question was whether he had told the president about Lt. Col. Oliver North's illegal diversion of funds from the arms sales to the Iranians in the Middle East to the contras in Central America. Swept away in the confusion and chaos, the president and his chief of staff, Donald Regan, made a dramatic move to institute three short-term remedies.

First, the president asked for the resignations of Poindexter and North—that is, he fired them.

Second, the president set up his own bipartisan board of three eminent individuals: former senator John Tower, former national security advisor Brent Scowcroft, and former senator and secretary of state Edmund S. Muskie. This panel became known as the Tower Board, after its chair. The administration hoped the board could quickly turn out a report on what went wrong and provide solutions for the situation. This would take place while the newly appointed independent counsel, Judge Lawrence Walsh, and the two congressional investigating committees were proceeding at a more deliberate pace to investigate the matter.

Third, the president would not exert executive privilege in the investigation that would follow. This was an extraordinary move toward openness.

There was much press speculation about the identity of Poindexter's replacement as national security advisor, and, according to the newspapers, I was the top candidate. I was not too impressed since the press had speculated that I would become the new national security advisor when Dick Allen and Bud McFarlane each in turn moved out of that role, leaving one friend to quip, "Abshire—always a bridesmaid, never a bride." The names of Sen. John Tower; former national security advisor Gen. Brent Scowcroft; and the former deputy director of Central Intelligence, Adm. Bobby Ray Inman were also tossed about. One had to next consider political maneuvering. Senator Tower had already been named as head of the new board. Scowcroft was viewed as too close to Kissinger, much as Bill Hyland, another candidate, had been viewed. The CIA director, Bill Casey, vehemently opposed Inman. As a result, in all of the papers I was listed as the top candidate. One unflattering press account said they had scraped the bottom of the barrel, and there was I.[1]

From Europe, I phoned some friends in Washington to get the lay of the land. Charles Wick, confidant of the president, told me he had flown back from California on Air Force One with the president. It was circulated around the plane that I was it. I called Attorney General Ed Meese, who was very close to the president. I told him that I had two problems about being national security advisor. First, I did not want to be away from my policy institute so long; after all, it was my life's work as an institution builder. Second and more importantly, the press had now placed real focus on Don Regan, with a new negative story being printed practically every day. I felt that Don, while my friend (he certainly was at that point), was a real millstone around the president's neck. It was going to be very difficult for a new national security advisor to function effectively with him as chief of staff. If I had ever dreamed of being national security advisor at the completion of my career—and I certainly had—it was not under these conditions.

Ed Meese listened but responded that I had to appreciate the importance of Don's superb organizing abilities. Furthermore, Don himself was in front, pushing for my appointment as national security advisor. Others in Washington confirmed this information. They said I should hang in there.

My worries were needless.

Like a bolt out of the blue, Bill Casey made a swift move to supplant me (he had supported me over Inman) with Frank Carlucci, who had been deputy director at CIA and, so Casey argued, had the intelligence experience I lacked. Of course, I had served on the President's Foreign Intelligence Advisory Board (PFIAB) and on the Murphy Commission Subcommittee on Intelligence with Bill Casey. Perhaps Casey, because of some past arguments we had had, feared I might be a whistle-blower on the types of covert operations he and Lieutenant Colonel North had created. I would hope that Casey's judgment of me would have turned out to be correct, but Frank Carlucci would never have tolerated wild operations such as Iran-contra either.

Whatever private concerns Casey may have had about me, his support for Carlucci was logical. In the past, Frank Carlucci had been a deputy to both George Shultz and Cap Weinberger, and the biggest problem in the functioning of the executive branch was that Shultz and Weinberger could not get along with each other. If Frank could close that gap between his two former bosses, he would render real service. In any event, Carlucci was an outstanding and tough foreign service officer veteran and had been involved in many foreign crises as an ambassador, most notably saving Portugal from communist control in 1974. The president wisely agreed with Casey's suggestion. Frank very kindly called me at NATO to say he was sorry if he had deprived me of the job. I told him he was clearly the man for this position at this time of multiple crises, and I assured him I genuinely had a CSIS commitment, but how nice of him to call.

Part of the regimen at NATO was that once a week a different ambassador would host the secretary general and his fifteen colleagues at a multicourse luncheon with three vintage wines. The justification for spending some of the ambassadorial representation allowances on expensive cuisine was to discuss affairs of the alliance more informally and confidentially than at the weekly headquarters sessions in the big NATO conference room, with vast mission staffs listening. Traditionally, the American ambassador hosted during Thanksgiving week. Our household Italian chef and sous-chef attempted with fair success the turkey, stuffing, and pumpkin pie routine. Thanksgiving of 1986 at my residence turned out to be quite different, not just for the departure from European cuisine but for what I knew the other ambassadors were saying to each other: "Can you imagine those self-righteous Americans scolding us for merely trading with the Iranians when they were in fact secretly selling them arms!"

To say the least, I was not looking forward to hosting this lunch.

However, our country residence outside of Brussels was still impressive for them to approach in their chauffeur-driven cars, despite our recent faded glory over arms deals. Their emissaries had to wind past Leopold II's little Versailles palace, the park and lakes, through iron gates with armed guards, up a beautiful planted hill and apple orchards, and then down the long avenue bordered by forty-eight double-rowed, buttonwood trees. At the far end stood our rambling Flemish residence, the official residence of the NATO ambassador. I never tired of the sweeping natural grandeur of these grounds, planned by a renowned European landscape artist.

As I would tell visiting members of the congressional appropriations committee, we were proud that we had bought this incomparably beautiful place for our taxpayers at a bargain price. The residence had belonged to the family that owned Côte d'Or, a Belgian chocolate company. The widow of the company's founder wanted the Americans "who had saved Belgium," as she put it, to have the estate and to have the mansion on the hill symbolize that the Americans, joined to NATO, were there to stay. When terrorism struck NATO in 1985 and 1986, this was the safest embassy residence and grounds in Europe. Visiting Vice Pres. George Bush could jog through its seven gardens and two mazes and over its walkways and grand lawns without his bodyguards. I was amused when my wife attempted to keep up with Barbara on her power walk and breathlessly try to make idle talk.

At a ceremony with all the NATO ambassadors and before receiving Washington's approval, I named this dormer-flanked, loaf-shaped mansion after the man who took us into NATO, Harry Truman. A fait accompli, before the State of Department could react, was having the Democratic name stick in a Republican administration. NATO was founded and had survived only through commitments by both Democratic and Republican leaders.

Standing in the marble-floored hall, I welcomed each ambassador to Truman Hall, and almost every one tried to be jovial by congratulating me on nearly becoming national security advisor. I quipped that I certainly did not need that job just now. After we settled at our sumptuous table and sipped the first of the wines, I spoke directly of the Washington crisis. The custom was to have a very small pad by each place setting for note taking, for the ambassadors always prepared a cable to their capital as to what had transpired. Most scribbled while

I talked: "I know your feelings and concerns. A terrible aberration has occurred, and we are all embarrassed. Several of you have asked me personally if we will see a repeat of Watergate and another president go down. The Watergate scandal involved an extended cover-up and obstruction of justice. Ronald Reagan is a very different personality from Richard Nixon, whom I knew quite well. If there has been a recent cover-up by staff, I believe such is now ended in this administration."

There were other comments, and many of the ambassadors thanked me for my reassurances. They did not eat as heartily as expected, nor did I. They were clearly shaken.

Don Regan had made ultraconservative Pat Buchanan the White House communications director to protect his right flank early in his tenure as chief of staff. Overwhelmed by the adverse press on Iran-contra, Buchanan wrote a memorandum that triggered events and soon changed my future.

Buchanan had an uncanny feel for public communications. He saw that the White House system could not effectively deal with the Iran-contra affair. He also knew from his days in the Nixon administration how a presidency could be destroyed by a cover-up. On December 12, 1986, he wrote the following to his boss, Chief of Staff Regan, who had had no such Watergate experience:

> This is a follow-up to our Wednesday meeting. At this time,
> I cannot conceive of a communications plan that will allow
> peak-period White House business to go forward in January,
> uninterrupted by Iran issues. No matter what we say, dissolu-
> tion will show. Current example: Final clearance is still pend-
> ing for guidance on the Iran issue. I offer instead a two track
> White House mechanism to get past [the] crunch of Budget
> and SOU [State of the Union].
>
> 90 Day Special Counselor—Appoint a Special Counselor
> to head a "Swat Team" to deal exclusively with the Iran/Con-
> tra issue. Goals: 1) Day to day management and tracking of all
> aspects of the Iran issue; 2) 10 points, restore the president's
> standing.
>
> The Special Counselor should have standing equal to
> the Chief of Staff and direct access to President; be able to

command White House resources; impact the President's schedule; shape events; oversee and sign off on statements and speech materials. He should come equipped to provide the President with sage advice on legal and legislative matters and external relations.

I believe this arrangement would be viewed as a positive development on the outside. It is difficult now, but soon will become impossible for you or anyone else on staff, likewise concerned with State of the Union and the Budget, to track all aspects of the Iran/Contra issue.

The person for the Special Counselor's job will be a rare individual—an intellectual power with energy to become consumed with the issue, a known and prominent Republican, and one who will not be tempted to use the 90 day detail as a springboard. Further, the Counselor should be provided three substantive detailees (White House experience) [legal advisor, legislative affairs, external relations], full time for 90 days, and staff support as necessary. The detailees should bring experience to accommodate the three areas of particular importance.[2]

Buchanan's clear-sighted plan soon became the Regan plan. Later, it became the Reagan plan, as an increasing number of advisors warned that the confused situation was deteriorating rapidly and that an outsider had to be brought in.[3]

Only days later, on December 19, I received a call at Truman Hall from White House chief of staff Don Regan, who said, "Dave, I am calling on behalf of the president, who'll be calling you very soon." Regan said that the president—and then he pointedly added the vice president also—was anxious for me to come to the White House for special duty. "Your commitment to get out of government is understood, and this'll be an assignment of only three months' duration. You're going to be special counselor to the president on the Iran-contra investigation. You'll report directly to the president. You're gonna have your own channel. I'll be free to run the daily business of the White House. You'll be Mr. Clean. You're not involved in the past events now under investigation. You have all the clearances. The transition can be immediate. The president will be calling you directly." He went on to say that these changes would show that the White House was not paralyzed.

"Hold up," I said to Don. "I've got to think this through. In the first place, you should be calling a distinguished attorney."

"All of these issues have been thought through," he replied. "You'll have attorneys working for you, and, of course, you have a great deal of governmental and congressional experience. You're the unanimous choice."

"Don, I want to think this process through. I'll phone you back very quickly. But please hold up on the president's call."

It was clear that there would be two distinct White House tracks—that of the chief of staff to run the daily business of the White House and that of the special counselor to coordinate with the investigation, restore integrity to the process, and report directly to the president. But how did I ensure that this process worked?

I made a number of overseas calls to some cherished personal advisors. I first called Anne Armstrong, chair of the CSIS Board of Trustees. She had been ambassador to the Court of St. James's, counselor in the second Nixon administration, and chair of the PFIAB. This accomplished Texan from Armstrong Ranch got right to the point: "Make sure the position is Cabinet rank and equal to Don Regan." I also talked to distinguished Chicago attorney, leader in the American Bar Association, Medal of Freedom winner, and longtime friend, Morry Leibman, who had advised me on many sensitive issues through the decades. Next I called Judge Charles Brower, who had been deputy legal advisor in the State Department while I was assistant secretary of state. There were a few others, too, including a couple of insurance executives from around the country, for they are often the world's best judges of risk, and I was dealing with a multitude of risks.

Out of these conversations and those with White House staff, I developed a framework for acceptance in order to ensure that I had the conditions to be successful and not become some kind of victim like Bud McFarlane. Then I called Regan back. First, I wanted to talk frankly with the president before any announcement. Second, to protect and symbolize my independence, I wanted to be special counselor with Cabinet rank. I did not like saying this because I never liked people that fight over status, but Armstrong was right. Third, I wanted a charter worked out precisely for the protection of all of us with regard to the mission and scope of my responsibilities. Fourth, because I am not an attorney, I wanted a very distinguished legal deputy, namely Judge Charles Nelson Brower—then sitting as a judge on the Iran–United States Claims Tribunal in The Hague. Fifth, I might want a small consultative group of "wise men" from the outside to prevent my isolation. Sixth, I would need strong administrative support because this was a new, unfunded office. Seventh, I was being abruptly called from NATO to the White House and believed it would be smoother for me to continue carrying the title of NATO ambassador as well as counselor to the president. I proposed that in late January I briefly return for a farewell meeting with the full NATO council and demonstrate an orderly departure. After all, this alliance was at the heart of winning the Cold War and should be treated with care. I was embarrassed that the list was so long, but I felt it necessary for my successful performance.

Regan was noncommittal on Cabinet rank and did not jump with joy about any outside advisors but promised strong support for my office and wanted to talk further about my deputy. He was decidedly unenthusiastic about bringing in another senior attorney not on his team.

I was prepared for the president's call, which came on December 26. His words turned out to be historic in the saga of restoring a presidency.

"David, I want your help in carrying out my commitment to get out all of the facts. There is no holding back through executive privilege. I want to get to the bottom of things. I want to ensure that there will be no cover-up." Those words were permanently etched in my mind.

"Mr. President, you've brought the presidency to new heights. Above all, as NATO ambassador, I understand the need for having a strong president as our world leader. We're at a historic moment in the Cold War. I'll do all that I can to keep the presidency strong. I look forward to serving you and will be back in early January. Mr. President, I had a good talk with Don." Noting that the president had not mentioned Cabinet rank, I added, "Since there is considerable speculation about Don and his role, I think it is important that I be in the Cabinet. I need that symbol of independence."

"Approved to Cabinet rank," the president snapped, as if making an important note on his talking sheet. Don Regan never subsequently contested the issue. I later attended all Cabinet meetings as a full member. It really gave me a tremendous advantage in achieving my mission.

I think both the president and I concluded the phone conversation feeling good about our future together. Reagan confidant Charlie Wick very quickly called me to say how pleased the president was with the conversation. I told Charlie that I deeply appreciated his frankness and that I felt my judgment of his basic honesty was being validated. I reflected on the 1973 summons from a besieged President Nixon and my fear that he might be leading a cover-up. Nixon in many ways was more brilliant than Reagan and was an artful schemer and global strategist. I believed that Reagan had probably been very naïve in this past affair, but I felt he was incapable of leading any kind of conspiracy. Of course, I did not know the facts or the chances of finding a smoking gun somewhere.

As for Don Regan, I felt that we had no serious rupture at this point although he noted the following in his book *For the Record:* "At Abshire's insistence—and after much dickering—he was invested with Cabinet rank and broad authority."[4] I'm sure my seven points or conditions could correctly be called dickering. Regan tried to drag his feet on the Brower appointment, saying that he would furnish me my entire legal staff. I stood my ground. After all, I was Regan's best ticket to survival, that is, his hope to separate the Iran-contra scandal from his role as chief of staff.

On the same day as my conversation with the president, the White House released the following statement:

> The President today announced the appointment of Ambassador David Abshire as Special Counselor to the President. Ambassador Abshire will serve on temporary assignment as the White House Coordinator for the Iran inquiry. He will assume his duties here January 5, 1987, and will continue with some NATO duties until his successor is confirmed. In that capacity, which will have Cabinet rank, he will head a team that will coordinate White House activities in all aspects of the Iran matter. He will coordinate White House responses to Congressional and other requests for information·in a timely manner, working with senior members of the White House

staff, assisted by representatives from key White House staff offices.

The President is pleased and grateful for Ambassador Abshire's willingness to undertake this important special assignment and looks forward to working with such a talented and educated public servant. Ambassador Abshire has served at NATO with the utmost distinction and success. He has a well deserved reputation as a respected and articulate advocate of our foreign policy goals.[5]

The press descended upon Truman Hall in droves. Within an hour, a call came from Frankfurt: CNN was sending a team to our residence. Other networks and journalists followed the next day with video and newspaper photographers. One shot went across American newspapers of our magnificent Truman Hall Christmas tree, our golden retriever, my wife, Carolyn, and me. Interviews were conducted in the library. Although questions were phrased in different ways, they united into one chorus:

"How are you going to deal with Don Regan?" "He's the prime minister." "How do you keep Regan from squeezing you out or keeping you down?"

"I've known Don for many years, going back to when he was head of Merrill Lynch. He wanted me in this job. But he fully knows I'm gonna be independent, get the job done. I've a pretty good reputation for that in Washington without getting into needless personality conflicts."[6]

Pat Buchanan, White House communications chief, had made a statement that carried over the wires: "This is the president's man. He's going to look into it and he's loyal to the president of the United States. But he's going to provide this information. He's got to be the president's man if you're going to work with the president's communications chief, his press secretary, and his chief of staff."[7] As the publicity from the Truman Hall interviews hit the wires of all networks, a flash message came from Pat Buchanan: All interviews were to be cleared in advance. "This is the standard procedure for White House personnel of which you are now a member." Pat was too late. The press army had departed.

★

Far away in Brussels, I already knew one thing: The second Reagan administration had trouble with congressional relations. Bob Dole, visiting Truman Hall two years earlier, had warned me insofar as possible to do all my NATO congressional relations as they related to the Defense Department part of our budget directly with the Hill. Cap Weinberger was unpopular with many in Congress, he said, because they felt he seemed never to listen. Furthermore, Dole said, the White House and Departments of State and Defense were not coordinated in their congressional interface.

Dole's concerns were validated by a *Wall Street Journal* article of June 5, 1986, headlined "Lobbying on Hill Is Foreign to Reagan's Team." House Foreign Affairs Committee member Henry Hyde was quoted as saying, "Amateur night is what leaps to mind when I watch the State Department and the White House try to coordinate policy." Even house Republicans complained that the administration ignored them. In the foreign aid area, including Central America, the administration "often does too little too late to advance its case on Capitol Hill," the article notes, on the basis of a wide range of interviews. "And aid for anti-government Nicaraguan rebels is being withheld because the administration is unable to build a consensus for a clear-cut policy in Congress, or even within its own ranks." The article goes on to say that the administration seemed uninterested in advice, even from a wise, mild-mannered senator like Dick Lugar.[8]

I knew I had to obtain congressional advice, listen as well as talk, and restore trust. I had to call upon all the lessons learned from my twenty-odd years working with Congress. The Democrats had just won both houses of Congress, so they were especially important. Here, the friendships I made as assistant secretary of state for congressional relations and as former head of CSIS would be valuable.

I immediately began to contact my friends in both parties on Capitol Hill. On the house Democratic side, I phoned the spunky, wise chair of the House Foreign Affairs Committee, Florida Democrat Dante Fascell.

"My big question," he said, "was whether this was really a rogue elephant unauthorized expedition or something more. In any event, it was a clear effort to bypass all institutions." I talked with the influential Georgia senator Sam Nunn, who spoke of the damage done by the president's speech and press conference, with all of the inaccuracies, which surely the staff could have avoided. Wyoming Republican congressman Dick Cheney feared we were starting to see another Watergate. With an unusual background, he had served as White House chief of staff in the Ford administration in the wake of Watergate and had coauthored with his wife, Lynne, an exceptional book on congressional leadership.[9] He offered me four conflicting procedures for the key witnesses: (1) Unilaterally give up protection; (2) offer presidential pardons, "which would be dumb"; (3) obtain from Congress limited immunity for key witnesses like Poindexter and North (he favored that option); or (4) delay committee investigations until the newly appointed independent counsel completed his work. Needless to say, Judge Walsh would like that last option, but the Congress would not wait.

I also talked with Indiana congressman Lee Hamilton and Hawaiian senator Daniel Inouye, chairs of the respective House and Senate Special Investigations Committees. Both were very concerned about the damage to NATO by the involvement of the leader of the alliance in such a scandal. And I had a long conversation with majority senate Republican leader, Bob Dole, to hear his latest senate perspective on things, which was very gloomy.[10]

During those last gray December days at my NATO residence, I sized up the tricky situation in Washington. How could I substantively prepare myself for the arduous and perhaps treacherous task ahead? I had to be on top of a lot of information quickly, develop some kind of narrative or framework, and learn what had transpired over the several years leading up to the revelation of the scandal. I would arrive at the White House on January 5, knowing the least of anyone there about the issues under investigation.

I did not have any documents related to the Iran-contra events. Clearly, my first need was to develop some kind of chronology and comprehension of who had done what and when. I was given a point of contact in the White House legal staff, Jay Stevens, who was deputy legal counsel to the president. After the crisis had developed, he had been moved into the Iran-contra case essentially full time. I sent a message to him requesting a chronology of events and a clear statement of the principal issues.

Adm. Arleigh Burke, my shrewd mentor and cofounder of CSIS in 1962, had given me a formula about how to approach tough public policy questions. First, get the facts straight if they are known; second, precisely define the several key issues with which you are dealing; and, third, look at them from all angles. This was the Burkean analysis I wanted from the White House. Consequently, I emphasized in my communications that I was anxious to have at least these basic documents for the plane trip to Washington so that I could use those precious hours for study. Days passed. Nothing came. I was mystified. Because the crisis had been continuing for some time, I assumed the information I sought was available. Why was there no quick response? I suspiciously wondered whether they were stalling. As I became more educated about this crisis, I came to understand the delay. Simply put, the White House staff did not know the truth. It was the same as the Kremlin's figures on the Soviet economy—there had been so much lying within the White House that no one could know the real truth. There had been too much shredding of documents and too much falsification of records. Truly, it was an inconceivable mess, and we were all standing on quicksand.

I later learned about the period from November 5 to November 20, 1986. Beginning with the first inkling that a major scandal was about to break, the national security advisor, Vice Admiral Poindexter, had invited Bud McFarlane back to work with Oliver North in preparing a chronology. All three had apparently put aside their U.S. Naval Academy honor code about truth. They created perhaps more than a dozen versions of a chronology; none were accurate. Their intention was to prepare a version that would best protect the president and the White House, thus wrongly moving the administration into a cover-up. Bud McFarlane, who later had an aching conscience that the self-righteous Colonel North never shared, described his process to the Tower Board as an attempt to create "a chronology that obscured essential facts." McFarlane confessed that this chronology did not present "a full and completely accurate account" of the events, and he admitted that he knew that the account was "misleading, at least, and wrong, at worst."[11] Soon after this, Bill Casey gave misleading testimony on Capitol Hill, which infuriated Secretary of State George Shultz because it was so blatantly inaccurate. Shultz began to threaten resignation.

If these attempts to shield the president and gild his motives were aimed at helping him, they did exactly the opposite. The deliberate distortion of the record made the president's press conference of November 19 disastrous. Story lines had already been changed by the staff so often that they compounded the president's confusion and soon made him publicly appear incompetent or even dishonest. Part of the president's confusion was driven by Poindexter's and North's impassioned plea to him that the lives of the hostages were at risk and the truth could thus not be told.[12]

I encountered the legacy of this incompetence and distortion along with a shell-shocked White House staff. The legal staff was not at fault because it had been cut out of things. They were dealing with a pile of manure, and it was clear to me that a lot of the people at the White House would be happy to dump that pile into my lap. I read a *Wall Street Journal* editorial that states, "In preparation for the next Iran, perhaps Mr. David Abshire's appointment as special counselor should be made permanent. Secretary of Scandal, we'll call it."[13] I picked up a day-old copy of the *Washington Post,* dated December 31, 1986, to read an Evans and Novak column. It was titled "The Reagan Presidency Is Dead." I had a sinking feeling, for I had no desire to be an undertaker.

On January 3, 1987, without a chronology, I left a rainy Brussels and my NATO embassy for my new White House assignment in Washington. Behind me, Europe was clearly eyeing America for "what next" in an unwinding drama.

CHAPTER 3

The Leader of the Alliance

On my Pan Am flight to Washington, I thought about the president under whom I would be serving. A dozen years earlier, I had first chatted with the tall, dark-haired governor of California at a reception at the American Embassy in Paris. He was on a delegation trip to Europe. I did not see Governor Reagan again until early 1980 at a small dinner hosted by *Washington Post* columnist George Will. The guests included notables such as Katherine Graham, publisher of the *Washington Post*; Lane Kirkland, head of the AFL-CIO; and Georgetown University professor Jeane Kirkpatrick. Will wanted to ensure that Reagan, as a presidential candidate, became acquainted early on with Washington power brokers, the so-called establishment. Not doing so had been one of Jimmy Carter's mistakes.

After dinner, I tried to engage this prospective president in a discussion on the importance of congressional relations and Carter's mishaps with Congress. With a head tilt and wink, Reagan quipped, "It'd be best to just lock 'em all up!" I had a humorous sense of failure about my effort to educate a potential president of the United States on my self-assumed specialty, handling the Congress.

The following November, Ronald Reagan won a stunning victory with 480 of the electoral votes compared to Carter's 49. To my surprise, Bill Timmons telephoned me in New Orleans during a CSIS conference on the Caribbean that I was cochairing. Timmons, a fellow Chattanoogan, had been the highly regarded White House deputy for congressional relations to Bryce Harlow during the 1970s while I was the congressional liaison for the State Department. Bill was a key Republican operative for running conventions and getting results, and he had been placed in charge of the governmental transition of all departments and agencies. He said I had been selected to head the changeover of the departments and agencies in the foreign policy, defense, international security, and financial areas. My younger friend from the early days of CSIS, Dick Allen, also had a role in my selection. Dick was to be the new national security advisor. I, of course, accepted this unexpected call with keen anticipation.[1] As head of a bipartisan CSIS, I had in no way been involved in the campaign, contrary to others in the transition team.

Over the next two months of the transition, I learned more about the president-elect. I immensely liked this leader of upright stance and purpose. He brought to a discouraged nation a sense of almost incredible optimism, a can-do attitude, and a pride in American exceptionalism—that the United States had a special purpose in the world. From my study of history and philosophy, this was a concept with which I could identify, and one need not be arrogant to believe in it. Like Reagan and Lincoln, I believed we were the world's last, best hope—as Lincoln put it, "God's almost chosen people"—and that the destruction of that hope would be unthinkable. Thus I was a happy member of the Reagan team although in no sense an original Reaganaut, as the long-time loyalists were called.

At the end of the Reagan transition, I wrote a preemptive letter turning down full-time government service because I was not prepared to take another early leave from CSIS. I did, however, accept an appointment as a member of the President's Foreign Intelligence Advisory Board (PFIAB). The only board that reports directly to the president, it was set up by President Eisenhower to examine the quality of our intelligence. It was a part-time job I relished, and I chaired a task force on the "user-producer" relationship in the intelligence process. I also visited all the CIA station chiefs in the capitals of the Warsaw Pact to do a report.

A year later, when my friend Richard Allen was being unjustly pushed out of the national security post, I was announced in *Time* magazine as his successor. *Time* got it wrong, and the job went to Judge William Clark, Reagan's close friend and chief of staff when he was governor. Newly elected President Reagan had named Clark deputy secretary of state despite his lack of foreign policy experience. I had been asked to coach him for his initial senate confirmation. We became friends, and he developed the habit of calling me at CSIS to discuss problems. No expert on Washington, he relied on his common sense as a California rancher. I remember one call, his voice cracking:

"Dave, it's not working."

"What isn't working, Bill?" I asked.

"The government. The antagonisms are too great. Haig and Weinberger and the White House. What do I do?"

"Talk to the president, Bill."

He did, but nothing came of it. Early on, I learned that the man for whom I would later be working, Ronald Reagan, would not confront those below him who were quarreling and would not force the system to work, and thus he would often seem aloof and unengaged.

Meanwhile, in 1983, Bill Clark, among others, became very concerned that NATO's weak coalition governments in Western Europe were losing political support for counterdeployments of intermediate-range Pershing 2 and cruise missiles. These deployments were needed tactically to checkmate Soviet SS-20 missiles targeting Western Europe and politically to convince the Soviets to negotiate rather than try to blackmail our allies and excite the so-called peace movements in Europe. The support of every NATO country was needed in the counterdeployment decision because NATO operated on the principle of consensus.[2] A new campaign had to be launched to win public opinion and political support across Western Europe—a campaign to win the hearts and minds.

Clark believed I knew Europe and its politics. He was aware that, as the first chair of the Board for International Broadcasting, I had renegotiated the basing agreements for broadcast transmitters in Spain, Portugal, and Germany amid some prejudice owing to the U.S. radios' CIA origins. As head of CSIS, I had conducted public conferences and seminars in Europe that had involved American luminaries such as Henry Kissinger, Zbigniew Brzezinski, and James Schlesinger as well as many members of Congress. Clark convinced the president that I—not the traditional foreign service officer that the State Department was pushing—would be their best point man to manage missile deployment and help change attitudes in Europe. With that mission, I arrived in Brussels in the summer of 1983 as Reagan's ambassador to NATO.

As NATO ambassador, I had a still closer look at President Reagan when, on several occasions, I escorted Sec. Gen. Josef Luns and his successor, Sec. Gen. Lord Peter Carrington, to the Oval Office. Carrington's first visit demonstrated to me how this president was driven by his dreams, which often had vital meaning and reflected his drive for far-reaching change in rigid policy areas where others thought change was unfeasible.

On the way to Washington for his first visit, Lord Carrington had complained to me about an article written by Undersecretary of Defense Fred Iklé, published prominently in the prestigious quarterly *Foreign Affairs* and titled "Nuclear Strategy: Can There Be a Happy Ending?" This brainy, longtime RAND Corporation strategist answered the question with an emphatic "no." He questioned our deterrent strategy of nuclear escalation when we no longer had superiority or so-called escalation control. Iklé's critique of what amounted to nuclear theology etched in stone, the Mutual Assured Destruction (MAD) doctrine, must have seemed to Carrington like a Church of England vicar questioning the Holy Trinity. Faith in the deterrent was what was important, and if there was enough faith, it would work. Iklé's apostate alternative was a robust defense: the strategic defense initiative (SDI).

Once in the Oval Office, after we settled into our chairs and enjoyed an exchange of jokes, Carrington brought up the *Foreign Affairs* article with Reagan. After all, he said, "Iklé is a high-ranking defense official, not a college professor." Carrington then argued that SDI would destabilize NATO's sacred mutual assured destruction strategy.

I am sure that Reagan had never read Iklé's erudite article, but he had more than wet his feet in the subject of nuclear strategy long before becoming president. By 1977, Dick Allen, while at the Hoover Institution, had become the ex-governor's informal defense advisor. He persuaded Reagan to become a member of the newly formed Committee for the Present Danger, of which the venerable veteran of our initial Cold War strategy, Paul Nitze, was a leader.[3] As governor, Reagan had often met with the father of the hydrogen bomb, Edward Teller, who had himself become concerned about the unfeasibility of our nuclear strategy once we lost nuclear superiority and needed to deal with escalation control. Finally, in 1979, Reagan visited the North American Air Defense Command (NORAD), the massive command post underground in Cheyenne Mountain. He was appalled. Although the Soviets were building heavy SS-18 missiles, each with ten independently targeted warheads, we had no plans to build defenses.[4] It was as if Reagan had been preparing his response to the new secretary general of NATO for six years.

"Lord Carrington," said Reagan, with his hot button pressed, "the problem with that nuclear strategy is that it won't work in a crisis." He continued, "The strategy was viable when we had nuclear superiority, but it's dangerous now that we've lost it. We do not want mutual assured destruction but rather mutual assured security. That's the purpose of SDI."

Carrington was visibly shocked that Reagan was questioning NATO strategy. After all, he was talking to the leader of the alliance, the president of the United States. "But the Soviets take this as provocative, as do the NATO allies," protested Carrington. "The Soviets won't have it!"

"If we get the SDI technology," retorted Reagan in one of his inspired moments, "we'll give it to 'em."[5]

Carrington then heard the full Reagan dream of avoiding nuclear Armageddon, replacing past arms control strategies with mutual nuclear disarmament and perhaps ultimately eliminating the weapons altogether. On the latter score, I thought hawkish Secretary of Defense Caspar Weinberger was about to fall off his chair.

But Reagan was basically correct in his assertion that the MAD doctrine was now that mad. The way the NATO deterrent strategy was supposed to work was a nightmare. A NATO-wide war exercise was conducted every other year between "red" and "blue" forces, where the red forces (that is, the Warsaw Pact), which were forward deployed in East Germany, attacked. Within days, they cut through the Northern Army Group of ineffectively deployed Belgian, Dutch, and some German forces. Soviet operational maneuver groups then raced for the English Channel. This was very much like the blitzkrieg of May of 1940. This scenario, by the way, was not a highly fictional one but instead what NATO military authorities expected would happen as a result of realistic war games.

At that point in the exercise, the Supreme Allied Commander in Europe (SACEUR) requested the authority for a limited nuclear release from the NATO Council. However, the theory was that this was not "nuclear war fighting" but "political signaling," as it was conveniently termed in the soothing NATO parlance. The hypothesis was that this very limited first use of nuclear weapons would show the Kremlin our will to continue escalation.

We ambassadors in the NATO Council would approve the request and, with subsequent authorization from the heads of the two nuclear powers, the United States and the United Kingdom, SACEUR would execute the limited nuclear strikes. Next in the exercise, as U.S. ambassador, I would be informed by Washington that the Soviets had not responded to this "political signaling." SACEUR would request authorization for another, more severe strike. It was not "nuclear war fighting," it was explained again, but another "political signal," the ambassadors would reassuringly mumble. After the devastating volley, I would then boldly and joyously announce to the NATO Council that I had received word from Washington that the Soviets had accepted the signal of our determination. They were actually withdrawing their attacking forces.

Mischievously, I always wanted to announce instead, "The Soviets say that they received the political signal of our determination and they are responding with their own political signal. This, they say, is not war fighting, mind you, by a limited nuclear strike in the Boston area. Just a signal!" Had I done so, the secretary of state might have fired me as a brash ambassador. But President Reagan would not have fired me. I fully understood Reagan's motivation for taking on this issue of MAD. Indeed, in 1979, at a CSIS-sponsored Brussels conference, I had sat next to the master strategist Henry Kissinger when he crafted newspaper headlines throughout Europe with these comments: "Therefore I would say—what I might not say in office—that our European allies should not keep asking us to multiply strategic assurances that we cannot possibly mean or, if we do mean, we should not want to execute because if we do execute, we risk the destruction of civilization."[6] Kissinger and Reagan had it right.

Again I witnessed Reagan's character and charisma in the wake of the 1985 Geneva Summit. NATO heads of government assembled for the highest-level NATO Council meeting in Brussels to hear our president's overview of the summit. It was quite an experience for me to see sixteen heads of government with their respective foreign ministers, ambassadors, and military representatives in one place. But most importantly, there was our tall president. Stories were already circulating that at Geneva, Gorbachev, more than twenty years Reagan's junior, had been stunned by Reagan's vigor. This was displayed physically in their brisk walks together and mentally in their discussions.

In the huge NATO conference room at a U-shaped table for heads of government and foreign ministers, George Shultz sat to Reagan's right and, a bit too obviously, on the edge of his seat as the president spoke. Shultz was noticeably worried that the president might slip.

He need not have worried; the president's presentation was clear and exact, followed by a graceful and deft handling of questions. It could have been a grand movie setting for the leading man.

On the way out, one after another, numerous NATO ambassadors and indeed several prime ministers said to me things like "What a leader of our grand alliance!" Even French president Mitterand himself, who was often derisive of Reagan behind his back, spoke his praises.

At no other point during the Reagan presidency were events as well handled as at the Geneva Summit and the following NATO heads-of-government summit.

The following year, at the 1986 Reykjavik meeting, there was a very different summit that tested Reagan's mettle in a different way. This summit had been encouraged by Gorbachev as a "preliminary working meeting" prior to a major summit in the United States. While a bit mystified by Gorbachev's desire for such a meeting, Reagan was eager for another personal encounter with the Soviet leader on almost any basis. He now reveled in person-to-person diplomacy.

The White House was thus led into a summit with too little preparation. Fun-loving Kenneth Adelman, head of the Arms Control and Disarmament Agency (ACDA), later wrote that the president brushed aside the issue with a favorite story from his early career in Hollywood: During a recess in a negotiation while he was president of the Screen Actors Guild, Reagan had produced a negotiating breakthrough. It happened at a chance meeting with his management counterpart in the men's room over the urinals—something Adelman mischievously labeled "urinal diplomacy."[7] While funny, it is a telling story.

Gorbachev opened the Reykjavik meeting with what was quite the opposite of such casual diplomacy.[8] He had some very clear and in no way casual objectives. He had returned from the Geneva Summit bearing a new rapport with Reagan but little else concrete for his side. For financial and political reasons, he needed disarmament, but he also wanted Reagan to give up SDI. From the Geneva experience he knew Reagan's nuclear allergy, so at Reykjavik he prepared to offer appealing proposals and concessions.

When the Reykjavik meeting convened, Gorbachev immediately transformed it from a preliminary meeting to a blitzkrieg of papers and proposals targeting his unprepared opposite. He correctly declared that the proposals were bold and unorthodox, aimed to limit intermediate-range weapons, strategic arms, and missiles in space. Most stunning was his offer to cut strategic weapons by 50 percent and eliminate all intermediate weaponry in Europe. He even made a shocking major concession to Reagan's position by not requiring the elimination of British and French missiles. Amid much startling progress, the negotiators even worked their way to the elimination of all ground-based ballistic nuclear missiles. Reagan's dreams appeared to be coming true.

Gorbachev, baiting and seducing Reagan, thought he knew his man. Having dazzled and mellowed the president, Gorbachev played his ace: The Strategic Defense Initiative had to be confined to laboratory research.

Reagan was caught short. Sensing a trap, the president's demeanor suddenly switched. With tension rising in his voice, he announced, "I've said again and again that SDI isn't a bargaining chip. I've told you if we find out that SDI is practical and feasible, we'll make the information known to you and everyone else so that nuclear weapons can be made obsolete. Now, with all that we have accomplished here, you do this and throw in this roadblock, and everything is out the window."

Some haggling followed. Reagan closed his briefing book, rose, and—standing tall—angrily snapped, "This meeting is over. Let's go, George [Shultz], we're leaving." And he did.[9]

This time Gorbachev was shaken, but so were George Shultz and others in the U.S. delegation. Two thousand members of the press were hovering outside. From faraway NATO headquarters I watched a mini-press conference on CNN that displayed an upset, defensive George Shultz, without the stony composure that had gained him his nickname—Buddha. His demeanor reconfirmed that the conference had broken up in abject failure. Reagan was receiving the blame.

Lou Cannon, a *Washington Post* reporter, was there. He later described it to me: "Here was the scene: Most of the correspondents filed holding stories, then waited in a crowded room for hours to be briefed on the final events. Shultz was emotional, more so than I had ever seen him. Max Kampelman was in tears. We were given (mostly by Shultz) a vivid picture of a conference that had come to the brink of success, then collapsed. Added to that was the angry statement by Don Regan at the airport. I'm a frequent critic of media accounts (my own included), but the portrayal of Reykjavik as a failure was almost entirely the work of the Reagan administration."[10]

Then came a remarkable turnabout. The Reagan team huddled, recomposed itself, put its act together, and took a totally different and positive public approach. The new line was that our leader, Ronald Reagan, had stood tall and not sold us out. He had not fallen into a crafty trap or compromised his principles. Now the Reagan team had to propagate this new line publicly and politically. One might say that the team had finally caught up with their president.

Secretary Shultz flew from Iceland to Brussels to report to the hastily assembled NATO foreign ministers and ambassadors. When he walked down the steps of his huge air force plane, his tune was in contrast to his anguished press conference. He greeted me: "Unlike some previous secretaries of state and national security advisors, we've stood firm. We didn't compromise and appease. We didn't give up our interests."

Meanwhile a stubborn, reenergized President Reagan was flying back to talk to a joint session of Congress. His line would be the same: We had held our ground; we had not conceded SDI; we had experienced not defeat but victory.[11]

If one looks back on the history of the Cold War, this reasoning—that it was a victory—turned out to be correct. Nevertheless, despite the new White House spin and the truth of the matter, most of the news continued to dwell on the Reykjavik blowup, a new Cold War standoff, and the almost complete breakdown of negotiations. Very soon this situation was mudded up for the United States by the Iran-contra affair and investigations of the White House itself. As I flew to Washington from Brussels, what I understood was that, at this decisive point in the Cold War, everything depended on the Reagan presidency's regaining its strength and leadership. It depended upon Gorbachev's clear recognition and acceptance of that fact. The Reykjavik happening, however, only reinforced my appreciation of how stubborn Reagan could be when his basic beliefs were challenged, as they were on SDI.

CHAPTER 4

The Prime Minister

If, in the drama unfolding before me, President Reagan was the leading man, Chief of Staff Don Regan was the runner-up and, some even thought, his stand-in. Soon after the Iran-contra affair broke, Regan became a principal target for journalists, editorial writers, and especially congressional Republicans. The press had labeled him "the prime minister." Lou Cannon wrote in a *Washington Post* article, "numerous Republican officeholders think that Regan has become too big for his britches."[1] In December, the *Post* included many headlines that reflected the ever-increasing sentiments of those within the Beltway: "The Stormy Siege of Don Regan; Critics Are Out in Force against the Autocratic Chief of Staff" and "Top Aides Say Regan Should Quit."[2] Nancy Reagan and her friends were part of this drive, but they were not alone.

It was clear to everyone except Don Regan and some of his immediate staff that he was now a burden to the president. Yet, he dug in his heels. As he saw it, he was not going to be driven out of the White House for something he had not done, and he certainly had not known about the diversion; he was not the national security advisor. But the press remembered his heyday and his boasts about his total command of the White House, and, therefore, this would not appear to permit him to renounce responsibility for what had happened on his watch.

Added to this, he had clearly supported the arms-for-hostages initiative unlike Shultz and Weinberger. As for Nancy Reagan, she believed that Regan was trying to barricade the White House and shut out other advisers. She was terrified by the thought of the president's isolation. In December, 1986, she attempted a breakout. Behind Regan's back, she sneaked in two sets of outsiders to meet with the president. She had them escorted to the White House through a secret, underground tunnel from the Treasury Department for meetings in the presidential quarters. In the first set were the old Reagan staff hands from the first term, Stuart Spencer and Mike Deaver. They argued that Regan had to go. Deaver took the lead in the attack.

"This is difficult, but you're not the first president to face difficult decisions," Deaver said.

"I'll be goddamned if I'll throw somebody else out to save my own ass," Reagan responded.

"It's not your ass I'm talking about," said Deaver. "You stood up on the steps of the Capitol and took an oath to defend the Constitution and this office. You've got to think of the country first."

"I've always thought of the country," Reagan said, throwing his pen so hard it bounced off the carpet.[3]

In the wake of this unsuccessful meeting, Deaver, along with Nancy Reagan, organized a second meeting, this time of two "elders." One was the lifelong Republican, former Nixon secretary of state, and Eisenhower attorney general, William Rogers. The other was Democratic Washington power broker Bob Strauss, who never hesitated to operate with some enjoyment across party lines when he felt duty called. Needless to say, Don Regan later had a fit when he heard that the former chair of the Democratic Party and head of Carter's reelection effort had been brought into the living quarters by Nancy to advise this Republican president.

Bill Rogers was the esteemed, handsome lawyer for so many in the eastern establishment. He laid out the problem for the president but indicated that it was not major. I suppose he may have told the president what he told me a month later: "There would be no convictions, for no laws were violated." To Nancy Reagan's chagrin, Bill Rogers's comments did not move Reagan to consider removing Regan. I believe Rogers was resting his argument on the fact that the Boland Amendment cutting off aid to the contras contained no civil or criminal penalties, even if the law was violated.

In disappointment, Nancy Reagan turned to the highly political Texan Bob Strauss. The president was in deep trouble, he announced. He recounted to Reagan a story of the Lyndon Johnson administration. Strauss was called to the White House as part of a group of so-called wise men. The Vietnam War was not going well. Strauss knew Johnson did not want criticism, so Strauss fell in line and gave only what

Johnson wanted to hear. In a vintage remark, Strauss told Reagan that when he walked out of the White House he in fact had "felt like a common prostitute, a two-dollar whore."[4] Looking discreetly at the president, Strauss retorted that this night he was not going to walk out on that lawn feeling like a two-dollar prostitute again.

With that opener, Strauss pulled out from his pocket a list of what was wrong. He characterized Reagan's November press conference as a disaster "because you didn't have your facts right and looked bad and you got bad advice."[5] Strauss said the obvious: The problem was not what Reagan knew about the Iran-contra affair but what he did not know.

"Bob is just saying to you, Ronnie, that he thinks you're telling the truth as you see it and, number two, it's inaccurate," Nancy said. "And he's saying to you that that's the worst of all worlds. If you're telling the truth and know it isn't the truth that's bad enough. But when you tell what you believe is the truth and it's inaccurate, then you're really in trouble."[6]

Nancy then moved the conversation to what needed to be done: replacing the chief of staff. Bill Brock, Howard Baker, and Drew Lewis were three Strauss suggestions. Reagan listened, but despite all this talk, he was still unmoved and, indeed, sided with Bill Rogers. Rogers's soothing advice was that there was no big problem.[7]

With these December initiatives having failed, Nancy's replacement offensive was blunted, and Don Regan remained the powerful but besieged chief of staff. This was the perilous and awkward situation I confronted upon my early January arrival.

Who was this Don Regan, the one who was being called the millstone around the president's neck? Truly, he was a man of extraordinary ambition, accomplishments, and intellectual quickness. If he had never gone to the White House in a chief-of-staff job mismatch, he would have been much acclaimed for his service as secretary of the treasury. He came from a less than modest Irish Catholic background in South Boston. His father was a police officer and later a railroad security guard.[8] He had won a partial scholarship to Harvard, graduated fourth in John Kennedy's class, and then, in a patriotic move, volunteered for the U.S. Marine Corps' officer candidate school. He had nearly two years of combat duty as an artillery officer, rising to the rank of lieutenant colonel. He fought in World War II battles from

Guadalcanal to the Solomons, Guam, and Okinawa. He possessed the warrior spirit that the Marine Corps exemplified.

Handsome, dashing Colonel Regan had done well, and he knew it. He entered Merrill Lynch and aggressively worked his way to the top. Once there, he completely transformed the company from simply offering securities to providing a range of services: checking, real estate, credit cards, and consulting. Well before the Reagan election, I remember visiting Merrill Lynch for a private lunch with CEO Don because the company's foundation was a financial supporter of CSIS. While I was waiting in the small reception room, I saw a herd of men double-timing toward the CEO's office. With a half smile the receptionist apologized. The CEO had called a sudden meeting, she said, only a short one. I knew Don really had that place in jogging shape.[9]

Don Regan was no more involved in Reagan's presidential campaign than I. The transition advisory team came up with a ranking of candidates for key posts. Bill Casey suggested the first three: Bill Simon, Walter Wriston, and Don Regan. Simon demanded not only to be treasury secretary but also to be put in charge of all economic policy. This was rejected, and Simon, quite testy, withdrew. When Wriston balked at the financial disclosures required, Regan was the surprise choice for secretary of the treasury despite the fact that Ronald Reagan hardly knew him.

Once in the treasury position, Don Regan gave an impressive performance; by the end of the first term, Regan was proposing a far-reaching plan to simplify the entire tax code so that, as the president said in the 1984 State of the Union address, "all taxpayers, big and small, are treated more fairly."[10] This Regan initiative emerged to produce the celebrated Tax Reform Act of 1986.

By November, 1985, Chief of Staff James Baker was frustrated that he could not pursue other positions in the Reagan White House like that of national security advisor. He happily surprised Treasury Secretary Don Regan by proposing that they swap jobs. Nancy Reagan was on board before the proposition went to the president, who amazingly accepted the idea without any discussion. From this experience, the new chief of staff should have realized that he must maintain a strong relationship with the first lady, who perhaps had preordained the switch.

Under the new regime, the White House culture changed quickly. It was not just the entrance of a more autocratic and aloof chief of staff but also the exit of the team that had created the successful White House culture of the first Reagan administration: Ed Meese, by now attorney general; Jim Baker, a chief of staff examining the Congress and cultivating the media; Mike Deaver, with his own media and image savvy and very close liaison with the first lady; Ed Rollins, with his acute political skills; and David Gergen to spin the issues on background with the press.

Regan brought his team from Treasury. This group of loyal subordinates became known unfairly in the press as Regan's "mice"—Peter Wallison, David Chew, Al Kingon, Dennis Thomas, and Tom Dawson—just because Regan was soon perceived as so dominant. Regan added Pat Buchanan to fill the slot David Gergen once held. To put it mildly, Buchanan and Nancy Reagan were political opposites.[11] Contrary to their media nickname, this group was quite able.

Over the next several months, tensions between the first lady and the chief of staff increased, with one adverse happening after another. She had a cold fury after the Reykjavik Summit, when Regan was quoted as being in charge of the "shovel brigade" to clean up the president's disaster. When the Iran-contra mess and Reagan's disastrous press conference followed, Nancy Reagan concluded all the more that Don Regan himself had to be shoveled out.

CHAPTER 5

Covert Master Strategist

CIA head Casey would play an important but complicated and controversial role in the Iran-contra events. By the time I reported for duty in Washington, he was incapacitated from a seizure that had occurred at the agency headquarters. The cause was lymphoma, a form of cancer that had spread to the lining of the brain. A five-hour operation had ensued, but his survival was questionable, and the CIA deputy director, career officer Robert Gates, was made acting chief. Casey, the famed spymaster, had been struck down just before he was to testify a second time as Iran-contra criticism against him reached a crescendo. Now it was clear that he would take his Iran-contra secrets to the grave and not get dragged through humiliating inquiries and inquisitions. This was a true blessing for this indefatigable cold warrior.

William Joseph Casey Jr. had a remarkable career marked by high risk. A son of Irish Catholic immigrants and trained by the Jesuits at Fordham University, he had been an idealistic social worker but soon turned against the New Deal approaches. He next received a law degree from St. John's Law School in 1938.

Then came his first big break, made possible by an unusual individual, Leo Cherne, who would become Casey's lifelong partner of sorts. Of Russian Jewish descent, Cherne the entrepreneur had cofounded a research institute (later the Research Institute of America) to help businesses deal with the myriad tax problems created by the New Deal. Cherne met and hired Casey and soon found that he was a genius at synthesizing tax law and writing best-selling manuals explaining the federal tax code.

In a sense, these two were the odd couple. Cherne later described Casey at that time as very much a Long Island boy—tall, thin, stooped, carelessly dressed, poor public speaker, all belying Casey's deftness with the pen and furious drive. On the other hand, Cherne was dapper, with a finely chiseled face, appropriate for his later renowned skill as a sculptor, and possessing brilliant oratorical skills. He was also an idealist and later became one of the finest speakers in America. Together they prospered; Casey was soon turning out more and more extraordinarily popular tax handbooks and guides. When the war clouds gathered and mobilization began, new guides for businesses were needed, and Cherne and Casey prospered even more.

However, patriotic Casey was anxious for action against Nazi Germany, and he wanted to work for the most highly decorated World War I hero, Gen. "Wild Bill" Donovan, another Irish Catholic. In mid-1941, over bureaucratic opposition, Roosevelt boldly made Donovan head of our nascent civilian intelligence agency organized separately from the army and navy. A year later, the organization was named the Office of Strategic Services (OSS). As a navy lieutenant, Casey was detailed to London with General Donovan. "I was just a boy from Long Island," Casey later said. "But never had I been in personal contact with a man of Donovan's candle power. . . . We all glowed in his presence."[1]

Lieutenant Casey went ashore at Omaha Beach the day after the D-day landings; later he called it "the most exciting moment of my life."[2] By year's end, Casey was chief of the OSS secretariat in the European theater. Donovan wanted to penetrate the Third Reich with sabotage operations as well as espionage. Casey, now just thirty-one years old, was put in charge of the latter, and he argued for the "immediate penetration of a fighting Germany"—dropping teams of agents directly into the country as had been done in France.[3] He daringly did just this.

After the war, Casey returned to Leo Cherne's institute, made more money as his renowned tax and financial adviser, and then, in 1950, set up his own business.[4] Casey made a run for Congress, but it resulted in a smashing primary defeat. He latched on to the 1968 Nixon campaign but was disappointed by being awarded only an appointment in 1971 as chair of the Securities and Exchange Commission (SEC). The appointment of the conservative Casey was blasted in the liberal press and even *Business Week*.

Nevertheless, Casey was confirmed by the Senate and astounded his critics by becoming a reformer looking after the "little person," not big business. He accomplished this by making a highly talented thirty-nine-year-old, Stanley Sporkin, his watchdog in the Enforcement Division of the SEC. Later Casey became undersecretary of state for economic affairs.

Before then I knew Casey only slightly, but he sought me out for knowledge of the State Department, and our paths crossed regularly when we were both appointees, as noted earlier, to the congressionally initiated Commission on the Organization of the Government for the Conduct of Foreign Policy, chaired by Ambassador Robert Murphy.[5]

During commission proceedings, I had firsthand exposure to Casey's viewpoint, and he mine. We soon became good friends. However, we had serious differences on the intelligence subcommittee, which consisted of Bill Casey, Murphy, and me. My senior cofounder of CSIS, Adm. Arleigh Burke, had influenced my view on covert operations. Burke believed in clear accountability, second judgments, and benchmarks. His career low point involved the poorly executed Bay of Pigs operation, when extreme CIA secrecy and compartmentalization prevented the Joint Chiefs of Staff from fully auditing the soundness of plans as many changes were made.[6] I soon learned that Bill Casey's penchant for operational secrecy during the OSS days made his philosophy quite the opposite of Burke's, and this explains why Casey was so comfortable a decade later with his freewheeling protégé, Lt. Col. Oliver North.

In our most dramatic argument on the Intelligence Subcommittee, Casey said that placing covert personnel in any government agency should be allowed. I objected fiercely. I gave an example in my own backyard: an independent government agency, the Board for International Broadcasting, which I happened to chair. Placement of undercover agents in this once CIA-funded operation would directly violate the public law setting up that public board.[7]

Bill responded, "Come on, Dave, you should have been with us in the OSS days; after all, CIA set up these radios." My response was, "After all, in the congressional battle to preserve them, we nearly lost Radio Free Europe and Radio Liberty, and we're not going to jeopardize them again by breaking the public law that created their rebirth under the public board." In a somewhat heated exchange I held my ground. For me, the conversation was a shocker, and I believe that it stayed in the corner of Casey's mind when my name came up for key appointments. During his later career, I know he thought of those glorious days in OSS where means needed not be restrained in accomplishing great ends.

Actually, I merely was being realistic while Bill remained in a dreamlike world politically. During the period when the Murphy Commission was working on its final drafts, the agency was being investigated as a "rogue elephant," as one senator called it. Congressional investigations by both houses resulted from a front-page *New York Times* article by Seymour Hersh headlined "Huge C.I.A. Operation Reported in U.S. against Anti-War Forces" (December 22, 1974, pp. 1–2).

Hersh's new information was a product of the Watergate investigation that revealed the ugly fact that the break-in at the office of Daniel Ellsberg's psychiatrist (Ellsberg had exposed the Pentagon papers) had been aided by equipment and technical help from the CIA. The agency's outgoing director, James Schlesinger, was understandably alarmed that there might be other violations of the CIA charter, which bars involvement in domestic law enforcement and other activities of dubious legality. When Schlesinger ordered employees to report other cases to him, he was swamped. This produced what the agency labeled the surrender of the "family jewels." The stories ranged through all Cold War administrations but arose dramatically during Operation Chaos in the Johnson administration, which involved surveillance of antiwar activists. Some material was leaked, and this produced the Hersh story involving agents worldwide.

In 1975, the senate select committee chaired by Sen. Frank Church and a house select committee chaired first by Rep. Lucien Nedzi, a Democrat from Michigan, and later by Rep. Otis G. Pike of New York held extensive hearings that not only examined the CIA's domestic abuses (which for the most part were actually under presidential direction) but also exposed a range of worldwide covert operations. The investigations of overseas activities produced further leaks that led to the abrupt loss of intelligence sources. Most flagrant was a *Counterspy Magazine* article that published the names of covert agents worldwide. As a result, the CIA station chief in Greece was assassinated. This was a terrible time for the agency.

In 1974, even before these congressional committees were established, President Ford appointed his own commission under Vice Pres. Nelson Rockefeller to review intelligence operations in the

United States. A range of reforms emerged, but in his heart of hearts Bill Casey remained unreformed.[8] He was, however, correct in his view that much damage had been done to the security of CIA agents because of leaks from congressional committees.

The final draft of the Murphy Commission report reflects the conflict between Casey and me because it does not address that issue. Yet, it strongly notes that an essential test of intelligence is "to function in a manner which commands public confidence." It contains the following two paragraphs in the executive summary on covert action:

> *Covert Action.* Many dangers are associated with covert action. But we must live in the world we find, not the world we might wish. Our adversaries deny themselves no forms of action which might advance their interests or undercut ours. In many parts of the world a prohibition on our use of covert action would put the U.S. and those who rely on it at a dangerous disadvantage. Covert action should not be abandoned, but should be employed only where such action is clearly essential to vital U.S. purposes and then only after careful high level review.
>
> Present practices for review and approval of covert action are inadequate and should be strengthened. Covert actions should be authorized only after collective considerations of their benefits and risks by all available "40 Committee" members. In addition, covert action should be reported to the proposed Joint Committee of the Congress on National Security or to some other appropriate congressional committee.[9]

Along with the rest of us, Casey signed the commission report. When he became director of Central Intelligence, I wish he had framed the paragraph and hung it on his wall beside his revered photograph of "Wild Bill" Donovan. He could have avoided much grief and would have left a far more balanced legacy as director of Central Intelligence, which included many noble accomplishments. We would have been spared Iran-contra.

Despite such occasional disagreements between Casey and me, my wife, Carolyn, and I saw much of Bill and Sophia Casey at their French-style mansion on Massachusetts Avenue and on a trip on the

Queen Elizabeth II. One day Casey presented me with his manuscript on the battles of the American Revolution to be published in 1976, the bicentennial year. It was titled *Where and How the War Was Fought: An Armchair Tour of the American Revolution.*[10] He asked for my endorsement for the back cover of the book: "I consider it to be an indispensable guide for touring the Revolution." The book, in the tactical field, shows the kind of command of detail and simple exposition that had made the multifaceted Casey a multimillionaire in the tax and finance field. To Casey's disappointment, it did not sell as well as expected, but it was a hit with me.

For this analysis of Casey's emerging strategic approach to the Cold War, in retrospect Leo Cherne's blurb on the book cover was far more significant than mine: "This is not a George-Washington-slept-here excursion. It is as vital as Casey's insights on the intelligence and guerrilla warfare aspects of the American Revolution are new and fascinating." We had lost in Vietnam as the British had lost in America. Both wars were fought conventionally against opponents using guerrilla and revolutionary tactics. In the American Revolution, the French had been clever with covert aid and provided America with money, supplies, and ships but not manpower on the ground. The Russians had done the same with North Vietnam. Bill Casey later drew from these lessons the covert Cold War strategy, appropriately known later as the Reagan Doctrine, that he boldly employed in directing the agency.

In 1974, during the Ford administration, Casey's friend Leo Cherne was named chair of the President's Foreign Intelligence Advisory Board (PFIAB), succeeding Adm. George Anderson.[11] Cherne promptly persuaded the president to appoint Casey a member. Former PFIAB chair Admiral Anderson, who by then had had several mild strokes, nevertheless remained a board member. Anderson told me he could never understand my infatuation with Casey because at meetings he could never understand what Casey said.

It was no wonder that the admiral was mystified by Bill Casey's difficult articulation. One subordinate said the problem was that Casey's "brain was so far ahead of his mouth."[12] A speech coach once said, "Part of the reason he mumbled and spoke half-words was because he was speaking to his own mind. He wasn't thinking about the listener."[13] In any event, this frustrating trait was to play a role in the drama of Iran-contra.

Casey sized up the 1980 presidential election and became a leading financial supporter and fundraiser for Ronald Reagan. After the presidential candidate suffered a surprisingly early setback in Iowa, a decisive Nancy Reagan took the lead in having campaign manager John Sears fired and backed Ed Meese in the belief that Casey should be brought in. Nancy was right, and Casey helped turn things around. Following the smashing Reagan victory in November, Casey confided to Reagan's national security campaign advisor, Dick Allen, how much he wanted to become secretary of state.

"It's not going to happen," responded Allen openly, while thinking, "Bill Casey, you don't look like a secretary of state. You don't talk like a secretary of state. You only think like one."[14] In the latter part of December, President-elect Reagan phoned Casey to ask him to become director of Central Intelligence (DCI) with cabinet rank.

Casey was deeply disappointed about not obtaining the leadership of the State Department, but the DCI job was a more appropriate reward for this OSS veteran. In a sense, it was a later fulfillment of his heroic World War II career. Thus, in late January, 1981, William Casey took over from Adm. Stansfield Turner as the director of Central Intelligence. Casey's new deputy, replacing Frank Carlucci, was Adm. Bobby Ray Inman, who had risen remarkably to four stars through a naval career that emphasized intelligence and attaché work. Inman had also headed the National Security Agency, which sat on our opponents' communications worldwide. Inman, with his broad toothy smile, was a popular networker on Capitol Hill and had the articulation, suaveness, and bearing Casey lacked. In fact, the artful Inman was the candidate of Senate Intelligence Committee chair Barry Goldwater for the DCI job and was pretty much imposed on Casey as his number two by this powerful conservative Republican icon and others.

As already noted, in the Reagan presidential transition, I had been asked to take responsibility for what was called the national security cluster: State, Defense, CIA, international organizations, and so on. I had visited Turner and Carlucci individually for transition briefings. From talking to station chiefs around the world, I had found that morale was extremely low and the agency was shell shocked from the various mid-1970s' investigations. Director Turner had eliminated 820 positions in human intelligence—the covert operators. To make matters worse, Stan Turner, the intellectual admiral who had done so well at reforming and enriching the Naval War College as its president, turned out to be a poor communicator within the sprawling agency.[15] As the transition director, I learned from my investigations that the shaken intelligence agency had nowhere to go but up.[16]

Although Casey was director of Central Intelligence, he aspired to be shadow secretary of state and go on the offensive against Communism. In 1953, when President Eisenhower came to power, he considered the Cold War strategy of "roll back" but decided it was not practical and could be dangerous. Not so with Casey. As he conceptualized the Reagan Doctrine, he planned to challenge the American containment doctrine and the Brezhnev Doctrine, which emphasized the irreversibility of Communist geopolitical gains. Casey, soon convinced that government did not conduct much strategic thinking, especially at State, thought he could fill the vacuum.[17] If he could not have himself appointed secretary of state, he could be a self-appointed "master strategist," seize the intellectual high ground, and dictate America's Cold War strategy from his CIA headquarters in Langley, Virginia. For the master spy, this doctrine was a mixture of his OSS experiences, his lifelong study of Communist tactics, his enormous reading, and the lessons he had learned from the American Revolution. In the midst of all this, a restless Casey astonishingly continued to write his OSS memoir.

Casey's strategy involved covert U.S. support in pivotal areas of the Third World, an arc running from Afghanistan to Nicaragua, to roll back the Soviet tide.[18] He was particularly concerned that the Sandinista government of Nicaragua was becoming another Communist Cuba in our hemisphere. Therefore, he sought to increase aid and other support to the contras, the "freedom fighters." Cuba was also supporting the Salvadoran insurgents, who were dedicated to setting up a Communist government in El Salvador. Casey proceeded to implant a new activist strategy in this Central American battleground.

Indeed, Central America became one of Casey's passions. He directed Duane "Dewey" Clarridge, a colorful and aggressive station chief in Rome, to take charge of the Latin American division even though he did not speak Spanish. For Casey's money, what Dewey lacked in language and background, he made up for in aggressiveness. By year's end, Casey had Reagan's commitment for a major rebuilding of the CIA, especially the covert side, to implement a newly formulated aggressive strategy of dealing with the Soviets.

Real problems promptly developed on the operational level in Central America and on the congressional level on Capitol Hill. Gradually, the contra army under Casey's plan was becoming so large that it lost its covert character and took on an overt military function. Capitol Hill and White House Chief of Staff Jim Baker worried that another Vietnam was in the making. Furthermore, Casey's new man, Dewey Clarridge, called by some CIA employees "General Patton," had a style that put off the senate committee. To make matters worse, Casey's reluctant new congressional liaison, Clair George, was from the covert side of the CIA, unaccustomed to courting members of Congress, and could not smooth over Casey's Hill problems.

Casey was increasingly losing his patience with the oversight committees, and they in turn were irritated with his mumbling. In the House, the result was a secret session meeting of the full House where the chair of the House Permanent Select Committee on Intelligence, Ed Boland, charged that the committee had been misled on Casey's plan. They took it as a limited plan that blocked arms to Salvadoran rebels, whereas in reality the enlarged contra forces were working to overthrow the Sandinista government in Nicaragua. Boland called for an amendment cutting off military aid to the contras. The amendment was approved by the full House a few days later, but the Senate did not go along, and $24 million was finally approved for the contras. However, the congressional support was running out.

Despite Sen. Barry Goldwater's increasing dislike of Casey, it was Goldwater's leadership that had saved the administration's effort in the Senate. Perhaps it was understandable that a conservative anti-Communist like Bill Casey might be abrasive, impatient, and misleading with some of the Democratic liberals, especially in the House. But he did this in the Senate as well, not only to Intelligence Committee chair Goldwater, the founder of the conservative movement, but also to the vice-chair, Sen. Daniel Patrick Moynihan, who was pro-CIA and a Democratic neoconservative. He finally declared, "Casey was running a misinformation operation against our committee."[19]

Thus, a great tragedy was in the making because of Casey's ego, intellectual pride, and uneven conduct. On the other hand, this innovative director of Central Intelligence continued to make improvements within that agency, including its intelligence assessment process, and he revived covert operations. Outsiders may not have understood Casey, but those at the agency could. Casey's stock with the agency's personnel was high, and morale shot up. Levelheaded John McMahon, the top professional and now deputy director (who had succeeded Inman), had Casey awarded the Distinguished Intelligence Medal for "restoring the credibility of the agency and pumping life back into it."[20] This he had surely done in his tenure of contradictions.

During this period at NATO, Lord Peter Carrington replaced Joseph Luns as secretary general. The protocol was that I, the NATO ambassador, would escort Carrington back to Washington to meet with the president and other notables. I feared Carrington, like my father-in-law Admiral Anderson, would not understand Bill Casey, so in advance I phoned Casey's deputy, Robert Gates, a careerist and outstanding Soviet expert. Lord Carrington did not have the best hearing. I suggested that when we met with them, Casey might just introduce Gates with a few preliminary words and Gates could then—loudly—give the actual brief. Gates phoned back to say the director was happy with this arrangement and quite understood Carrington's hearing problem, which I am not sure really existed. To avoid driving to CIA headquarters at Langley, the two of them would meet us in the director's downtown office in the Old Executive Office Building (OEOB).

A few days later, we duly arrived in Casey's high-ceilinged, ornate Victorian office— number 345 at OEOB. As we entered, I commented to Carrington that, as chair of the Victoria and Albert Museum in London, he should feel at home. This quick-witted sixth baron could match Casey's illustrious history. As a young major and tank commander in World War II, he had won the military cross for gallantry; he had subsequently served as defense minister and a decade later as foreign minister.

Our meeting opened with some pleasantries. Then Casey announced that I had phoned Robert Gates and asked whether Bob could do the brief while he, the director, would give only a few words of introduction. We all nodded assent. With that, Casey proceeded to give an introduction that soon turned into an unbearable thirty-five minutes, while Carrington and I leaned across the table, hands cupped to ears, trying to pick up a bit of substance. When Casey finally announced that now Bob Gates would give the brief, I apologetically said, "Bill, I fear that we're out of time. It's been great to be with you. Peter and I must head for the Oval Office." Bowing and scraping, we made our departure.

On our way to the West Wing, the short Carrington hitched himself up to my 6 ft. 3 in. frame. I tilted my head as he mumbled in a deep voice, perhaps mimicking Casey a bit, "David, if Bill Casey, who holds your intelligence, rang up the president and said we're about to be attacked, would the president know the war's on?" "Absolutely not," I quipped. Carrington seemed lost in thought as we trudged toward the White House. And I was not going to add to his distress by telling him that the president was nearly deaf in one ear.

From what we could glean from his scrambled briefing, Casey had spoken of various issues and strategies of a rollback of Communism in the Caribbean, the Soviet leadership, Eastern Europe, especially Poland, where Casey was very interested in the pope's role, and, finally, the tormented Middle East. In the months ahead, it was the Middle East, not by choice but by necessity, where Bill Casey would be forced to focus. This is where he would become entangled in what became the Iran-contra scandal, which ultimately connected the arms trade in the Middle East with the contras in Latin America.

Casey also had his problems within the executive branch, arising in part from his conflict with the White House chief of staff, Jim Baker. Casey's White House allies had been Dick Allen and then Allen's successor, Bill Clark, along with UN ambassador Jeane Kirkpatrick. When a worn-out Clark moved to become secretary of interior, a White House caucus of Baker, Mike Deaver, and Dick Darman convinced Reagan that Baker should be the new national security adviser and Deaver should take over as chief of staff. Casey heard of the proposal and, accompanied by Clark, rushed to see Reagan to urge the appointment of Jeane Kirkpatrick as national security advisor.

This former Georgetown University professor was an authority on the Third World and a brilliant neoconservative political scientist. Kirkpatrick fitted Casey's strategies but had a balance Casey lacked. This was not the way Secretary of State George Shultz saw it, however, and when he got wind of the deal, he threatened to resign. In a compromise, Robert McFarlane was selected. He was Clark's deputy, a former State Department counselor, and NSC staff member during the Nixon administration. Later, in his memoirs, Reagan regretted this decision not to appoint Baker.[21]

Casey had two things against Baker: First, he labeled him a manipulator by leaks; second, he believed Baker would moderate the hard-line policy toward the Soviet Union. For Casey, the prime example of a leak was the story about more than fifteen hundred marines that had been sent to Beirut as peacekeepers. As deputy national security advisor, McFarlane—himself a former marine lieutenant colonel—had visited to survey the situation firsthand. Upon return, he arranged a secret meeting in the West Wing situation room to obtain President Reagan's approval for the exposed marines to have authority for calling air strikes.

Two days later, the story appeared on the front page of the *Washington Post*. In Casey's opinion, Baker was surely the guilty party. Without naming Baker as the one at fault, Casey, with the soon-to-depart Clark, persuaded Reagan to authorize the use of polygraphs in other parts of the executive branch just as in the CIA. I was with Secretary of State Shultz at a NATO meeting when he received the cable announcing this new lie-detector policy. Shultz shot back that he would agree to take the polygraph once and then resign. Ultimately Reagan backed Shultz.[22] That was a setback for Casey in what was developing into a full-blown Casey-Shultz power struggle. (I was worried about Shultz's frequent threats to resign.)

As for the marines, the joint chiefs and the secretary of defense wanted to pull them out, contrary to McFarlane's and Shultz's opinions. Early on the morning of October 23, 1983, a disguised terrorist truck was able to penetrate the marine headquarters building and detonate a bomb, killing 241 marines. By February, the marines were withdrawn, "redeployed to sea," as the president rephrased it. Nevertheless, the extended American tragedy of Lebanon that would ultimately precipitate the Iran-contra scandal was just beginning, and Bud McFarlane and Bill Casey were to play the lead.

The drama had begun in the spring of 1983, when George Shultz initiated a major diplomatic campaign to dissuade other countries from selling arms to Iran. As noted in the introduction to the book, this effort was labeled Operation Staunch. Upon my arrival at NATO, I was instructed by the State Department to become the lead spokesperson of this antiterrorist policy at plenary meetings of the North Atlantic Council. There was no better way to communicate to fifteen other allied nations simultaneously: The unequivocal message was "absolutely no dealings with terrorists," and that was directed toward all of the countries represented around the NATO table.

After the bombings of the marine barracks and, later, the U.S. Embassy in Beirut, it became clear that those responsible were Lebanese Shiites—Hezbollah terrorists financed by Iran. On January 18, 1984, Iran was placed on the State Department's public list of terrorist states.[23] Then the Shiites began a campaign of kidnapping Americans, and on March 16, they hit the jackpot by seizing CIA station chief William Buckley. Casey had personally picked Buckley for this sensitive role. The news shook Casey, a veteran spymaster. This was his own man who held a sacred bond to the agency Casey loved.

Three months later a videotape was passed to an American journalist in Beirut that, in turn, was secretly sent over to the State Department. In it, three kidnapped Americans, including an emaciated, tortured William Buckley, pleaded for the release of seventeen Muslim (Da'wa) terrorists held by Kuwait.[24] Casey took the tape to the White House for a tearful Ronald Reagan to see. It contained images of an abused, weakened, but courageous Buckley. In total contradiction to stated policy, Ronald Reagan was setting the emotional stage for the trade of arms for hostages. Reagan, like Jimmy Carter, seemed to be powerless in the face of Middle East hostage taking—a crippled giant, to use Nixon's phrase. Casey was distraught, and Reagan, too. Why should the strongest nation on earth tolerate such acts?

Now I must piece together the full mosaic that led to the contra part of the scandal. This drama involves Oliver North, the person who would connect the two distant fronts in an operation he referred to as a "neat idea." Oliver North, a charismatic and enterprising U.S. Marine Corps lieutenant colonel, became one of Bill Casey's favorites.

CHAPTER 6

The Nightingales Sing

An Annapolis graduate turned journalist, Robert Timberg wrote a fascinating book about five famous fellow Annapolis graduates and the impact of their Vietnam War experiences on their futures. In the Iran-contra saga, the three graduates of concern are Oliver North, Robert McFarlane, and John Poindexter; the other two graduates were prisoner-of-war hero and now senator, John McCain of Arizona, and novelist and former secretary of the navy, James Webb. Timberg chose the title *The Nightingale's Song* because the nightingale has a template in the brain that has to be programmed by a prior singer. Timberg implies that the prior singer—the programmer—for these Vietnam War–era Annapolis graduates was Ronald Reagan himself, whose song in the wake of the Vietnam defeat was to restore America's strength and win the Cold War by any means.[1]

Oliver North was the handsome son of an army colonel who won the Silver Star in World War II and then returned to the family milling business in Philmont, in the Hudson Valley of New York State. After entering the Marine Corps, Oliver North won an appointment to the U.S. Naval Academy. While a midshipman, he was in a bad car accident but went through a remarkable rehabilitation and became the middleweight boxing champion for the brigade. After graduation in 1968, he soon became a combat platoon leader in Vietnam and matched his father's record by receiving his own Silver Star. Later, after he left Vietnam, an incident occurred in the village of Son Thang, where one of his former marines was court-martialed for the murder of sixteen women and children. North thoughtfully paid his own way back to Vietnam to defend his men and, in a preview of his televised congressional performance more than two decades later, turned around the court with his stellar pleading.

In December of 1974, North had a near breakup with his wife, and a psychological breakdown landed him in the psychiatric ward at Bethesda Naval Hospital. He allegedly removed the evidence of that event from his personnel file.[2] Later, the aggressive young navy secretary, John Lehman, met North at a Naval War College affair and was deeply impressed. Lehman recommended North to his close friend, national security advisor Richard Allen, who took him on his staff and assigned him to Latin American affairs. Initially he had menial jobs, but, as a self-starter and a promoter, he soon gained influence and became known for relating how he met alone with the president.

His office was on the third floor in what became known in the OEOB as "spook alley," which ran from Bill Casey's corner office, down the hall past the President's Foreign Intelligence Advisory Board and the Intelligence Oversight Board, and past North's office, number 392. Casey increasingly came to know and admire the young, gung-ho, can-do marine. North wanted to get things done and could think outside of the box.

In the meantime, Casey had a new problem. A new version of the Boland Amendment came to vote in Congress, and this time it passed both houses in the wake of the fury over what congressional members termed the unauthorized CIA mining of the Nicaraguan harbor and charges that Casey had dissembled to the Senate Intelligence Committee. The amendment stipulated that no appropriated funds for the CIA or any other "department, agency, or entity of the United States involved in intelligence activities may be obligated or expended for the purpose or which would have the effect of supporting directly or indirectly military or paramilitary operations in Nicaragua by any nation, group, organization, or individual."

As befitted a clever tax attorney, Casey was adept at spotting loopholes. The NSC was not involved in intelligence activities—the prohibition of the amendment—and therefore it could be the coordinating body for the contra effort. The Intelligence Oversight Board's lawyer was willing to support this unique logic in order to support and save the contras. Casey saw North as the type to organize the other means. Casey went to the president and received his approval. Of course, North would not—could not—officially be working for Casey, which would then have constituted breaking the law. He would be working for the national security adviser, who at that time was Bud McFarlane. It was a "neat" arrangement to outfox the Congress.

At this point, Bud McFarlane had become a major player as national security adviser. He had grown up in Washington culture as a son of a Texas Democratic member of Congress. An uncle and his brother had graduated from the Naval Academy and had served the navy with distinction. McFarlane, a self-described runt, never made it at football or basketball but did become something of a gymnast. The Presbyterian faith touched him so deeply that he almost switched to the ministry, but his navy family talked him into staying the course at Annapolis, where he became a high-ranking midshipman, a "four-, striper," as it was called. But McFarlane wanted moral purpose in his life.[3] He failed the eye test for becoming a naval aviator, entered the Marine Corps, and married Jonda Riley, also of strong Presbyterian faith. In 1964, as a member of the Third Marine Division, he led the first battery to land in Vietnam, where he served two tours of duty.

McFarlane was chosen to serve as a White House fellow in 1971 and 1972, next door to Kissinger's office in the West Wing of the White House. The junior McFarlane later wrote that Kissinger was an "iconoclast, unapproachable, demanding, imperious."[4] McFarlane was in awe. From my association with the seventh floor of the State Department, I came to know Bud as I coordinated much of our interagency work for issues dealing with Capitol Hill. I knew him as a good guy, self-effacing, dogged, with a marvelous skill to mimic Henry Kissinger's German accent. Bud could practice this skill even more when he joined Kissinger's own staff in 1973; McFarlane notes that this was a year after the brilliant Kissinger-Nixon secret diplomacy led to the opening of China and the reordering of the world balance of power. As early as 1971, secret exchanges had begun. McFarlane later wrote admiringly in his memoirs about this diplomatic model: "Once again, had Congress known about these exchanges [the secret ones with China], there is no doubt it would have immediately curtailed or ended them. . . . Kissinger took a risk and clearly withheld information from the Congress. Yet, in so doing, he undeniably nurtured a relationship of profound importance to our security."[5]

During the Carter years, McFarlane went to work for Sen. John Tower on the Senate Armed Forces Committee staff. Thus, unlike Poindexter, North, or Casey, he had congressional experience, and, after all, his father had been a congressman.

In late December, 1981, as director of the national security group for the Reagan presidential transition, I had joined others to recommend that Bud McFarlane be offered the job of State Department counselor. I was in the transition room with my codirector, John Lehman, when Secretary of State Al Haig offered the position to Bud McFarlane, a job for which McFarlane had superb training.[6] Haig, who had served with McFarlane in the White House, called him "an old and trusted acquaintance." Later on, McFarlane frequently talked to me about his concern that Haig was becoming isolated from the White House. When Judge Bill Clark became national security adviser, Clark realized that he himself was still in a foreign policy learning stage and warmly took McFarlane as his deputy. Here McFarlane helped develop something of a conceptual framework for a Reagan foreign policy. McFarlane's credentials were expanded in July, 1983, when he also became special envoy to the Middle East. Then, with Clark's departure, McFarlane became national security adviser—everybody's second choice.

However, McFarlane, who was a self-effacing operations officer and coordinator, was unable to move the State and Defense Departments and the NSC into a unified effort. He became as frustrated as Clark. He had only limited rapport with the president, often did not speak up to his commander in chief, and, as Mike Deaver wrote, drifted into "Bud speak, the deep voice, the twenty dollar words, the stultifying monotone."[7]

McFarlane's power struggles with Regan became increasingly frequent, with Regan noting in front of Reagan that he, Regan, had become a lieutenant colonel in four years, whereas it had taken McFarlane twenty years. The comparison, of course, was unfair, for Regan's faster promotions were made possible by the magnitude of the World War II conflict. Outside of the White House, McFarlane increasingly received favorable press and won a reputation as a balanced and competent national security adviser, though not a brilliant one. His considerable successes include the Caribbean Basin Initiative, the Kissinger Commission on Central America, and the finely honed 1985 Geneva Summit. It was the Middle East and his misjudgment of people that were to do him in, plus his effort to comply with the president's statement, after the passage of the Boland Amendment, that the contras must be held together "body and soul."[8]

Unlike Casey and the counsel of the Intelligence Oversight Board, McFarlane believed that the Boland Amendment really did cover the NSC. He repeated Reagan's words about the contras having to be held together "body and soul" to zealot Ollie North and thus launched a dangerous effort. To North, this meant that anything goes—laws be damned. The nightingale had sung.

McFarlane was also preoccupied with Iran. He became involved with a colorful cigar-smoking scholar, dazzling writer, and relaxed operator named Michael Ledeen. A former young college professor in Rome and the first editor—and an able and imaginative one—of the CSIS's *Washington Quarterly*, Ledeen's specialty was European socialists who were anti-Communist, and he later became a consultant to both the State Department and the NSC on the subject. However, Ledeen portrayed himself to the Israelis as McFarlane's official representative, and he had meetings with David Kimche, director general of the Israeli foreign ministry.[9] Kimche theorized to Ledeen that there was a more "moderate" cabal in Iran, and this theory eventually evolved into the idea of hostages being released to show the clout of the "moderate" faction in Iran in return for arms being shipped from Israel and replaced by the United States. In a follow-up, Kimche visited McFarlane in July, 1985.

That July, Ledeen appeared again in McFarlane's office with new, very specific information. He had received a roundabout message from the Iranians suggesting the hostage-release deal as a sign of their bona fides if the United States would do the same with U.S. weapons transfers. This would signify to the Iranian military positive U.S. intentions toward the friendly Iranian faction. Ledeen said the Iranian side wanted one hundred state-of-the-art TOW antitank missiles. Ledeen then brought up the name of the principal Iranian contact in all this, a former member of the shah's secret police named Manucher Ghorbanifar, who represented himself as a key Iranian middleman. He was the one, by the way, who had convinced Kimche of the feasibility of the arms-for-hostages idea.

Ghorbanifar was supposedly involved with opposition leaders in Iran. An impressionable Ledeen, with no experience in the intelligence field, described Ghorbanifar as a "genius" and a mastermind of Iranian politics.[10] The CIA had a different view: Ghorbanifar was a criminal and a liar who could not pass a CIA polygraph test. Lacking caution or probity, McFarlane met with Reagan while the president was recuperating from prostate surgery at Bethesda Naval hospital and imprudently brought up the so-called opportunity to ship arms to support the moderate Iranian faction and thereby gain the release of the seven hostages.

Reagan wisely said, "We can't do it. . . . We don't have any firsthand experience with these people . . . but tell them again we do want to talk."[11] At a subsequent National Security Planning Group meeting at which, irresponsibly, no notes were taken, McFarlane, strongly backed by Bill Casey, pushed the arms idea against the opposition of the other principals. Although Casey's own CIA operatives knew that Ghorbanifar was a discredited character, Casey—the director of central intelligence—did not reveal this critical information.

This omission was disastrous and truly inexcusable, for the primary mission of the director is to fairly represent the intelligence community and its findings to the president and not twist or omit critical information to fit the director's personal views on U.S. policy. It is one thing for a freelancing, untrained Ledeen to be taken in by Ghorbanifar but quite another for the head of the CIA to permit the president to be so misled when Ghorbanifar had in fact been blacklisted from CIA contact. One CIA profile on Ghorbanifar as early as 1984 reads as follows: "He had a history of predicting events after they happened and was seen as a rumormonger of occasional usefulness. In addition, the information collected by him lacked sources and detail notwithstanding his exclusive interest in acquiring money."[12]

The CIA's only fluent Farsi-speaking expert on Iran, George Cave, not only thought Ghorbanifar was motivated "to make a lot of money" but also believed Ghorbanifar's Israeli sponsors had goals different from those of the United States in the Iran-Iraq War. The official U.S. policy was to see neither side win and dominate, whereas the Israelis, so close to the shah's Iran, wanted the Iranian revolutionary government on top and in a new relationship with Israel as it had been under the shah.[13]

The hostage issue played on Reagan's conscience until, tragically, he relented on his principled opposition. He gave in to McFarlane's idea. Soon thereafter, Kimche came to McFarlane with the clever idea that the Israelis ship the weapons and the Americans replace the shipped Israeli weapons. McFarlane liked it, as did Casey. Both soon tangled with Secretary of Defense Weinberger, who argued that the transfer of U.S. weapons to a recipient country, which would then transfer the weapons to a third country, had to be reported to Congress in accord with the Arms Export Control Act.

Casey disagreed. He argued that the CIA could do it as a covert action authorized by a "finding" in accordance with a provision (section 501) of the National Security Act. Casey always had a way around a problem, but he did not add that such a finding had to be reported to the Congress "in a timely fashion." Secretary of State Shultz expressed strong opposition and retorted that it sounded like trading arms for hostages. The president's diplomatic policeman, Mr. Operation Staunch himself, for once agreed with Weinberger. After all, he was declaring at NATO and elsewhere that no country should sell arms to countries, including Iran, which supported terrorism.

While McFarlane favored the initiative, he wanted the NSC to provide the president with all opinions related to the situation. This occurred at a White House meeting on August 6. First, McFarlane offered his update that included a report from David Kimche, his Israeli counterpart, citing Iranian sources (chiefly Ghorbanifar) that stated that political conditions in Iran were ripe for building opposition elements through the arms transfer. An inconclusive discussion followed in which the president failed to take a clear position. Shultz felt that after his "strong argument" against the initiative, the president was inclined to his (Shultz's) direction.[14]

According to McFarlane's account, later that same day Reagan called him to hear the Israeli proposal again. After discussion, Reagan announced, "Well, I have thought about it and I want to go ahead with it."[15] McFarlane further says that, later that day, in a secure telephone call after a discussion about issues related to Colonel Qaddafi of Libya, he related the president's decision on Iran to the dissenting Shultz and Weinberger.[16]

The die was cast for the Iran-contra embroilment. In the various liaison activities, Michael Ledeen continued his lone-ranger role, driven by his infatuation with Ghorbanifar, and—to make things much worse—Ollie North soon joined him. For McFarlane, the only positive note out of this episode was that the president himself had approved the deal and his secretaries of state and defense had been informed.

The initial arms transfer of 100 TOW missiles by Israel on behalf of the United States occurred on August 20, 1985. On September 14, an additional 408 missiles were shipped. Officials were disappointed when only one hostage was released. Then the Iranians demanded more sophisticated weapons. A second shipment in November, 1985, of 80 Hawk missiles followed. Once again, the president expected that all of the hostages would be released, but this did not happen. Clearly, the U.S. government was being bamboozled and blackmailed.

This fiasco was taking its toll on Bud McFarlane. At NATO head-quarters in November, 1985, following the Geneva Summit, as the presidential party arrived, I was shocked when I greeted a haggard Bud McFarlane. We had a triumph at Geneva, so I knew that, for Bud to be so unhappy, something had to be wrong personally. We had no time to talk. I now know that, first, he recognized that his Iranian policy was a failure and, second, that his conflicts with Don Regan had become overwhelming. Bud soon decided it was time to resign.

On December 4, as I went into a North Atlantic Council meeting, my ambassadorial colleagues began to congratulate me on becoming national security advisor. They had heard the BBC and CNN report this misinformation. However, within days, Vice Adm. John Poin-dexter, McFarlane's deputy, was named for the position. A spate of newspaper stories in the *Washington Post*, the *New York Times*, and others said McFarlane had lost struggles with Regan. As Lou Can-non and David Hoffman describe it, "Often the conflict concerned what senior officials referred to as 'process issues.' McFarlane . . . was annoyed by Regan's insistence that he be part of decisions on which he had little expertise, in McFarlane's view."[17] It also notes that McFarlane was irritated by small slights. For example, Regan insisted that he sit next to the president in meetings concerning for-eign affairs and pushed for the release of a photograph from a Geneva meeting in which he is seen leaning over the shoulders of Reagan and Gorbachev. The article goes on to state, "Officials said yesterday that the position is likely to be diminished further after McFarlane leaves because neither Regan, Shultz, nor Weinberger is anxious for a powerful policy-making competition in the White House."[18] Several articles note Regan's resentment of McFarlane's access to the president and his attempts to curtail it.

The *Washington Post* also said that McFarlane had become weary, much like Judge Clark had before him, "of trying to referee a series of disputes" between Shultz and Weinberger. The *Washington Post* and the *New York Times* both reported Poindexter and me as the leading candidates for the position along with Eagleburger and Kirkpatrick.[19]

By December 4, the principal staff and the president had settled on John Poindexter. In his biography on Reagan, Lou Cannon con-cludes that the president "may also have realized that the secrecy of the Iran initiative recommended staying within the inner NSC staff circle."[20]

Though Bud McFarlane had stepped out of office, he could not step out of the Iran-contra mess. A botched Israeli attempt to send Hawk missiles to Iran—the wrong ones were sent—led to a review of Iranian policy. This review ended with a decision to ask the just-resigned McFarlane, as former national security adviser, to go to London with Ollie North and the retired Maj. Gen. Richard Secord. They were to meet with Ghorbanifar and an Israeli official. McFarlane traveled to London but came out of the meeting believing that Ghorbanifar was untrustworthy and interested only in arms deals and their profits. Again learning the hard way, he concluded that the initiative should definitely be closed down. On the contrary, North emerged from the same meeting with renewed determination to try to open up a bold new initiative: have the Pentagon itself do the arms shipment.

There was, however, a silent witness to the London hotel meetings: British intelligence. Operatives had bugged the hotel suite, and the resultant recording shocked the few high-level UK officials who heard the highly restricted tape. English eyebrows must have twitched as they realized that Ronald Reagan, who had led a Tokyo summit of heads of government in May that condemned terrorist countries, seemed to be exporting arms to a major terrorist nation. One British commentator later wrote the following: "[T]he evidence seemed to those who did get it to be both incontrovertible and unbelievable. How could the Americans possibly be doing what they appeared to be doing? How could they behave in a way that was so contrary to everything they were saying?"[21]

The distressed and puzzled foreign office sent high-level emissaries to visit with the new national security adviser, John Poindexter. The admiral promptly dissembled to these representatives of our closest ally. Ironically, within two months, the U.S. government was asking the British government to use U.S. bases in Britain to make an air strike at the terrorist nation Libya while continuing to trade with terrorist nation Iran. Margaret Thatcher, with her affection and admiration for Ronald Reagan, was surely biting her lip. One wonders why she did not broach the subject directly with her friend Ronnie the way she later talked to President George H. W. Bush at the time of the Iraq aggression. Had she done so—or had Bud McFarlane's advice been followed and the operation closed down as of January, 1986—there would have been no Iran-contra scandal.

One cannot fully understand the great shock of the British eavesdroppers without moving our story to my perspective in 1985 and 1986 as NATO ambassador. So great were the various terrorist threats that I was allowed to drive about only if accompanied by two bodyguards in my armored car and three more in a chase car. In these years, terrorism in various forms struck all over NATO Europe. The U.S. NATO support center was bombed, as were the NATO pipeline and the North Atlantic Assembly headquarters. A three-star NATO French general was shot in Paris. Palestinian terrorists hijacked the *Achille Lauro*, an Italian cruise ship, and an elderly American, Leon Klinghoffer, was slain in his wheelchair and thrown overboard.

In line with Operation Staunch, Secretary of State Shultz continued to instruct me to scold the weaker allies at NATO meetings—allies like the Greeks, the French, and for a time the Belgians—for not being tougher on terrorists and permitting "pass throughs" and "safe havens" in their countries. In April, the last straw occurred for the U.S. government when a bomb exploded at the West Berlin discotheque La Belle. One American was killed, and fifty more were wounded. Our intelligence intercepts disclosed convincing evidence of Libyan involvement. On April 15, thirteen F-111 bombers based in the UK and twelve A-6 attack aircraft from the Sixth Fleet made a major eleven-minute strike on Libya. At the NATO council, some representatives criticized us for attacking another sovereign nation. I delivered a strong rebuttal that we would under no circumstance appease terrorism from any country or group, certainly would not trade with them, and expected our allies to follow suit.[22]

Back in Washington, Vice Adm. John Poindexter was assuming the role of national security advisor. This third Annapolis graduate of the nightingale saga, by far the most accomplished, was a self-contained, highly disciplined naval officer. He was not a loose cannon like Ollie North. He had stood first in his class at Annapolis and was a brigade commander. He received a graduate scholarship and used it to pursue a doctorate in nuclear physics. He was part of the navy's new Arleigh Burke Scholar Program designed to develop more promising leaders with a background in science and engineering. Admiral Burke became a role model for Poindexter, who aspired to be a chief of naval operations like Burke. One fellow officer quipped, "John says his prayers every night: Our Father, who art in Heaven, Arleigh be thy name."[23] Poindexter, however, lacked the shrewdness, warmth, sense of accountability, and outreach that had helped make Burke a beloved legend.

Poindexter held important assignments at sea and also became an assistant to three secretaries of the navy. Despite these political experiences, he never developed any sort of affinity or feel for the Congress or the political realities of Washington. When he replaced McFarlane as national security advisor, his reaction to the NSC battles with the Pentagon—especially with Weinberger—was simply to bypass the entire Defense Department chain of command.[24] Furthermore, he was at ease with Ollie North's maneuvers to bypass the State and Defense Departments. As for Congress, why not bypass it, too? He disliked politics and began to show a reclusive nature, with the door to his office usually shut.

All this seems astonishing for such a highly trained and patriotic three-star admiral. To make things worse, Poindexter did not have a deputy for five months, and North was able more than ever to carry on without close supervision. Despite all this, as NATO ambassador, I knew Admiral Poindexter favorably as deputy and then as the full national security advisor. In my few contacts, I found him easy to deal with and would never have imagined him secretly enabling out-of-bounds mischief.

Under John Poindexter, the Iranian initiative continued, and, indeed, contrary to the advice of the disillusioned, outgoing McFarlane, he pushed it into a new phase. The United States began to sell arms directly to Iran as Oliver North had proposed. Direct sales were made from the Defense Department through the CIA to Iran, and no systematic notes or records were maintained. Hence, no authoritative review or accounting existed of this super-secret, hip-pocket exercise. If Poindexter so admired "Arleigh be thy name" Burke, he should have had the same discussion I once had with the revered chief of naval operations as to the reasons behind the failure of the Bay of Pigs operation: too secretive, too compartmentalized, no accountability or review, no notes. Ironically, with Secretary of Defense Weinberger and his military assistant, Maj. Gen. Colin Powell, opposing the transfers, the Pentagon was now required to undertake the arms deliveries.

This new procedure for arms sales required an organization that North had set up with retired Maj. Gen. Richard Secord and a former Iranian businessman, Albert Hakim. The organization included Swiss bank accounts, and the ingenious North conspired with an Israeli, Amiram Nir, to divert some of the profits of the Iranian sales to the contras.[25] Poindexter was privy to this diversion operation. This is the illegal act of diversion that would have become the smoking gun if the president had been informed and had thus been a part of the decision. Quite plainly, it could have led to his impeachment.

As for Casey, what did he know? Later, under investigation, Casey denied that he knew about his protégé's operation, but Bob Woodward asserts that, on his deathbed, Casey signaled that he did know.[26] Leo Cherne told me it would have been almost impossible for Woodward to enter the secured ward of the hospital and bypass Casey's family to talk with Casey. To Cherne, it seemed unlikely that Woodward met with Casey alone in his hospital room. This is also the position taken by Casey's biographer, Joseph Persico.[27] North testified that Casey knew, and he supposed the president did, too. Of course, North was a congenital liar, and Casey was not around to defend himself.

The operation to return all of the hostages continued to fail, and yet the controversial Ghorbanifar remained in the middle of it. Then came the colossal folly: Ghorbanifar and North developed the idea of convening a high-level meeting with Iranian leaders, led by former national security advisor McFarlane. The idea was to cover issues beyond just the hostages. However, it turned out that more arms would be a part of the deal. On April 22, 1986, Poindexter approved this ill-fated plan for late May and gained the president's backing. In a huge lapse in judgment, McFarlane agreed to lead it because, as he said, he could not refuse the president.[28] When McFarlane's delegation arrived in Teheran, senior Iranian ministers did not meet with them, the hostages were not released, and a former national security adviser had made himself vulnerable to being taken hostage. The whole affair was incredible, and once again Ghorbanifar had grossly misled our government.

Yet the affair continued to grow. In October, Colonel North opened up a second channel to Iran, carrying a Reagan-inscribed Bible to the Iranians in exchange for a Koran. Then came the public bombshell. On November 2, 1986, a pro-Syrian magazine in Beirut broke the story of the McFarlane mission, and the next day the Iranian Majlis speaker, Hashemi Rafsanjani, publicly confirmed the story, which ran in the American press on November 5. Senate majority leader Bob Dole publicly proclaimed that the Reagan administration, contrary to policy, appeared to reward terrorists. Senate minority leader Robert Byrd called for an investigation. The White House stonewalled.

On November 13, Vice Admiral Poindexter had North and McFarlane begin to prepare a misleading chronology. Soon the Justice Department became concerned that laws had been violated. On November 19, Reagan had a disastrous press conference because records were so poor and North and McFarlane were preparing a misleading backup. Casey gave misleading testimony to Congress, at times including direct lies.

When Attorney General Meese started an informal investigation, North heard about it, took a cab to Michael Ledeen's house, where Ledeen and McFarlane were meeting, and brought McFarlane back to the White House. North told him that he was commencing a shredding operation before Meese could get his hands on incriminating papers.

While North's shredding was highly successful, Meese's investigators nevertheless discovered a smoking-gun memorandum dated April 4, 1986. The document revealed that millions of dollars of profits from the arms sales were being diverted through Swiss bank accounts to sustain the contras. Initial estimates ran from $10 to $30 million. The shocked attorney general recognized that, if it could be shown that the president had been in the loop, it could be grounds for impeachment. Meese hurried to the Oval Office to see the president and inform him of the startling memo. As Regan, who was in the Oval Office, describes the scene, "The President, in person, is a ruddy man, with bright red cheeks. He blanched when he heard Meese's words. The color drained from his face, leaving his skin pasty white."[29] Don Regan, former investment banker, naturally was stunned by this reference to the diversion of funds no less than the president.

This calamitous revelation and its implications appeared to finally break the octopus-like hold that the Iran-contra faction had on President Reagan. Indeed, the day after Meese's bombshell, Meese and Regan pushed for the resignations of Poindexter and North, and the president agreed. The Tower Board investigation was soon authorized, and Meese held a press conference to disclose the diversion and to request that a three-judge panel appoint an independent counsel.

One would assume that, with North and Poindexter fired, all Iran-contra initiatives had ceased. Amazingly, that was not the conclusion of the indomitable Bill Casey, who went on the offensive in the executive branch. He had written a confidential message to the president criticizing Shultz for failing to support Reagan's policies and calling for Shultz's replacement: "If we all stand together and speak out, I believe we can put this behind us quickly." He added, "You need a new pitcher! A leader instead of a bureaucrat." He suggested Jeane Kirkpatrick or Sen. Paul Laxalt "to give your foreign policy a new style and thrust and get the Carterite bureaucracy in State under control."[30]

Just before the disclosure, Reagan had grown angry at his secretary of state for being so publicly critical of the Iranian initiative. Immediately after the November 25 disclosure that linked that initiative with the illegal contra diversion, a disillusioned and shocked Reagan did a complete reversal in favor of Shultz. Reagan gave the secretary of state assurances that he (Schultz) would report directly to the president whenever he desired without the presence of the national security advisor. Furthermore, said Reagan, the State Department would henceforth control U.S. Iranian policy. A vindicated and re-empowered Shultz immediately announced his new authority to the press.

This turnabout did not stop an ever-determined but clearly physically ailing Casey. He in no way gave up. He even visited the contras—the "freedom fighters"—in Central America to buoy spirits, including his own. Israeli go-betweens were to continue to discuss hostages, and even the discredited Ghorbanifar was moving back into the act. CIA's George Cave, at Casey's direction, was offering assessments of new Iranian attitudes and continuing the CIA-Iran liaison even without Ollie North.

In an October meeting in Frankfurt with the Iranians, Cave had discussed a new nine-point program for U.S.-Iran collaboration. This involved Iranians pressing Kuwait for release of Da'wa terrorists from a Kuwait prison, which would supposedly help trigger the release of American hostages in Beirut. When this plan got back to Shultz, he was livid and again marched into the Oval Office to confront an even more shaken Ronald Reagan. George Shultz was later to write that the nine-point agenda was "a shocking document: dangerously amateurish and totally at odds with the rigorously stated policies of the United States of America." Noting that this effort was being pushed even after Poindexter and North had been fired, he concluded that "Casey, the street fighter, had been clearly driving this catastrophic effort."[31]

That very same day Bill Casey was rushed to the hospital, very ill, and Robert Gates became acting director of central intelligence. Obviously, Casey's illness predated his collapse and no doubt contributed to his loss of judgment in his final weeks and perhaps months.[32] Only with Casey's seizure did the Iranian initiative finally die. This would weigh heavily in favor of George Shultz's final judgment on the affair.

In December, as an innocent NATO ambassador in Brussels, I knew nothing about a nine-point agenda or a second channel to the Iranians until I had a long-distance phone conversation with House Foreign Affairs Committee chair Dante Fascell. It became clear to me that, at this dizzying point, few people trusted what came out of the White House. Thus, I sought information about the confusing Iran-contra affair from Congress instead.

CHAPTER 7

The Darkest Hour

On Saturday, January 3, 1987, I took up temporary residence at the University Club on Sixteenth Street, about four blocks from the White House. St. John's Episcopal Church, a yellow-colored building with white columns, the famous "church of the presidents," was just north of Lafayette Park between the club and the White House. Sunday morning, the longtime rector, John Harper, greeted me after the service and added that I had his prayers. "I need them, John." The president, of course, needed them more. On that cold day, I walked through the park around the equestrian statue of my fellow Tennessean, former president Andrew Jackson. At the base of the statue is etched, "The Union, it must be preserved." It was now the presidency of that Union that had to be preserved.

For my new role in furthering this preservation, I knew there was only one overarching principle: the mantra of that wise aide to presidents Bryce Harlow—"Trust is the coin of the realm." The restoration of trust was essential in restoring this presidency in the face of the tremendous mistrust that permeated Washington. I needed to build an operation that would restore trust within the White House, the departments, the Congress, the independent counsel, and, I hoped, the press. I especially needed to think back and draw on my earlier experiences working with the Hill.

January 5, 1987, was day one of my ninety-day mission to help restore the presidency. Things could hardly have been worse. On that day, the seventy-five-year-old president of the United States underwent prostate surgery for forty-five minutes. He would not be fully recuperated for six weeks.[1] As one key White House staff member later wrote, "the White House itself came nearly to a dead stop as a functioning institution."[2] The president's director of central intelligence was on his back at George Washington University Hospital following a five-hour lymphoma operation. By contrast, Mikhail Gorbachev was at the height of his glamour and power as a dynamic world leader.

Yet things did become worse. On Tuesday, January 6, 1987, the 100th Congress would be sworn in, and for the first time Reagan had to face a Democratic-controlled Senate and House; this was to be a totally new political experience for him. On January 6 and 7, Congress authorized, under their formal titles, both the Senate Select Committee on the Secret Military Assistance to Iran and the Nicaraguan Opposition and the corresponding House Select Committee to Investigate Covert Arms Transactions with Iran.

Fortunately, much of the Congress was still back home on recess until the third week in January—the time of the State of the Union address. I was grateful for even the smallest of blessings.

On January 5, I became the beneficiary of what I thought was my only tangible perk as a member of the cabinet. Even though the University Club was only a few blocks from 1600 Pennsylvania Avenue, the White House, as it did every day for the next ninety days, sent a Chrysler and an attentive chauffeur to fetch and return me at the end of the day.

On the early morning of my first day, as I passed the doorman on the way out of the University Club, he said with a broad smile—and to my surprise—that there was not only a car and driver but also a large greeting committee just beyond the front door. It was a hazy morning with some snow left on the ground.

As I stepped into the brisk morning air, I found that the committee consisted of dozens of cameras and reporters who commenced peppering me with questions. "How are you gonna deal with that all-powerful chief of staff, the prime minister? The first lady? Their feuds? What is the president's medical condition? When will Bill Casey resign? When will the Tower Board report be completed? When will the president meet with the board? Is he stalling? Is he running away from meeting with the board?"

Not wanting to offend the White House communications department again, I popped into the car, waving, smiling, and saying only that I looked forward to my first day at the White House.

My first day began with a meeting with Director of Administration Jonathan Miller. I needed a pass, credentials, office designation, and staff billets. With regard to my office location, I had known before I left Brussels that I had three choices: a small office available in the West Wing of the White House near the chief of staff and the national security advisor; a large suite on the fourth floor of the Old Executive Office Building (OEOB), just across from the White House; or a still larger suite in the New Executive Office Building, across Pennsylvania Avenue. The staff that I had begun to put together and other advisers strongly urged me to pick the White House West Wing office, for location reflected power, they said, and most of Washington would have agreed.

I went against their judgment for two reasons. First of all, I did not want to be cut off from my staff. While I would have a small staff, it was very important that it be coordinated as one powerful and effective team. Part of a general problem with the national security advisor has been that the advisor's offices are housed in the West Wing and are thus cut off from the larger staff. In that position, proximity to the president at cost to staff was necessary, but for mine, I was convinced that it would be a great mistake. Whatever power I had needed to come from effectiveness and not location. After all, I had the overriding advantage of being able to meet with the president alone.

The second reason was Don Regan. Isolated from my staff, I could have fueled the impression that I was being subsumed under the powerful chief of staff. I did not want him breathing down my neck every time I stepped into the hall. I needed distance and privacy. Therefore, I told Miller that I would take the Old Executive Office Building suite. Soon a *New York Times* writer characterized my location as relegation to Siberia.

When I departed Miller's office, I dropped by to see Deputy Assistant to the President Dennis Thomas, who had been exceedingly helpful to me in a range of areas. Then I went to see his boss, the chief of staff himself.

I was familiar with the history of White House chiefs of staff. President Eisenhower was the first to have one. The five-star general believed that "organization cannot make a genius out of an incompetent," but "disorganization can easily lead to disaster."[3] From my study of history, the skillful organizer of victory in Europe was also the best organizer of the growing White House staff of any president in the twentieth century. However, he could err in judgment about people: He placed former governor Sherman Adams in this position. Adams was extraordinarily efficient. He built tremendous power, controlled access to the president, and, after Eisenhower had his heart attack in 1955, developed as much prominence as Don Regan later did.[4] Adams's arrogance eventually alienated members of Congress, valuable campaign contributors, and political allies. These factors along with ethics charges resulted in Adams's departure from the White House and replacement by an opposite personality: the humble, retired Maj. Gen. Jerry Persons, who immediately opened up the White House to people and exposed the president to more diverse sources of information.[5]

Presidents Kennedy and Johnson did not have true chiefs of staff and often seemed to enjoy the more chaotic atmosphere they had learned on Capitol Hill. There was certainly a cost for such chaos. Nixon went back to the Eisenhower model with another dominant chief of staff, Robert Haldeman. A milder Jack Watson served Jimmy Carter. In the first Reagan administration, a troika reigned: Jim Baker, Ed Meese, and Mike Deaver. This resulted in an open White House and served to draw out the president into policy discussions. Then came Don Regan. Presidential scholar James Pfiffner notes in his study of chiefs of staff that a domineering approach to the job "is a likely prescription for disaster."[6] He was referring to Bush's chief of staff, John Sununu, as well as to Adams, Haldeman, and Don Regan.

Don Regan's office was located on the southwest corner of the West Wing and overlooked the south lawn, but it was certainly not the grand office he had occupied as chief executive officer of Merrill Lynch. However, it was strategically placed, with only a small staff office between it and the Oval Office.

If I were casting a movie and picked an individual to play the role of an imposing prime minister of another country, it would have been Don, with his handsome looks, standing next to an ever more good-looking president. One White House staff member describes Regan this way: "He favored light plaid business suits that seemed to enhance his ruddy Irish complexion, with French-cuff shirts and collars with heavy starch, highly polished black shoes and stylish ties that indicated that he kept up with the trends, which he did. Swept-back gray hair was the final touch . . . high cheek bones, a long, angular nose, and darting, mischievous eyes, always the eyes . . . he was elegant and strong."[7] That he was. Then there was charm. A member of Regan's staff had the job of producing a new joke that his chief could use with the president each morning to increase the charm.

With the chief of staff's warm greeting, the meeting started well. I detected no resentment because of my firmness over the phone from Brussels. After all, he had wanted me to be the NSC advisor and then the special counselor to the president, and we had traditionally had good chemistry. I saw no reason that such would not continue over the next three months. We began our discussions by reviewing the terms of my office and the way that it would operate. No issue arose there.

Then came the subject of my meetings with the president. He made it clear that it was my prerogative and authority to meet with the president whenever I felt it was necessary. Indeed, he said that it was important that I spend a great deal of time with the president so that Reagan would gain a better understanding of the complexity of the issues with which we were dealing. He felt I could build a good relationship with Reagan. He reiterated that I would be the one reporting directly to the president. The chief of staff was, in effect, in charge of the first track, the ongoing business of the White House; I was clearly in charge of the second track, dealing with the investigations. When we met with the president, I was the spokesman and responsible individual for my track, not Don Regan.[8]

I quickly caught the "we" that he explicitly added: When questioned, he said he meant that he would merely "sit in."

I responded gently but firmly.

"Don, you're the person who first came to me on this two-track approach. You're the person who said that I, Mr. Clean, had to come back and deal with the investigative side, the second track. You said it had to be independent of your track. Like it or not, justified or not, we both know that the press has made your role a point of contention. That's why I have been brought back. Every day the press is watching our every move. They watched me getting into my car this morning. The first time I have my meeting with President Reagan, if you're present, that's gonna be the story. The story is going to be that nothing has really changed. Your presence in the Oval Office would undermine the image of my independence."

"All right, David, we'll do it your way," he responded with a touch of irritation. "But we'll do it under the condition that you stick to your agenda. You don't get into my agenda. If you intend to get into my agenda in any meeting with the president, then you will ask to take me with you."

I liked Don's directness and replied, "Absolutely."

Then he stipulated another condition. "If in a meeting you ever intend to recommend to the president that I not be retained as chief of staff, I want to know about it in advance."

I replied, "Agreed." Nothing wrong with that.

I also emphasized to Don that I had elected to take the Old Executive Office Building location. I felt it would be much better for this three-month period to keep close to my staff. With that he seemed very happy, and I was, too.

I departed, pleased that Don Regan had respected another unwelcome position that I had taken. It helped that I liked Don Regan, even admired him, and somewhat pitied the position in which he now found himself.

That same morning, I met with Peter Wallison, the legal counsel to the president. I had known Peter to some extent when Nelson Rockefeller, through his foundation, set up a mammoth study on the future of the United States called the Commission on Critical Choices for Americans. Wallison, also working with Nancy McGinnis (who later became Nancy Kissinger), was involved in the coordination of this study. Peter was a person of charm, conscience, and ideals as well as legal competence. I came to realize that he stood out as a bit of pure gold during this dark period for the White House. He was concerned about the number of strange happenings but was unable to adequately exert his influence. He was clearly a part of Don Regan's team from Treasury, but I found out he was also my ally, which is to say that, if there was any conflict of interest between serving the president and his chief of staff, his loyalty was with the president.

What I did not know until much later was the heroic role that Wallison had played in the early stages of the Poindexter-North cover-up. At the time, Wallison was counsel to the president and was trying to determine what laws might have been violated in the arms shipments. Poindexter was blocking him from the facts. Wallison came to realize that the developing cover-up was not to protect the president but to protect Poindexter and North. There were blunders and irregularities, and they were drawing the president into supporting their falsification in his speech on November 13. Wallison had been the first in the White House to appreciate the depth of the emerging scandal. As the scandal worsened, he recommended that the president forswear executive privilege and that he also appoint an outside commission of inquiry. Wallison's recommendations were not taken seriously until the North diversion memo was discovered and Don Regan got behind them.[9]

In my meeting with Peter Wallison, he also introduced me to Jay Stevens, his deputy counsel, with whom I had already talked several times from Brussels. Wallison indicated that Stevens, along with his associate Peter McGrath, could spend much time in supporting our efforts.

I then marched across the parking lot of the West Wing into the OEOB, through its marble halls, past many mosaics, under high-molded ceilings, and by a brass-railed grand stairway to an elevator to my fourth-floor suites. Unfortunately, my office faced Seventeenth Street rather than the historic White House. Thus I embarked on a difficult job without a staff in place. Fortunately, the cavalry was on its way, disguised as Judge Charles Brower, Capt. Peter Soverall, and Elise Callaghan. Elise was my longtime assistant at CSIS, NATO, and the State Department; she maintained my Rolodex, could translate my writing, and could read my thoughts before I had them. Captain Soverall was Captain Competence of the U.S. Navy.

In this mix, Judge Charles Nelson Brower was the legal bulwark. A tall, imposing man whose dark, chalk-striped suits contrasted with his pale blond hair, he could deftly guide me—a nonlawyer—over the treacherous ground I trod. We had worked closely together in the early 1970s on matters such as the Okinawa reversion agreement with the Japanese and the 1972 Quadripartite Agreement in Berlin. Brower had a rare ability to take the measure of shifting political power and build a base of strength for us serving a delicate cause. A Harvard-trained, longtime partner at White and Case, he had recently been sitting in judgment on the dispersal of $6 billion of frozen Iranian assets at the Iran-U.S. Claims Tribunal in The Hague. I would be greatly reinforced by Judge Brower.

I hardly was seated at my desk when phones began to ring. Sen. Ted Stevens of Alaska, a key Republican on the Senate Appropriations Committee, expressed his deep concern but wanted to be helpful to me. Fortunately, I had worked closely with him as NATO ambassador, and he had been involved in CSIS meetings even when he first came to Congress. The next call was from Democratic congressman Sam Stratton, an influential Armed Services Committee member, with whom I had again dealt at NATO. We exchanged views and advice. I also talked with the politically savvy former member of Congress and defense secretary, Melvin Laird. I learned from him that he was one of those who suggested that I be brought to the White House. Former secretary of state and attorney general Bill Rogers phoned and this time with good advice: "Don't let yourself become a point of controversy." He felt this was at the heart of my success as assistant secretary of state working with the Congress in the difficult war years of the early 1970s. Then I spoke with Congressman Lee Hamilton of the House Investigating Committee. Ebullient attorney general Ed Meese was on the phone with a hearty welcome and his update. There were others as well.

The next day brought an array of phone conversations involving Senators Rudman, Inouye, and Mattingly and, the following day, Senators Warner, Roth, and Cohen. Bill Cohen said the president was making a big thing of the fact that he did not know what was going on. "This misses the point," Cohen added. "When you have an institutional mechanism in the State and Defense Departments and the Congress and cut them all out and relegate operations to the White House, the president must take responsibility. The president took responsibility for the marine deaths in Lebanon." I assured Bill I would emphasize his point to the president. I had a conversation with Congressman Henry Hyde about his newspaper quote that the president should now apologize to the nation. I said, "Let's hang on until we receive the Tower Board report and have the facts."[10]

As these conversations continued, an overall theme emerged. Members, whether Republican or Democrat, were telling me that they did not want to lose another president. They were concerned about leadership in the Cold War. Nonetheless, the president had to take responsibility—full responsibility—for what his administration had done, and he had to admit trying to trade arms for hostages.

After my second day on the job, I returned to my suite at the University Club and turned on the evening news. There on the screen was Oklahoma Democratic senator David Boren, the new chair of the Senate Select Committee on Intelligence. He vehemently charged that White House representatives had tried to censor the committee's document on the Iran-contra controversy. Sinister CIA personnel were even invading his committee quarters, he asserted. Congenial David Boren was widely respected in both parties and not known as a partisan. We had a new problem whether or not we needed it, and the next morning I made an appointment to call on him.

Also on day two, my just-arrived assistant, Elise Callaghan, received an intensely interesting call. The gentleman on the line introduced himself with some fanfare as Brendan Sullivan, the attorney for one Lt. Col. Oliver North. Elise did not know it, but he was by all odds one of the sharpest attorneys in Washington. Knowing that I had the president's ear, he asked her for a meeting with me alone. With considerable charm, he attempted to humor Elise by rambling on about their common Irish background. The Irish brogue thickened until she finally asserted, "You know, Mr. Sullivan, my husband is Irish. I am of English descent." Very well, he much liked the English, too.

Obviously, Sullivan hoped to persuade me to circumvent the president's legal counsel and staff and ask the president to pardon North. I agreed to meet with him accompanied only by Charles Brower, my deputy, and Alan Raul, the able associate counsel to the president who had been assigned to my staff. We met with him a few days later.

When we met, Sullivan spoke with passion. He characterized his presentation as his "opinion of how the matter could be resolved in the best interests of the President and concluded that of course his suggestions would also benefit his client."[11] Sullivan suggested that the president should grant a full pardon to Admiral Poindexter and Lieutenant Colonel North in order to facilitate their full disclosure of what they knew about the Iran-contra affair. He argued, first, that the congressional committees would move slowly, and, second, limited immunity would not work as a way to uncover the full story. Sullivan noted that North had received twenty thousand letters, only eight of which were critical of North. The public believed North to be a hero. Speaker Jim Wright himself had suggested a pardon. Such a pardon would be viewed differently from President Ford's controversial exoneration of former president Nixon because Nixon was perpetually viewed as a villain.

After his emotional plea, I thanked him for the presentation but emphasized that I did not have an investigative role. I explained why

I did not want to meet with anyone involved in the Iran-contra events or their representatives. I told Sullivan that this was the reason for my reluctance to have the meeting with him. In response, Sullivan emphasized that he was not making a formal request but only giving his opinion on how this matter could be resolved. I thanked Sullivan for his visit and his opinion.

North's extensive and now much-publicized claims about meeting alone with the president concerned us, but I did not mention this to Sullivan. We therefore did some careful research on this issue and found that he had met with the president nineteen times, and four of these meetings involved hostages. But North had never met the president with fewer than six people present. He had never met with the president alone. He was never at Camp David with the president as he had claimed. The president spoke to him only once over the telephone, when he was fired on November 25, 1986.[12] On balance, this episode cast a deep shadow on the veracity of Ollie North but left me convinced that if I ever got into trouble, I wanted Brendan Sullivan as my lawyer.

On day three at the White House, I delved into the Boren controversy.

"What were those agents doing in the committee staff room?" I questioned the CIA. I learned that in the previous Republican-controlled Senate, Sen. David Durenberger had chaired the Intelligence Committee, which had completed an examination and preliminary report on the Iran-contra affair.[13] Obviously, it was done in haste, and there was agreement only to declassify and publish items such as a factual chronology, which, as I had found out, was pretty hard to come by. They had the best chronology I had seen, and I was delighted to see others putting their credibility on the line as to what was correct in view of the previous, fabricated White House chronology. The new controversy with the executive branch, however, came about not over this issue but as a result of the declassification process.

The true circumstances, however, were different from Senator Boren's perception of his strange and sudden encounter with shadowy CIA agents in his committee office. Durenberger's chief of staff had asked the White House counsel to put together an interagency team for the purpose of clearance. It was this group that had entered the committee offices to carry out the requested clearance. When the new chairman passed through the area and encountered such executive-branch representatives, he apparently took them to be spies, poring over their reports. This drove the good-natured senator to unaccustomed anger and to storm the evening network news programs.

Judge Brower had just arrived in Washington, so on January 8 we went to Capitol Hill for a chat with the Oklahoma senator. After some helpful banter about several good mutual Oklahoma friends, I moved to my rather detailed explanation of what had transpired and apologized for it having caused all this trouble. The review of documents, I emphasized, was intended to protect sensitive sources and methods essential to our foreign intelligence activities. There was no intention to remove material that would be embarrassing to the administration or have legal implications for investigators. The agents had to thoroughly examine these materials and had been invited to do so by the previous chair. Boren not only listened closely and fully understood. He also allowed with a smile that it would have been very nice if all this had been explained to the new chair in advance. I gave an agreeable nod; indeed, he was right. We then had a discussion of the mutual damage that was being done by the day-by-day NBC leaks of the draft report of the previous committee.

Some weeks later, I was happy to read Senator Boren's inspiring article in the *Washington Post* about the need for bipartisanship in executive-legislative relations. I hoped our visit helped inspire that op-ed. In any event, Boren became a staunch ally in our efforts to keep our process nonpolitical, fair, and objective.[14]

Every Democrat with whom I talked in these early days, including Boren, continued to ask my view of the condition of the Atlantic Alliance and the possible damage of this new scandal to our leadership of that alliance. It was helpful, indeed, that for the time being I was double hatted and still greeted as "Mr. Ambassador." Time and again, members of Congress informed me of their concern about another president being suddenly eliminated, like Richard Nixon, and what that would do to our world posture at this critical stage of the Cold War. The bipartisan support was impressive and continued through my three-month tenure. I recalled, however, that this bipartisan support was totally conditioned on the new two-track system and the integrity of the president's promised open investigative process.

It is difficult for anyone who has not been through our experience to understand the difficulties of setting up a new operation in the White House. One would expect unlimited resources, but exactly the opposite is true. The White House has a very limited budget, and new requirements are not budgeted in advance. Part of the way out of this for any new White House operation is to temporarily borrow people from other agencies. This process can work, but it takes time. We did not have time. We were counting the days.

The White House administrative office had been told that I would have a team of five people, so anything beyond that was subject to further clearances by the chief of staff. Of course, this was laughable. There was no way that five people could coordinate the general counsels of all departments and agencies, the collection and processing of thousands of documents to go to congressional committees of jurisdiction, to the Tower Board, and to the independent counsel. The latter office, I learned, had a staff of fifteen to twenty aggressive assistant prosecutors and twenty FBI agents.[15] As the early days passed, my small staff felt besieged, fenced in, and increasingly suspicious of Don Regan for possibly plotting to keep us small and inconsequential. I tried to maintain an easygoing attitude to avoid early confrontations but brought steady pressure to expand the staff.[16]

Slowly my staff began to shape up. In addition to Brower, Callaghan, and Soverall, we borrowed Razvigor Bazala from the U.S. Information Agency (USIA); Aileen Giglio and Kathleen Fitzpatrick from the State Department; Lynn Withey for congressional relations; Linda Green from the intelligence community; Judith Hydes from the Arms Control and Disarmament Agency (ACDA); Deborah Curtiss from the Department of Defense; and Dennis Kloske, a young deputy undersecretary of defense and Rhodes scholar who had previously served with me at NATO and CSIS. Able Dean McGrath from Peter Wallison's office was freed up full time. A lively, humorous foreign service officer and, indeed, a class act, Roman Popadiuk, was assigned as our liaison to Larry Speakes, the White House day-to-day press spokesperson;[17] and the already-mentioned Alan Raul from the White House counsel's office joined our staff full time. The joke was that Raul seemed to work all throughout the night as well as the day, and his eyes often showed it. All of my staff members, however, were hardworking and quite agile and possessed a sense of mission. I was lucky. What we lacked in numbers, we had in quality.

CHAPTER 8

The President Himself

Throughout my public career, I had dealt with the media, but never before had I been the personal object of massive attention by networks and journalists. I had had a slight taste seventeen years earlier, the day after I became assistant secretary of state for congressional relations. Minority leader Hugh Scott phoned to say that he had a letter to the secretary of state, signed by most of the Senate, about war planes for Israel.

"Could you come to the State Department lobby for a personal meeting, David? I haven't really congratulated you on your new job." I was complimented. When we met in the lobby of many flags and a huge globe, I found myself surrounded by press cameras and reporters whom Scott had alerted. Not I but he was the one being congratulated, with publicity to his constituency that painted him as a hero for Israel. Thus, I learned that the press was a major, perhaps *the* major, part of the political power game in Washington. Even back in prehistoric 1970, Douglas Cater had christened it the fourth branch of government.

I was nevertheless surprised by the dominance of the press when I attended the first 8 A.M. staff meeting in the Roosevelt Room in the White House West Wing. When first notified of the regular morning meeting, I questioned myself as to whether I should attend since it would give the impression I was a part of the White House, where Don was the "chief," the chief of staff. But I soon realized there was no other way either my staff or I would know what was happening elsewhere in the White House. So I showed up. Handsome Don Regan sat at one end of the long conference table. Near him hung a dramatic equestrian portrait of roughrider Roosevelt over the carved wooden mantel, and on an adjoining wall hung a portrait of Roosevelt's cousin

Franklin. At the opposite end sat short and wiry national security advisor Frank Carlucci. Staff were along the sides in no particular order. I slipped in, conscious of my peculiar and unorthodox position in the White House. The chief of staff began the meeting by calling on Larry Speakes, the press spokesperson, who reported on the overnight breaking news on TV and in the print media as it affected the White House. White House events coming up during the day were then analyzed with relation to the media. I came to realize that the media were setting the White House agenda for much of that day. We were being reactive to the media even before the events occurred. For that matter, governing had become increasingly reactive to television imagery and commentary, and shaping the agenda was becoming far more difficult.

I was even more surprised by press demands when first attending the noon White House press briefing. After the press spokesperson's update, Peter Wallison, legal counsel to the president, gave an account of the Iranian episode. It was in effect a special feature, fresh meat, it seemed to me, for the lions in the den. It was not what he knew, but what he did not know: He attempted to respond to every new allegation from leaks on the Iran-contra scandal.

As already noted in the Boren incident, the Senate Select Intelligence Committee had a helpful unclassified chronology; it also had the unreleased classified report, over which the committee was split. However, the entire report had been leaked to the press, and it was dribbled out night by night on the NBC evening news. In 1986, viewers learned that there were repeated warnings that the U.S. initiative toward Iran had "gone wrong" and that the CIA had major misgivings about a key Iranian intermediary, the discredited arms dealer Manucher Ghorbanifar. Reagan's aides had overlooked such warnings, it was announced, and this was big news. The report also faulted CIA director Casey for his testimony before that committee on November 21, 1986, just several days before the public announcement that the Iranian arms sales funds might have been diverted to the contras. Casey's prepared testimony, the committee staff wrote, "contains several misleading statements and omitted certain significant points." This made bigger news, yet the committee noted that Casey did not mention the diversion of funds. He had certainly been aware of the diversion for more than a month—if he did not know all along.

The report also cited a range of inaccurate public statements including Reagan's November press conference. It added that several of Reagan's own 1981 guidelines for handling covert operations were violated. One investigator commented to the *Washington Post* that the Senate committee's Iran-contra history "showed the characteristics of Mark Twain's *Innocents Abroad* in the leading U.S. actors."[1] Much later, on January 19, 1987, the *New York Times* carried twenty-three pages of the staff conclusions. The newspapers and networks overflowed with harrowing Iran-contra tales, all the more juicy because they were leaked in small, dramatic bits.

Thus, new issues emerging each day would produce a barrage of questions at the next noon press conference. The White House spokespeople would bravely stand before the podium, attempting to respond. This was all a prescription for disaster. No one in the White House had accurate answers, and it was better to say so and simply shut up.

Using my newfound authority, I abruptly terminated this noon circus that the press so adored. Publicly, I stressed that we had two newly constructed investigating committees on Capitol Hill, the two intelligence committees, the Tower Board, and finally the independent counsel. Our role was to aid these committees and the board. They, not we, could make the best judgments based on my office's dissemination of all relevant documents. We were no longer going to respond piecemeal in ways that would later produce contradictions and destroy more credibility. The cancellation of the noon press conference did not initially increase my popularity with the press corps, which loved its daily red-meat feeding.

Luckily, my press officer, Roman Popadiuk, had good judgment, marvelous situation humor, and great expertise on the Iran-contra affair. In talking with him, I realized that in calling off the press it was very important to set up some kind of alternative press activity. We started regular one-on-one, in-depth meetings with select members of the media. We pointed to the fact that Congress was increasingly accepting the credibility of our efforts. Reporters were urged to verify what we were saying with members of Congress.

Over the coming weeks, therefore, a number of positive stories on our operation emerged. Steven Roberts, in a profile in the *New York Times*, describes the delicacy of the job: "Mr. Abshire has been placed in a tricky position. While his mandate is to get all the facts out, he is working for an administration that has a deep interest in its own survival. What if his investigation turns up a 'smoking gun,' a document that could severely damage the administration he is serving?" Roberts wrote, "The 60-year-old diplomat and academician said he had learned the lesson of the Nixon years and would turn over the evidence . . . and let the chips fall where they may." He also quoted me quite correctly as saying, "I did not request the job."[2]

In another article, which appeared in the *National Journal* on January 24, 1987, titled "The Diplomat in the Trenches," the authors wrote the following: "[By choosing Abshire,] Reagan is playing a desperately needed Congressional card. The president side-stepped Capitol Hill in his dealings with Iran, and Abshire's experience and contacts, he was congressional liaison in the State Department during the Nixon administration, lend credibility where it is most needed. In a recent interview, Abshire said a strong presidency ultimately . . . depends on good Congressional relations."[3] The article goes on to say, "Abshire could help the White House with the press. Because he has nothing to hide, this personable, almost affable veteran of the ways of Washington is a natural to summon groups of reporters to his office to explain how the president is getting all the facts to Congress and to the independent counsel. If favorable news stories result from these sessions, Abshire will have gone a long way towards creating the perception that the crisis is being dealt with adequately by Reagan."[4]

Despite these positive developments, it is hard to imagine the massive number of Iran-contra newspaper stories that soared around the White House and the Congress, often from unannounced sources. From the beginning of November to the end of January, Peter Wallison counted 555 such stories in the *Washington Post* and 509 in the *New York Times* alone. These numbers were only a small slice of the journal articles, editorials, commentaries, and line media coverage nationwide.[5]

Among some of the more rambunctious press members were those who attempted to create misunderstandings. At one point, a columnist wrote that we were furnishing too many documents to Capitol Hill and that some of the Republicans were concerned that we were too forthcoming. To one of them I quipped, "You won't be satisfied until there is another obstruction of justice as occurred in the Watergate."

For me, it was day seven, January 12, 1987, when a recuperating president Reagan returned from the hospital to the White House. The doctor allowed him to leave the second-floor family quarters to be in the West Wing Oval Office for only one and a half hours in the morning and then, after a rest, another one and a half hours in the afternoon. I had twenty minutes, and at 3:00 P.M. I was ushered into the historic office by the president's secretary, Kathy Osborne, after Jim Kuhn, the president's personal assistant, and Fred Ryan, his devoted scheduler, had greeted me.[6]

When a first-time visitor enters the West Wing and goes beyond the reception area with its magnificent paintings and then moves down a narrow hall with low ceilings past some cramped rooms, the visitor may feel disappointed. But then suddenly the door to the Oval Office opens into the beautiful curved room with large regal windows behind the presidential desk. As I entered, a bright afternoon sun shown across the well-kept lawns. I was always in awe of this magnificent room.

It deserved awe. Dating back to 1909, the Oval Office is a place filled with history and imposing architecture: the attractive pediments over the doors, the shell canopies above floor-length windows, the presidential seal in low relief set in the ceiling, over the fireplace the magnificent reproduction of Charles Wilson Peale's portrait of George Washington in his Continental Army uniform, the east wall mahogany clock ticking history, near it Remington's bronze "Bronco Buster," the bust of Benjamin Franklin, and the huge gold seal repeated in the wool carpet.[7] I had seen the Oval Office many times before, but I had never been alone with a president, except briefly with President Nixon, when I was leaving his first administration as assistant secretary of state.

My appreciation of the setting changed to shock. Behind the desk sat a frail, pale, and thin Ronald Reagan, dreadfully different from the vigorous, commanding presence I had last seen at the NATO heads-of-government summit. Certainly this fatigued condition reflected his recent operation, but I wondered how much it also reflected this normally incredible optimist suddenly being placed on the defensive with his public and with himself. The president stood to extend a welcoming hand as I seated myself at the chair to the side of the desk. At the beginning of any Oval Office meeting, the White House photographer snaps pictures for the historical record. When the photo from this meeting was developed and printed, Reagan looked so weak that the chief of staff and the first lady ordered that it not be publicly released.

Quite worried, I settled into my chair as we focused on one another. There was a bit of banter and light talk, and then I said, "Mr. President, my doctorate is in history." It was a little repeat of the Brussels telephone conversation the day after Christmas. "History's always been my great interest. As I said over the phone when you called me in Brussels, I want to see the strength of this presidency fully restored. When you took over, the presidency had been at a low point. It was stalemated, lacking effective leadership. You know, President Carter's counsel, Lloyd Cutler, wrote an op-ed piece that we might have to revert to a parliamentary form of government. Cutler believed strong presidential leadership was no longer possible. You've shown that a president can lead in Washington and lead the nation. You have demonstrated how an American president could lead the great alliance in this critical stage of the Cold War." He responded in a soft voice but with genuine appreciation and warmth.

In the back of my mind, I knew that the initial problem was the president's unwillingness simply to say that, while he had not intended it, it *was* arms for hostages. So I decided to join the issue and not repeat Bob Strauss's mistake with Lyndon Johnson. Regardless of the president's health, I felt I had to move in on this central and controversial issue. In retrospect, maybe I rushed in too soon. But I was determined that these sessions not turn into small talk. I started by telling him of my conversations with members of Congress and how they kept saying the president must take responsibility. How could he do so if he kept concluding he had not traded arms for hostages?

"Mr. President," I said, "we have a severe perception problem. Please look at these polls, sir." I placed a clipping in front of him on the desk. "Sixty to 65 percent of the American public believes that there's a cover-up in the Iran-contra affair. They believe we've traded arms for hostages. I know that you don't believe we traded arms for hostages. But the majority of the American public believes that. We must recognize that this perception problem is a major one. I think your honesty is attested to when you phoned me in Brussels to say 'get all of the facts out.'"[8]

In his gentle but firm way, President Reagan responded: "The press has been exaggerating these problems. Certainly there've been many mistakes in carrying out our policy. But the original goals in dealing with Iran were justified. We're trying to make a breakthrough. I don't believe that we were trading arms for hostages. We're dealing with one group in Iran. They were dealing with another group in Beirut." He said with his voice rising, "It was not government to government."

"But, Mr. President," I responded respectfully, "the American public doesn't see it that way. This wasn't your intention, but it's the way it ended up. If we could clear the air on this issue and say that, while it wasn't your intention, it ended as trading arms for hostages, we wouldn't have such a credibility problem. We could put this thing behind us." I remember him leaning forward in his chair. He asserted with passion, "Dave, I don't care if I'm the only person in America that does not believe it—I *don't* believe it was arms for hostages." I'm sure that I stared back in amazement.

If this exchange showed his naïveté, it also confirmed to me Ronald Reagan's basic honesty even when it was clearly to his disadvantage. Even if he felt that political expedience was the only reason to give up his stubbornness and say this was unintentionally arms for hostages, he could not bring himself to do it. A shrewder Nixon or Kennedy would have so responded, if only for tactical reasons. Reagan's refusal to admit what happened convinced the public that he was lying. They supposed that if he would lie about that, he would lie about the contra funds diversion.

I realized that I was not making headway. I was struck by how this stubbornness, which at the Reykjavik meeting helped win the Cold War, was now deeply destructive to his presidency. Of course, Ronald Reagan believed that trading arms for hostages was immoral. He could not bring himself to say that he had done something so morally wrong. For him, it was neither a public relations nor a tactical problem. He could not believe that he, Ronald Reagan, had violated his personal honor.

Concealing my exasperation, I moved on. I noticed how firmly his eyes were fixed on me. Despite his physical condition, the president not once showed impatience or agitation. In one-on-one meetings, especially when I am in the lead, I tend to raise my voice. (I had been an infantry sergeant before going to West Point.) This compensated for his deafness in one ear. He could clearly hear me; he did not have a problem understanding me, as he did Bill Casey. My next strategy was to reinforce in Reagan's mind the role he himself had given me. This also enabled me to move to the positive high ground. I told him that, while I understood that I was to be neither the investigator nor the defender of the president, almost everyone else, including some of the press, was distorting that role. Therefore, I reinforced his original concept of my role: "Mr. President, I want to confirm to you again the wisdom that you've had in establishing my unique role here at the White House. It was certainly necessary to restore our credibility. If I'd jumped into my job and functioned as a judge, a juror, or an investigator of facts myself, I'd be in a mess already. We would be right back where we were in December." I stressed that we simply didn't know all the facts: "In the past month and a half, different members of the White House staff have been contradicting themselves and tying themselves in knots."

"You're sure right," he said.

I added, "One of the first things I did after my arrival on January 5 was to end the noon briefing sessions. They were a circus." I told of the daily leaks from the Hill and attempts to answer them at the White House noon press briefings: "I closed down that operation fast."

"That's a very smart move," opined the president. "You're right. We got ourselves into a big mess in November in not knowing what we were talking about. You're doing the right thing. Don't let anybody talk you out of it."

I continued, "You know, I haven't exactly won the popularity contest with the press corps by ending their noontime feeding. I find that I have to remind the press corps and, indeed, some of the White House staff and the people on Capitol Hill that I am the facilitator, not an investigator. This means getting everything out, getting to the bottom of things, as you put it in your telephone call to me in Brussels. We are substituting 'due process' for the 'flawed process' that got us into this damn mess. It is important that we get this process accepted before the State of the Union address later in January." Then I struck my central theme: "Mr. President, I cannot emphasize strongly enough that, in convincing the Congress that we're following due process, we'll build bipartisan support."

He nodded in agreement. I then touched further on the congressional situation and added that I was talking to dozens of members of Congress. I couldn't help but recall my meeting with the president at George Will's dinner before the election: "You said to me about Congress, 'It would be better to lock 'em all up.'"

Shaking his head, he cracked, "We sure can't lock 'em all up now. Too late!"

I added, "They're essential to our success." He signaled his agreement.

I felt it was very important to stress to this isolated president that the Republican and Democratic members of Congress with whom I dealt had a constructive attitude. I related the encounter with Sen. Dave Boren. I finished by saying, "I particularly want to keep you abreast of the situation on Capitol Hill because I think we're going to build a bridge of confidence. I will guarantee you that we will obtain bipartisan support. That will help us get through this storm."

Conscious of the time, I eyed the ticking mahogany clock standing against the east wall. I did not want to exceed my twenty minutes because I was talking with not only a highly scheduled president but also a very frail, recovering one. I rose to leave, extending my hand.

"Go to it," he said. Then, with great courtesy, he walked me to the door. We had covered much in a very short period.

As I moved down the narrow hall to exit the West Wing, I realized again how fortunate I was to be meeting with the president alone, with no other person in the room to interject or redirect the conversation. I totally controlled the agenda. I was also deeply confirmed in my original instinct. Unlike Nixon, this man was incapable of conspiracy.

But we were not home free. Amid this quagmire I found one island of strength: Ronald Reagan was with me in what I was doing. That, after all, was what I needed most. For me, this was just day seven of eighty-three to come.

The president later sent me the unreleased photograph of this meeting. The inscription read, "Dear Dave—I hope you know how welcome you are."

I subsequently had a dozen private conversations with President Reagan, and all were forthright and earnest.

One commentator later said that we spent our time cracking jokes. In fact, very few jokes passed between us during these one-on-one meetings. I went to this and each subsequent meeting with my points written on a legal-size sheet folded in half lengthwise.[9] I stayed with my outline. Of the time allocated, I employed every minute. I was gratified that he was never distracted, evasive, absentminded, frustrated, or nervous. I always had his full attention even as I talked about process. I know this does not fit his image or the experience of some others who were trying to discuss process, with all their talk of inattentiveness. All I can do is relate my firsthand experience.

Of course, I also cannot compare this Ronald Reagan with the younger one who was governor of California or who was president before the assassination attempt early in his first term. But for me the speculation about when Alzheimer's set in has never been a real issue. I never saw him faltering or failing, except in the egregious and stunning case of the second Tower Board hearing, which I describe later. Of course, he was never good with names and dates. True, there was this horrendous Reagan naïveté on arms-for-hostages deals. He could also compartmentalize out bad news and not face it. However, I reminded myself almost daily that this was a president in his mid-seventies, recuperating from an operation, with a confusing crisis on his hands. Yes, he was depressed. Although the flame burned low, he was a bit frail but still a president in command of himself. Character is best measured by how one gets through a crisis when the flame burns low.

CHAPTER 9

Winter Snowstorms

By late December, 1986, before my arrival, the early FBI investigations had identified three thousand documents in the White House and various departments and agencies relevant to the investigations by the independent counsel. In such a short time span, that was an impressive accomplishment. For me, the newcomer, there was a scary dimension in this horrendous number of documents. Conceivably, any one of them might contain a smoking gun—something incriminating of the president, some statement by Poindexter, North, or Casey, whether accurate or not, about something said to Reagan regarding the illegal transfer of funds. I was not the only party with that thought. The Tower Board and the two Hill investigating committees immediately wanted copies of those documents. Many of these were highly sensitive CIA papers requiring closer examination as to their appropriate security classification. This review had to be accomplished by special teams, and this took time. Therefore, we began to get complaints from Capitol Hill about the CIA "dragging their feet."

The house committee had us operating under a deadline, and its staff was telling the press that we were stonewalling when its imposed deadline was not met. I talked about the complaint to Robert Gates, acting director of Central Intelligence. He told me that the request could be met by the end-of-the-week deadline, but it would be impossible to complete the careful categorizations and clearances necessary to determine which were highly or less sensitive documents. Highly sensitive ones would be retained in the executive branch, Room 302 of the Old Executive Office Building, where cleared Hill staffers or members of Congress could review them. "Highly sensitive" documents were those that, if disclosed, would compromise intelligence "sources and methods"; that is, they could lead to the identification and indeed the murder of our covert intelligence agents or to the disclosure of the valuable, highly secret, technical means of interception.

There was the additional screening for relevancy by my committee, chaired by Judge Brower, of the general counsels of the State and Defense Departments and the agencies. In this process, there would still be documents that would prove deeply embarrassing to the executive branch if sent to the Hill, but not ones that disclosed intelligence methods and sources. All of the originals were kept in the executive branch, and careful records were maintained of what was sent where. The openness of this process was also helped by the fact that the president had already made it clear that he would not invoke executive privilege. The integrity of the search process was the essence of our activities, and Judge Charles Brower was the careful coordinator of that extensive interagency endeavor.

Lee Hamilton, the straight-arrow, crew-cut chair of the house investigating committee, was my longtime friend. I grew up a Methodist, and his father, in my early teen years, had been the inspiring pastor of the First Methodist Church in Chattanooga. As a teenager, I never forgot a forceful sermon the Reverend Hamilton gave on the character of St. Paul. Speaking of character, the reverend's son Lee had it as a college basketball star and throughout his distinguished congressional career. It showed in his chairmanship of both the investigative committee and the House Foreign Affairs Committee, where he was never highly partisan, always composed and purposeful, well expressed like his father, and a profile in political courage.

I phoned Chairman Hamilton to lay out the dilemma over the staff deadline. He responded bluntly and unequivocally, "Dave, you get the documents up here when you're satisfied that we don't have a security problem. Do it the right way. I'll tell the staff to keep quiet." His staff shut up.

The ranking minority committee member was Wyoming representative, Republican whip, and former White House chief of staff Dick Cheney. I knew Cheney well, and, in fact, he had been with me in 1981 on a CSIS trip to Tokyo when he had his second heart attack. A man of few words, he was cool, wise, and tested, and I was among many who expected him one day to end up as minority leader or Speaker of the House. My call on him was especially informative on Republican concerns, and I thanked him for his early analysis in our phone conversation, clearly the best I had received.

In the Senate, Chair Daniel Inouye had a sense of responsibility similar to Lee Hamilton's. This widely respected senator from Hawaii had won the Distinguished Service Cross in the World War II Italian campaign, when he served in the 442nd "Go for Broke" Japanese-American regiment. Charging up a hill in the Po Valley in Italy with one bullet in his abdomen, Inouye rushed a machine gun and hurled two grenades before his right arm was shattered. Like Lee Hamilton, Inouye was accustomed to bipartisanship almost as a requirement of patriotism. This was again demonstrated when he designated the ranking Republican, New Hampshire senator Warren Rudman, as vice chair (in place of the usual ranking member) in order to achieve, he hoped, bipartisanship equal to that of the senate Watergate hearings. Rudman was plainspoken and independent minded. Compared with the house committee, which had majority and minority counsels, Inouye and Rudman selected one chief counsel and a "unitary" staff.

After an intensive search, a fifty-four-year-old trial lawyer from New York, Arthur Lawrence Liman, was selected as chief counsel to the select committee. Judge Brower briefed me on his friend Liman's awesome credentials: Harvard College, first in his class at Yale Law School, counsel to the state commission that investigated the dramatic 1971 Attica prison riots, and supervisor of the 1985 examination of cover-ups of police brutality. His star-studded list of past clients included William Paley, Michael Milken, Carl Icahn, Felix Rohatyn, and Henry Kissinger. I was certainly happy that I had Judge Brower by my side.

At our meeting with Senator Inouye, Senator Rudman, and Art Liman, Inouye told Judge Brower and me in no uncertain terms that if we ever felt the committee was doing anything wrong—anything that might jeopardize intelligence methods and sources—he wanted to hear about it directly from us. He desired a fair and bipartisan investigation. He thought Brower and I were on the right track. We left the meeting inspired, as if we wanted to find and salute the flag somewhere.

During the first weeks in January my office remained overwhelmed with activity. On track one, the White House was preparing for the State of the Union address with fears about how the recuperating president would look before Congress. On track two, Judge Brower was in full action with his committee of departmental general counsels. Documents were being moved. The tempo of visits and telephone calls increased: Vice Pres. George H. W. Bush and John Tower frequently; Gates every day or so; Senators Inouye, Warner, Roth, Boren again; Cohen, McClure, Trible, Dole again; Byrd, Levin, Sarbanes, and Hatch; and Congressmen Broomfield, Courter, Hyde several times; Speaker Wright, Foley, minority leader Michel, Brooks, Stokes, Jenkins, McCollum, DeWine, Fish, and so on.

There was a mid-January rash of stories about the president being "in seclusion," running away from the Tower Board, and "having never met with Abshire." A January 20 *Washington Post* headline read as follows: "Senate Staff Report Finds Casey's Iran Testimony Misleading, Incomplete." Casey's role in Iran-contra and his illness were constantly featured, and there was controversy about whether he could ever be led to resign, especially with his wife clearly resisting. The press questioned why Reagan was so indecisive. Meanwhile, Bob Gates remained as acting director of the CIA, and I found him refreshingly steady and organized.

As I went from day five to day eighteen of my tenure in January, I also stayed in touch with my informal outside advisers: Mel Laird, Bob Strauss, Morry Leibman, Bill Timmons, Anne Armstrong, and the young Wayne Berman. They all were encouraging and as yet had no bad vibes. Nonetheless, they kept asking about the ailing president and the situation in a White House that from the outside seemed so inconceivably messy.

It was a snowy January 22 when we had a detailed briefing session with the president in preparation for the first Tower Board meeting, originally scheduled for January 26. No longer could it be said that the president was avoiding the board. Wallison and Regan, with George Bush sitting in, went through chronologies and events to refresh the president. As for me, I departed that evening for Brussels. I had left the alliance abruptly during the Christmas holidays, and I needed to do my farewells and reassure my NATO colleagues in a meeting of the North Atlantic Counsel, where I would make an address about restored leadership in Washington. Judge Brower would represent me in Washington. Although slightly awkward for me, I thought at the time that it was an impossible duty to ignore. The president agreed.

While my wife, Carolyn, packed us up at the ambassador's residence, I returned to Washington just after the president's State of the Union message. Although his physical appearance was now much stronger, I found that White House morale was at its nadir. Roz Bazala, on my staff, had written a memo for the record containing the following: "The president's State of the Union message . . . sadly mirrored the stupor which had settled over 1600 Pennsylvania Avenue. The president's uninspired reiteration of the standard points of his domestic and international agendas represented a backward look to better days. Coupled with the absence of any new approaches, current problems or references to Iran-Contra issues, the president's performance led many to conclude that the administration was 'dead in the water.'"

Bazala continued: "Given Don Regan's awareness of the utility of the second track at the White House, and his effective promotion of the idea, his inaction in keeping the engine of the first track stoked was incomprehensible. The State of the Union address . . . nothing creative or innovative . . . this was damaging enough for domestic perspective, but with Soviet General Secretary Mikhail Gorbachev increasingly seen as a dynamic force with increasing impact on the international scene, the perception of an administration unable to act in defense of its own foreign interest became very worrisome to U.S. allies around the world." Bazala added, "Whether it is justifiable or not, many attributed White House inaction to Regan, who seemed unable to cope with the Iran-Contra issue. His only response was to circle the wagons until the Tower Board issued its report. As a result, no one in the White House was working on a strategy to put the problem behind the president."[1]

Of course, the astute Bazala was an inside-the-beltway observer from the government and quite focused on substance—or lack thereof. The president's speech stayed away from Iran-contra except for forty-six modest seconds. Reagan conveyed his usual high spirit of patriotism, which helped him communicate outward. In a focus group in Atlanta, one forgiving soul said, "Nobody's perfect. If you get a dent, you don't throw out the whole car." Another Reagan Democrat said, "On this day and time, I'm not sure you can hold one man responsible." An anti-Reagan Democrat quipped, "Jimmy Carter would have been impeached." Reagan's own pollster found a "vein of forgiveness."[2]

The truth is that Reagan had received a temporary pass from the American people—until more was known about Iran-contra.

Meanwhile Herblock drew a cartoon of a stone wall being erected around the White House. He had another one showing me with a megaphone, saying, "Maybe we will call in Pat Robertson next."

Plainly, it was critical to get the president moving again. Somebody had to be thinking about how to take the release of the Tower Board report, then scheduled for February 19, as a jump off to move forward to some kind of dynamic strategy. This indeed was not emerging from the first track because Don Regan, in all of his efficiencies but also his lack of political skills, was not reaching out for ideas or bringing in outside advisers. He might have been Mr. Efficiency. He was not Mr. Creativity.

In midafternoon of January 30, I had another meeting with the president in the Oval Office. Outside of the ceiling-to-floor windows arched behind his desk chair was a snowy winter wonderland with fog.[3] We began our conversation by commenting on the picturesque scenery. I congratulated him on his State of the Union address because, despite Bayala's commentary to me, the address and especially the president's appearance were much better than expected.

I studied the president across his desk. His color had clearly improved, and his body movements were decidedly stronger. Then came my commentary. In a raised voice, I recounted my NATO trip and how Lord Carrington and the entire North Atlantic Council of fifteen other ambassadors sent their best wishes to the leader of the alliance. I then moved to the work of my office and our departmental teams. We had received the three thousand documents that the FBI had initially identified as relevant to the investigation. We had processed them and moved them all to Capitol Hill. It was quite a feat, I added, and Brower and his team should be congratulated. As for congressional relations, we had developed a very constructive relationship with Inouye and Rudman on the senate side and Hamilton and Cheney on the house side. Brower and I were calling on every member of these two investigating committees.

"Mr. President, I believe that even in the media we're winning the battle to build the credibility of our operation. Journalists are slow to understand that we're trying to restore 'due process' and to be the credible facilitator. A *Washington Post* article [January 19] kept the old line that my job was 'to assemble all the facts, which could take months.' It will take time to fully change the images of what we're doing with everyone." I went on to comment on the good work of Peter Wallison in reviewing documents in the White House's possession and of Judge Brower's committee of departmental legal counsels. The masses of paper were moving, yet we were being careful with sensitive documents. That was a very serious concern.

I knew that some White House staffers said that any discussion of process could bore him, but I felt it important to give him a feel for what was going on. I described what appeared to be the general thrust of the forthcoming final Tower Board report and noted that I understood that his first meeting with them had gone well. There would be a definitive chronology that Tower was finding difficult to assemble. One section would focus on the NSC conduct and operations during the Iran-contra episode, and the findings would be critical. Another part would look at what the future role and procedures of the NSC should be.

As was the case in our first meeting, his eyes never strayed from me. He did not fidget. He showed no impatience.

I had intended to use this meeting principally as an update on my activities relating to the investigations, but I also hinted at the urgency of developing a larger strategy for the full restoration of the presidency. I restrained myself, however, because I thought it would be better to reserve that discussion for a time closer to the release of the Tower Board report. I also recognized that in my excursion into the larger arena I needed to honor my agreement with Chief of Staff Don Regan, for larger policy was his responsibility. I had to sell Don Regan on a broader strategy before I could fully engage the president in discussing such a tactic.

Before I departed, the president took a few minutes to warmly express his full support for my activities, now that he understood them better. He reiterated what he had written on the inscribed picture to me, saying just how welcome I was.

As I left the Oval Office and ambled down the hall to exit into the snow to reach the Old Executive Office Building, I felt very reassured and believed I had something of a real bond developing with the president. I really hardly knew him upon arrival.

CHAPTER 10

The First Lady

In late January, the *Washington Post*, CBS's *60 Minutes*, and other media outlets carried a rash of stories increasingly critical of the president. Secretary of State Shultz's three-hour closed-door testimony to the House Foreign Affairs Committee made both the president and Bill Casey look bad, and the testimony was promptly leaked. It was especially damning that Reagan had made a public statement as early as November 19 that no more arms would be furnished to Iran, but, to Shultz's consternation and anger, CIA discussions on arms transfers continued into early December. With this as but one example, the talk increased about Reagan being "too old, too out of touch, and too dependent on aides," and many of those aides were still involved in making confusing statements.[1] In the wake of these many stories, I heard that a dismayed Nancy Reagan, from the isolation of the family quarters on the second floor of the White House, was saying, "When will Abshire get moving and clear the president?"

"Nobody up on the Hill is defending Ronnie on Iran," Mrs. Reagan complained to her antagonist, Don Regan. "We have got to get somebody in who will defend him. Larry Speakes [the White House spokesperson] should defend him more."

Regan later wrote, "I replied that someone else, namely David Abshire, was now in charge of the Iran-contra affair, as she had desired. I was supposed to be doing other things." She replied, "Tell both of them [Abshire and Speakes] they've got to do something."[2]

I had shied away from meeting privately with Nancy Reagan because I had believed that to arrive in my new job and immediately race up to the family quarters to see the first lady would antagonize my relationship with Don Regan. But now I faced a dilemma: Clearly, she did not understand my role as a truth facilitator as compared with a public defender of the president. Neither the president nor Don had fully explained it to her, and she was reading the misinformed stories in some newspapers about my role.

This is where my outside advisers were helpful, especially Charlie Wick and Bob Strauss. Charlie Wick and Mary Jane Wick were pals with the Reagans going back to the Beverly Hills days of the 1950s. Charlie, in his youth, had first rolled into Los Angeles as the pianist and arranger with the Tommy Dorsey orchestra and, when the band continued to tour, decided to stay behind and make his fortune in the entertainment industry and eventually in real estate. Through his wife, Mary Jane, Nancy's school chum, he early on became fast friends of the Reagans. Charlie had a fierce but intelligent loyalty to the Reagans and had the considerable virtue of being able to make the president laugh at the right moments. After the election Wick became Reagan's director of the U.S. Information Agency but was much more than that as a confidant to the president.[3]

In separate phone conversations, both Wick and Strauss advised me to start regular meetings with Nancy Reagan. I remember Strauss's Texas snarl over the phone: "Abshire, you're doing one thing wrong: Not seeing the first lady." Suddenly I realized that in a different way I might make the same mistake as Don Regan. I had to see her.

I called Wick back: "I've seen Nancy Reagan in receiving lines, but I really don't know her; I need a bit of introduction."

"I'll phone you in a minute," he said, and he did. "She invites you to visit her in the family quarters at three o'clock." It was February 3, 1987, day twenty-nine of my tenure.

Nancy Reagan was one of the most powerful first ladies in history. In this respect she ranked with Edith Wilson and Eleanor Roosevelt, but I learned that she was totally different from each. She was—as former senator and Reagan confidant Paul Laxalt recognized, but Don Regan did not—not only the president's closest adviser and best friend but also the "indispensable factor in his political life."[4] Reagan would most probably never have been president without her. Time and again, she had been a major factor, sometimes the key factor, in the crises of her husband's political career. Ronald Reagan once said, "In some ways Nancy and I are like one human being. When one of us has a problem, it automatically becomes the problem for the other;

an attack on one of us is an attack on both of us. When one suffers, so does the other."[5]

After graduating from Smith College, Nancy managed to break into Hollywood, ultimately with parts in eleven films. In 1951, she met fellow Warner Brothers actor Ronald Reagan, and they were married a year later. "My life began when I met Ronnie," she later declared.[6] Politically, she helped to facilitate his move from being a liberal Democrat to a Republican. This is an interesting fact when one considers the brickbats later thrown at her by the Republican right wing.

When Reagan's 1980 presidential campaign went off track under the management of John Sears, Nancy pushed to have Sears fired and Bill Casey recruited. She was a force in the run up to the New Hampshire presidential debate as she helped persuade her Ronnie to insist on having, in addition to Bush, who wanted a two-way debate, other presidential candidates on stage. From this stage came Reagan's now famous winning retort to the debate moderator, "I paid for this microphone."

Not only would she intervene in her husband's affairs to help a campaign turn around, but she also did likewise for her own faltering situation early in the first Reagan administration. Mrs. Reagan's social life in the White House involved wealthy women, expensive clothes, and the leaders of style. She set out to use her contacts to refurbish the White House. Jacqueline Kennedy did similar things with her innocent air—winning over the star-struck press—but not Nancy Reagan.[7] The country had moved into a recession, and Nancy was widely portrayed as a Marie Antoinette. One writer on first ladies notes, "Her timing was off—the announcement of $200,000 for new china came on the day before the administration publicized a plan to decrease nutrition standards for school lunch programs."[8] Her approval rating hit 26 percent, the lowest yet of any first lady.

With the help of her adviser and deputy chief of staff, Michael Deaver, she engineered a fast turnaround in her public image. She moved aggressively on her war on drug abuse, traveling one hundred thousand miles to fifty-seven cities and even seven foreign countries. At the black-tie Gridiron Club dinner in 1982, she walked onto the stage in rags, danced, and sang in a self-deprecating manner to a song titled "Second-Hand Clothes," a parody on "Second-Hand Rose." She ended up smashing a piece of china. There was a tremendous ovation.

In times of crisis, Nancy Reagan simply did not believe in standing still. In the snowstorm winter of 1987, she was locked in her own storm with the president's chief of staff. The beginnings of the conflict occurred in 1985, when Reagan was out of action for his cancer operation and convalescence. She resented the way Regan appeared to take over the president's role. As noted earlier, after the Reykjavik Summit, she was infuriated over Regan's remark about heading the "shovel brigade" to clean up after the president.

On the other hand, even the "good guy," the chief-of-staff-to-be, Howard Baker, was later to refer to her as the "dragon lady." The dragon lady and I were about to meet. She had bluntly said that I was supposed to defend and absolve the president. Could she be led to understand my role? How impatient would she be? Would I be caught in the crossfire between the West and East Wings of the White House?

An attendant escorted me to the small family elevator to reach the second-floor living quarters. We exited a few steps from the sweeping traverse hall of the family quarters. In Theodore Roosevelt's day, this central area was opened up to run the full length of the mansion between the grand fan windows on each end.[9] Later, on the west end, a closed-off sitting area had been created, with a couch against a stunning Palladian-style window that allows the golden afternoon sun to pour through to give a warm glow to the yellow-and-white room. The first lady received her visitors and friends here, as Eleanor Roosevelt had in her day.

She rose to greet me. I towered over her by almost a foot. She was fashionably dressed, and her almond eyes and bouffant hairdo set off her slenderness. She was animated, and I relaxed.

She didn't seem like a dragon lady after all. Following small talk, I explained how once again trust must become the coin of the realm. My role was to restore credibility and honesty to the White House's response to the investigation, to develop bipartisan support on Capitol Hill, and to get all the facts and documents out in accord with the second-track mission that the president himself had set up. We had to leave it to the Tower Board and, later, the other investigators to reach conclusions instead of jumping to an impromptu, incomplete defense of the president when we did not have all of the information analyzed. That process, by far, provided the best defense of the president. I also explained why it was essential to end the noonday press circus, where there was an attempt to defend on every issue—every day—when we did not really know the facts.

Yes, she repeated more than once, she now finally understood my role. She emphasized that for the first time she understood the whole concept, the entire strategy of restoring credibility to the White House's involvement in the ongoing investigation.[10] No one had bothered to explain this to her before, she said.

Later in the discussion, Nancy opined that I seemed to be the only one in the White House working for Ronnie and not for Don. (In my presence she invariably referred to the president as Ronnie.) Don Regan was intentionally walling off the White House, she said. He was squeezing out outside advice and contacts. Nancy Reagan said that her husband was being isolated and, therefore, weakened in his overall judgments. "The only other adviser with access is you," she said. There was a hopeful gaze.

"You must not let Don into your meetings with the president"— here for the first time she used the word "president" for emphasis.

Mrs. Reagan then complained vigorously that Don Regan wanted to push the president into travel and speeches too soon after the surgery. The first week in February was the president's first full-time return to the office. Regan argued that the president should undertake a speaking campaign out of Washington, around the country, on various issues ranging from the balanced budget to the strategic defense initiative, to take his messages "to the people" and to create "diversions." Mrs. Reagan had been told that, in similar operations involving older men, premature travel and activity had produced serious setbacks.

I agreed with Mrs. Reagan that, between his operation and more importantly the upcoming Tower Board report, such a strategy would be a mistake. To undertake such a campaign of speeches and press conferences when we were still unclear on some Iran-contra facts would be a formula for disaster, comparable to the charge of the Light Brigade. He would be hounded with questions that neither he nor even the investigators could now answer.[11]

Mrs. Reagan went on to say, "We need new ideas, imagination, and an invigorated agenda. Such has been lacking in the White House since Don Regan took over." I could feel her intense anger at the chief of staff and her utter frustration over the fact that he remained in his powerful position.

At that point, I felt it right to hint at a comeback plan that I had been turning over in my mind. I wanted to use the Tower Board report as the jumping-off point for a White House reorganization. Part of the purpose of the report had been to review the NSC structure and operations, not only to disclose what went wrong in Iran-contra but also to determine how to operate our national security process in the future. "All the publicity is painting the commander in chief as extraordinarily detached and not knowing what's going on. I, therefore, see the Tower Board release as a window of opportunity for the following 30 to 45 days. I'm going to propose a very vigorous president not running around the country but first moving around Washington, putting his fractured national security house back in order." I then outlined a more detailed plan for a major address to the nation followed by a display of unity including the Secretaries of State and Defense and a newly energized National Security Council staff. I added that "It is widely known that Weinberger and Shultz constantly fight and, therefore, split the national security process. It is a disgrace. Had they operated together, they might have prevented the Iran-contra scandal."[12]

Nancy vigorously nodded in agreement, "Of course they could have prevented it. There is no doubt about it."

"Let me use a military concept," I said, noting that I had started out in the military. "The first principle of strategy is to have unity of command. We were winning the Cold War because we had a unified NATO. We've not had unity of command in Washington, in what I call our national security process. Cap and George and, earlier, Bill Casey, were out of step, and the rogue Ollie North was off on his escapades."

Nancy commiserated that it had been a self-destructive situation. She agreed on the absolute need in both imagery and reality to communicate a new unity of effort. She interjected: "This is the first imaginative idea I have heard since Mike Deaver left the White House." She wanted me to present it to the president soon. "Make your next meeting much longer," she told me. "I will phone Kathy Osborne (the president's secretary) and insist. Don't you let Don Regan in the room." We agreed to stay in close touch through visits and by phone. I bade Mrs. Reagan good evening with a strong sense of not only relief but also elation.[13]

My initial meeting with the first lady soon was followed by others and by frequent phone calls back and forth.[14] Time and again, I sat with her as the afternoon sunrays lengthened through the Palladian window. She was deeply devoted to her husband and would do anything to ensure his place in history and in the affection of the American public. She did not want what she considered to be Regan's obstinacy and instincts for self-preservation to imperil her husband's legacy.

The week of February 8, day thirty-five for me, was an especially difficult one for the first lady. Years later I learned from her diary that she had had a bitter fight on the phone with Don. He was "arrogant" and "loud" and hung up, she wrote. She added in the diary that she talked to "Mike and David Abshire, who is so sound." It would come as a real blow to her when, just over a month later, Mike Deaver was indicted for perjury by a federal grand jury on matters that related to his business activity. Her world was coming apart, she confessed to me years later as she went through her diary with me. The Regan phone incident made its way into the press, and she was accused of leaking it.[15]

To make things worse, a public-relations man, John Koechler, had been hired at the White House. Nancy Reagan did not know him personally. Some derogatory information had come out, an assertion that he had been a boyhood member of the Hitler Youth. The Regan West Wing leaked the story that the Nancy Reagan East Wing wanted him hired. When Mrs. Reagan spoke at a very large meeting with youngsters at the Spirit of America awards, the press showered her with questions about this appointment and also about Iran-contra. Her mother was ill, and, on top of this, the Reagans were having problems with the children. Nancy noted to me that her husband, when he returned to the second-floor residence in the late afternoon, had lost his peppiness, his chattiness about what had happened that day. In other words, he was downright depressed.

During one of our meetings, though, there was a light moment. The president popped out of the family elevator. Seeing me, he joshed, "Caught ya at it," amidst our laughs. He was obviously very relieved that I was talking to the first lady regularly because he bore her pent-up feelings. The president then disappeared down the hall to the exercise room for his late-afternoon workout, an activity the staff guarded from the press to avoid him being labeled Tarzan because of his daily care for his superb physique. I believe that this exercise regimen was extremely important during this down period.

President Reagan's playful remark also reflected the essential romance of the Reagans. In the midst of this Iran-contra disaster, I came to respect this romantic aspect as something positive and beautiful. The president once explained to me while we were meeting in the Oval Office what he had said to others: "I can't sleep well when she isn't here at night." In a 1998 interview with *Vanity Fair,* Nancy Reagan explained her relationship with her husband as only she could: "Our relationship is very special. We were very much in love, and still are. Thank God we found each other. When I say my life began with Ronnie, well, it's true. It did. Forty-six years? Can't imagine it without him."[16]

This closeness never weakened, despite differences and arguments over the firing of Don Regan, despite the stresses of political campaigns, despite the demands of the presidency, despite the curse of the Iran-contra affair, and, ultimately, despite Alzheimer's disease.

CHAPTER 11

The Prosecutor

Judge Walsh

In the Iran-contra investigations the key player was seventy-five-year-old Judge Lawrence Walsh. Ironically—to me at least—he was Reagan's age. A Republican deputy attorney general under Bill Rogers during the Eisenhower administration, he had won his spurs under Gov. Thomas Dewey fighting crime as part of the New York district attorney's office. On December 19, he had taken his oath of office, so he was in place before me in dealing with the Iran-contra matter.

On the evening of January 20, dressed to the nines in vest and white shirt, the slender judge with intense eyes came calling at my office. For a time Judge Walsh had served in Paris as a diplomatic negotiator, so I greeted him in my best diplomatic style—the Tennessee version of it, that is. His sharp staff attorneys, Guy Struve and John Douglas, accompanied him. Judge Charles Brower, equally dressed in pinstripes, seemed to know the academic record of every attorney we met and briefed me on every detail of their school performance and law-firm ties. Struve was especially important, for he had been Walsh's closest colleague at the firm of Davis Polk and Wardwell and came with an especially outstanding academic record from Yale and Harvard Law School. I was out of my depth, surrounded by such an array of legal talent whose fraternities seemed to overlap, and I was doubly thankful for my early judgment that I needed my own judge as my deputy.

With Judge Walsh and his staff, we understood that everything was to be gained by establishing good personal relationships and avoiding confrontations over minor matters. As we went along, Judge Walsh more than reciprocated our attitude. Both of us bowed and scraped when we met. In my subsequent visits to his office, he would always whisk me over to the best chair—a large armchair, formal but comfortable—the place for "the ambassador," as he put it. We were off to a good start, no doubt about it.

However, the same experience did not happen in his relationship with John Tower. Judge Walsh, in his book *Firewall*, notes that his relationship with the Tower Board did not begin on a cordial basis.[1] Senator Tower had invited him and members of his staff to the New Executive Office Building, but "Tower kept us standing in the seemingly unheated building lobby for a half hour, waiting to be escorted past the security barrier." It was a cold, unpleasant day in the first place, Walsh noted. "Finally, as we were about to leave, a staff assistant rescued us."

Tower's message was brief and blunt. He wanted the independent counsel, as Walsh later comments, "to grant immunity and the power of our grand jury to subpoena witnesses and documents to get information for him so that he could publish the information in his report."

"My answer was even briefer," asserts Walsh. "What he proposed was contrary to law, and we would not do it. After exploring the possibility of sharing other information and, particularly, a joint appeal for cooperation by the government of Israel, we both saw clearly that we were pursuing different issues." Despite the unfortunate nature of the meeting, that conclusion was most probably appropriate. Walsh later remarked, "In their view, the role of the independent counsel was just to prosecute the crimes that they exposed. But I was not that kind of prosecutor."[2]

I was surprised at this chilly, almost rude reception, for former senate committee chair Tower, who, while never winning the popularity contest on Capitol Hill, was normally a man of great decorum, tailored in his London-cut suits and trained in senatorial courtesy, usually with a few flourishes. The reception was therefore both uncharacteristic and strange.

Walsh's visits on Capitol Hill also produced friction. In his first meeting with senate counsel Arthur Liman, according to Walsh, Liman recognized that Walsh could not furnish grand jury information to the committee or share Swiss financial records. Liman argued, however, that "to the extent that when the committees could not get the documents that they needed, there would be enormous pressure to immunize central figures in the scandal. The committees had to be able to trace the flow of money."[3] Walsh observes that "[c]onfidently, almost arrogantly, [Liman] predicted that by carefully insulating ourselves, we would be able to prosecute individuals who had received congressional immunity." With that, Walsh recalls that the only immunized Watergate defendants who were later convicted were the two who pleaded guilty. Thus, a major conflict was set up at the very beginning between the work of the congressional committees and that of the independent counsel.

In dramatic contrast to these conflicts with the Hill and the Tower Board, Judge Walsh told Judge Brower and me that he had made a major decision, and he said, "You will like it." He had decided to request but not to subpoena executive-branch documents. We were astonished and delighted. I think his decision was helped by his trust of the process we were creating. Brower and I had a feeling of success.

In his memoir, Walsh regrets this decision due to later controversies and obstacles that developed after Brower and I had left the White House. Walsh states, "[I]n relying on written document requests rather than subpoenas, I probably made a basic mistake. I was acting like a government lawyer who could expect honest compliance by a government agency. Although the threat to use subpoenas could be effective, I believed that issuing them would invite litigation as to the scope of our demands, which would delay me at a time when I was racing with Congress."[4]

Certainly in the three months of our tenure Walsh received honest compliance, as he recognizes in his book. However one may judge Walsh's work in the long, tangled later years of the investigation, he must be given credit for the way he began with the special counselor's office.[5]

During this period, Judge Brower's task force of departmental general counselors continued to review three thousand relevant documents identified by the FBI for the investigations. Each of these documents had to be carefully sorted, and the most sensitive had to be retained for safekeeping in the executive branch, where the committee staffs and others were invited to view them. This was one of the initial problems we had with the Congress—safekeeping. The CIA was very slow in replying to requests related to the contra supply operation because they had difficulty evaluating the documents. As for the Walsh team, we had to work out arrangements to have filing cabinets and space at the CIA headquarters in Langley, Virginia. This enabled the Walsh attorneys to see what the agency had blacked out as legally irrelevant but sensitive in terms of revealing sources and methods. Similar arrangements were worked out with the Treasury Department since it also wanted to follow North's money trail.

A very significant event occurred on February 24. Oliver North's attorney, the unstoppable Brendan Sullivan, aggressively challenged the very constitutionality of the independent counsel act itself and moved to file suit. This dramatic initiative threatened to put a cloud over the Walsh investigation while it was still in its early stages. Walsh reacted swiftly by proposing to Brower and me that the attorney general appoint him directly as independent counsel to ensure continuity while legal challenges went forward. I gave Walsh my approval of this proposal, and we immediately gained the support of the president. Walsh had done one for us in his no-subpoena policy, and we had done one for him in parrying the enterprising Sullivan.

CHAPTER 12

A New Initiative Attempted

The snowy winter wonderland lasted into early February, and much was going well for my group and me. First, we were working effectively with the Tower Board. Second, we were rapidly broadening and deepening our contact with the Congress. Names on my calendar included Representatives Fascell, Cheney, Hyde, Derwinski, and Stokes and Senators Mitchell, Heflin, and Nunn. Third, we were working well with the independent counsel. Fourth, with Popadiuk's help, we were convincing more of the press that we had an honest and open process to facilitate the investigations. Fifth, the first lady was supportive, and despite that fact, the chief of staff had remained cooperative with me. We were immensely helped by the fact that the new national security advisor, Frank Carlucci, and his talented deputy, Lt. Gen. Colin Powell, had brought competence and openness to that deeply wounded office.

But these positive aspects were outweighed by the grave Cabinet splits. The secretaries of defense and state remained at odds. The White House chief of staff and the new national security adviser could not remedy this flawed relationship as had initially been hoped. The Tower Board report was not yet out. Nancy Reagan remained distraught. Perhaps she alone sensed for her husband the true depth of this complex presidential crisis.

I had to remind the press and myself, however, that my job was the second track: handling the investigations, advising the president on these issues, and lifting the burden of the Iran-contra affair. Yet I wanted to move outside this reactive track to push a more dramatic and broader, proactive initiative that would reinforce a revived national security process and restore the leader of the alliance to his full strength. If I were to go beyond my authority, I could be successful through the power of persuasion.

For any new initiative, it was essential that I have Don Regan's support for my plans. I would be operating not within my area but within Regan's and Carlucci's. A few days later, I went to Don to review my strategy. I laid it out in detail. To my delight, he was very much taken with the proactive plan. He encouraged me to engage the president immediately. I left his office feeling that this was Don at his best.

On February 4, over lunch in the White House mess, I discussed the plan with the White House director of communications, politically astute Pat Buchanan. He wisely warned that my new plan cut across many peoples' responsibilities in the White House and would need broad staff support to sustain it. He was right.

Contrary to Nancy Reagan's advice, I invited Don to be in the Oval Office for my next meeting with the president. It took place on Friday, February 6, and lasted forty-five minutes. It was the president's seventy-sixth birthday.

When Don and I entered, the president was at his desk, and Don and I sat on chairs to his right. We joined in birthday salutations, Don withheld his jokes, and it was clearly my meeting. To Don's credit, he wanted it that way.

Conscious of my time, I moved rapidly through a diverse agenda before reaching my main subject: "Mr. President, as I've already told you, three thousand documents have been supplied to the house committee, and eight boxes of documents will go to the senate select committee at 4 P.M. today. This completes our first task. In our preparatory review, the various departments and agencies have cooperated superbly as part of the committee Judge Brower chaired. I am proud to say that our intelligence methods and sources have been protected"—unlike what happened in the Church and Pike Committee investigations of the 1970s.

Then I turned to the issue created by the Hill committees' hearing of Reagan's private diary. They wanted access. In this regard, I told the president, "You mentioned your diary at the first Tower Board meeting. Peter Wallison and I have had discussions with the committee leadership about their request on relevant portions of your private diary. We have reached a compromise by having Peter extract relevant portions. Senator Inouye and Congressmen Rudman, Hamilton, and Cheney expressed their deep appreciation to you through me. They recognized your desire not to set a precedent for future presidents.

They all noted the constructive role the White House was playing and that hearings are now planned for March."

I noted that Marlin Fitzwater had told the press the day before about the personal notes and the process by which these would be handled. Marlin's official line was that "the process will be a consultative one between the investigating body and the president, Abshire, and Wallison."

I then gave the president a more detailed rundown of the structure of the Tower Board report and what appeared to be some of the key findings. I went over what we expected in the various sections of the statement and stressed that it would surely say we traded arms for hostages.

This last point triggered the president to say again, as I almost sighed aloud, "This was not arms for hostages. They made overtures to us. There was no thought of arms until they brought it up. We talked hostages, but they brought up the arms need separate from our raising the hostages. I had no intention of getting into arms for hostages."

Then Don Regan made one of his two interventions in the forty-five-minute meeting: "What if you were hoodwinked by your staff on all this?"

"Possibly," he responded, "but it was not my intention."[1]

After some discussion, I made the argument that we had to use this report as a springboard for launching a new and broadly based initiative. Then I moved into some specifics of the proposal: "It's absolutely critical that the Tower Board report be accepted by you in its entirety, even things in it that we might not like. If you don't fully accept the report, if you start making disclaimers or stating reservations, that'll be the focus of the publicity, and we'll be right back where we started." Don nodded agreement.

I then suggested that, some days after receiving and digesting the report, the president make a major speech. "Mr. President, I believe that you should unequivocally accept the report, commend the Tower panel, but then state that it does not go far enough. You should go farther to truly refocus and recreate the national security process at this crucial time in the Cold War and publicly mandate its unity. As NATO ambassador, I experienced the past devastating disunities."

I then explained the plan: We had about a 30–45-day opportunity to seize the initiative and move ahead of both the Democratic Congress and Gorbachev. Our aim should be to greatly strengthen presidential leadership by developing a new unity and coherence for the last two years of the Reagan presidency. The president must be seen publicly in charge as the commander in chief. He should meet and talk things through with the National Security Council staff. He must instill a new coherence in the National Security Council and the departments and with the key congressional committees. The president should demonstrate the new unity in his own administration, where Cap and George, along with other departments, had frequently been out of step with each other on a wide range of issues. This could be demonstrated by taking Cap with him to visit George at the State Department, George with Cap and himself at Defense, and all three of them could go to the CIA together. He should call a special meeting of the President's Foreign Intelligence Advisory Board and vehemently proclaim that this board would never be bypassed again as it had been during the Iran-contra matter (something the Tower Board had missed). As for the Congress, the president should encourage the formation of a national security group of overarching committees to meet regularly with the president and his national security advisor. Finally, he should call a heads-of-government summit at NATO to give new direction to U.S. leadership in the alliance at this critical point in the Cold War.

"Mr. President, as I have said before, in successful military strategy throughout history, unity of command is the first principle. You have the opportunity to leave the Iran-contra episode in the dustbins of history and to have the next six months among your most brilliant."

I had held the president's full attention. "I want to do it," he exclaimed.

Don cautioned, "It's going to be a lot of work. You must make a commitment."

The president nodded, "I know. I do."

My time was more than up, so I rose to repeat "Happy birthday" and "Thank you for this support." Don and I departed very encouraged. In the next Cabinet meeting, when Secretary of Labor Bill Brock brought up the need for some fresh thinking in the presidency, Reagan nodded toward me and said, "We have such a plan."[2]

Don Regan had been very supportive of me in this meeting, but the open warfare between the chief of staff and the first lady was increasing daily. The Tower Board report scheduled for February would be a milestone on the road to Don's hoped-for departure. Rumors spread that he was determined to stay beyond it, restore himself, and eventually seek to be appointed chair of the Federal Reserve Board.

In mid-February, Don was even crosswise with the president's daughter Maureen Reagan—"nose to nose," as Nancy put it. Outspoken Maureen angrily went directly to her father to complain.[3]

It took various efforts to gradually unseat Regan. These ranged from the Bob Strauss December meeting at the White House; to the political director, Mitch Daniels, making *Washington Post* headlines on December 18, 1986, with the leak that he had suggested to his boss, Don Regan, that he resign; to the latest by Maureen. As did George Bush, Nancy Reagan urged me to try my hand since Regan-Abshire seemed to be going well. The overriding concern was that if Regan was still on board after the release of the Tower Board report, his continued presence would dominate the news.

I sought a time to talk with Don in a relaxed manner. It was at 5 P.M. on Tuesday, February 24, day fifty-one of my tenure, with thirty-nine to go. I opened up.

"Don, you remember when I first knew you and came to lunch with you at Merrill to talk about the Merrill Trust? You were recognized as a great CEO of an outstanding financial institution. You later had an equally fine tenure as Secretary of Treasury. You produced major tax legislation. The first part of your tenure as chief of staff at the White House was a time of domestic and international triumph. From the Geneva Summit meeting to Reykjavik, history was made. You had a role. You had wide recognition in the press. Now that same press is eating you up, bit by bit. Your achievements are being destroyed. You are losing the initiative. You are on the downward slope."

Regan was listening closely, I think with some pain. The atmosphere was friendly.

"Let me tell you the Lord Carrington story."

I related how, when Carrington was foreign secretary, the entire British press and much of the Parliament were down on him when the Argentine forces surprised the British and moved into the Falklands. It was an intelligence and defense ministry failure and not Carrington's. But all over Britain, Carrington, a brilliant former first lord of the admiralty, defense minister, and then foreign secretary, took the rap. The publicity and blame increased daily, and Carrington's position was deteriorating. I looked at Don carefully as I said, "Then Carrington made his dramatic move. He gallantly fell on his own sword. He resigned. You know, Don, what happened? Overnight, the villain was a hero. Later he went on to greater heights as NATO's secretary general. This all happened because Carrington seized the initiative—was not pushed out but dramatically stepped out. It was a class act." Don nodded.

I then told Don that he was certainly an organization expert with vast experience from his Merrill Lynch and Treasury experiences. He had often spoken to me about what he considered to be the organizational problems with the national security adviser and the first lady's office as well as the Cabinet problems.

I said, "Get out now, Don. Write a book. Tell how the White House should operate. Tell about how your other governmental experiences compared with the private sector. You could draw on these organization experiences and come up with constructive suggestions."

He brightened up. "I like that idea," he declared. "Would you give me a memo? Again, Dave, I've been thinking about stepping out, but not yet."

As I rose to shake hands and depart, I added wistfully, "Please don't wait, Don, until it's too late."

When I reached my office, I called both Vice President Bush and Nancy Reagan, and both received my unhappy report.

"He listened very closely but I don't think he's going."

Indeed, he wasn't going. Hence he gave up the chance to be part of the solution instead of being the problem.[4]

CHAPTER 13

Conflicting Memories

On February 17, 1987, we learned that the *Los Angeles Times* was about to break a story about how the president had dramatically contradicted himself before the first and second Tower Board meetings. At the first meeting, he told the panel he had given prior approval to the 1985 Israeli arms shipment to Iran, and then at the second, he said he had not given approval until afterward. The press was going to say that not only was there strong evidence of a faulty presidential memory, but it also appeared that the chief of staff had manipulated the president to change his testimony.

The issue did not involve the Boland Amendment or the diversion of funds to the contras but focused on the first attempted trade of arms to Iran for hostages. There had been a transfer of U.S. tube-launched, wire-guided antitank missiles (TOWs) through Israel to Iran in late August, 1985. That much was clear.[1] What was not clear was *when* the president had authorized it: by oral authorization before the transfer, as maintained by former national security adviser Robert McFarlane, which would have made it legal if the Congress were notified; or after the fact, as Chief of Staff Regan maintained. The transfer prior to presidential approval would have been illegal, and McFarlane would have been the culprit. It was widely known that Chief of Staff Regan was anti-McFarlane.

The emergence of this issue came in the wake of Bud McFarlane's attempted suicide by taking 25–30 tablets of Valium just two hours before he was to testify before the Tower Board. A shaken McFarlane had been under great strain and had been about to testify as to his failures before John Tower, his former boss on Capitol Hill, and Brent Scowcroft, under whom McFarlane had also worked—two men he much admired and whom he no doubt felt he had let down by his performance. It was a cruel time.[2]

However, regardless of whether the controversial transfers had been made before or after presidential approval, the deals still stank of trading arms for hostages—something Reagan publicly promised his administration would never do—and also violated the Arms Export Control Act. This act required that, if Israel made a transfer of the U.S. weapons to Iran, U.S. written consent was needed, and the president had to notify Congress, which was never done. Also, Iran was labeled a terrorist country and, therefore, under this act was ineligible for direct U.S.-Iranian transfers.

However, as already noted, the burning new issue that emerged from the second Tower Board meeting on February 11 was whether the increasingly vilified chief of staff, Don Regan, had overly influenced Pres. Ronald Reagan. Reagan's contradictions before the Tower Board were indeed dramatic. His first meeting with the board took place on January 26, 1987. Because I had briefly returned to NATO, Brower sat in for me. Of the many matters discussed, the president indicated he thought he had given his approval to the controversial arms transfer before August, 1985, but that he was "still digging." He revealed that he had kept a diary. In other words, he tentatively confirmed the McFarlane version and in fact had on his desk a copy of McFarlane's January testimony to the Senate Foreign Relations Committee. The Tower Board considered this first meeting, in contrast to the second, a very good one and found Reagan's account credible.[3]

Before the second Tower Board meeting of February 11 and after my return from NATO, I attended a White House preparatory session with the president. Vice Pres. George Bush; the president's counsel, Peter Wallison; and, of course, Chief of Staff Don Regan were in attendance. It was quite clear that all of the president's interlocutors were becoming exasperated with Reagan's lack of or confused memory and that he was indifferent about trying to figure it all out.[4] As we were reviewing the chronology with the president, Regan forcefully opined that he was quite sure that Reagan appeared surprised when informed that the arms transfer had actually taken place. Reagan lit up and announced that, yes, he had been surprised.[5] He had finally said something quite decisive. Wallison then added that if this was his best recollection, he should tell the Tower Board so at the forthcoming meeting.

As the newcomer to the White House, I had no view or personal knowledge on whether McFarlane or Regan had the correct position, and I had not been present at the first Tower Board meeting. But I did think we should help hold the president to his just-uttered conclusion since he finally appeared so certain about being surprised. However, I learned later that this was the second time the president had been asked this question; the first time had been on January 3, before my arrival. At that meeting between Peter Wallison, Jay Stephens, Don Regan, and the president, Wallison had been the one to put the question to the president, who remembered being surprised to hear about the arms shipment.[6]

On the way out of the session, I suggested to Wallison that he draw up what I call an aide-mémoire to hold the president to his just-stated opinion in case it came up at the next Tower Board meeting. Wallison's motivation—and that of all of us—was to keep Reagan from swinging back and forth. At the top of the memorandum, Wallison wrote, "On this issue of the TOW shipment in August, in discussing this matter with me and David Abshire, you said you were surprised to learn that the Israelis had shipped the arms. If that is your recollection and if the question comes up at the Tower Board meeting, you might want to say that you were surprised."[7] Writing this memo turned out to be a bad idea.

The second Tower Board meeting occurred in the Oval Office on February 11. The meeting began with the president reading points that Wallison and I had prepared about the appropriate functions of the White House national security process, with Tower then noting that his views were similar to those of the other former presidents with whom the panel had spoken. Chairman Tower asked about the discrepancy between Reagan's statement in the first meeting and the recent testimony that Don Regan had given to the board. The board was especially mindful of the fact that the chief of staff had already testified that in his view the president was clearly unaware of the shipment beforehand. This became the issue at the second full board meeting.

At this point, the president arose and walked to his desk, not so quietly whispering to Wallison, "Peter, where is the piece of paper you gave me this morning?" Finding the paper, the president—to the shock of all present—started reading, "If the question comes up at the Tower Board meeting, you might want to say that you were surprised."

At that point, Tower's jaw went slack, the faces of Scowcroft and Muskie drained, and my heart skipped. Wallison later wrote, "I was horrified, just horrified. I didn't expect him to go and get the paper. Much less read from it that way."[8]

Wallison was later to write, "[I]t was not only a terribly embarrassing moment but at a time when there had been much press attention to the canard that Regan was somehow interested in making sure that his view of this issue—rather than McFarlane's—was accepted by the president, it could reasonably have been viewed by the Tower Board as an effort to influence the President in the direction of Regan's view."[9] Meanwhile, public sympathy had moved toward McFarlane, with his attempted suicide, and, to boot, the panel contained two former bosses of McFarlane, who were fond of him. It was not a good day for Reagan or, for that matter, me, Wallison, and certainly Don Regan.[10]

The damage had been done. The Tower Board report, which was about to go to press, would contain this frightful discrepancy. There were some whispers around the staff, the White House press corps, and beyond. There were a few anticipated questions: Was the president, wounded once and recently operated on, incompetent? Was he being dishonest? If he was so confused, maybe he knew about Oliver North's illegal diversion of funds to the contras and forgot it. Was he being manipulated by the powerful chief of staff? Where was the special counselor in all this? No one seemed to be asking that question, but I was. I did not know at the time, but the Oval Office was outraged over the Tower Board meeting. As Clark McFadden, the counsel to the Tower Board, later explained it to me, the angry Tower Board members felt that "Don Regan, to save himself, had manipulated" the president into making McFarlane the villain. The president was unaware he was being used.[11]

Over breakfast indigestion on February 19, I read a three-column headline on the front page of the *Washington Post*. The lead story, "President Changed Statement on 1985 Iran Arms Approval," related Reagan's contradictions. In this piece, Bob Woodward and David Hoffman cite a source that said that "Regan redirected the president, went over the issues with him, and got the president to line up his recollections." The second headline read, "President Says Future of Regan 'Up to Him.'" Similar stories soon ran across the country on the problem of Regan as chief of staff, with many calls for his resignation.

During these tense days, the president reflected to me several times that, if he had only recorded in his diary that evening of August 6, 1985, he would not have caused all of this trouble. I was shocked by that comment. I blurted out, "Mr. President, if you asked me, as NATO ambassador, to come clean and tell you the conversation I had with NATO Secretary-General Lord Carrington in Brussels, on August 6, 1985, I'd tell you that I've no idea. But you know what? As ambassador, I had a note taker. He kept the record. I didn't have to remember everything. You had two national security advisors. They should've kept this record for you. They shouldn't have placed you in this intolerable position."

The president stared at me with those smoky blue eyes. There was embarrassment, but where was his anger? I was astonished by how he recoiled from bringing himself to criticize subordinates.

About this time, I had a little luck. I needed it. The Tower Board's date for going to press was delayed by a few days because a whole new source of the computer-stored, e-mail-like PROFS (professional office system) notes that North and Poindexter believed they had destroyed had been found.[12] I conferred with Peter Wallison about how to use this delay. Wallison and I decided to meet alone with the president to tell him bluntly that we had a major crisis with regard to his credibility. As an interested party in the dispute, Don Regan had to be excluded. Of course, I had the authority, as special counselor, to meet with the president at any time without the chief of staff.

As the three of us huddled in the Oval Office, it was a poignant moment as a deeply concerned president very quickly confessed that he had made a terrible mistake.[13] He unsuccessfully tried to stretch his memory. He had tried too hard to remember something that he simply could not, so he had grabbed at straws. Wallison and I both chimed in that a clarification had to be urgently made with the Tower Board before its report went to press. Wallison argued that I should talk to Tower as to how to clarify the record with the board. Reagan agreed.

Once back in my office, I telephoned Tower in his temporary quarters in the New Executive Office Building: "John, can we arrange a meeting or a telephone call between the president and the board? This would allow the president to make a final statement resolving the conflicted testimony."

"David, it's no longer possible or practical to have another encounter with the president," an exasperated Tower replied. I was stunned. It was a devastating statement about the president of the United States. "Dave, if the president has anything to add, he should do it in writing. But let this Texan offer a little country advice to his Tennessee friend. The president himself should write the letter. Not his staff!"[14]

"John, I get the point. John, I agree," I replied grimly.

By phone I updated Wallison and Brower as to Tower's remark about the futility of meeting again with the president and the board's loss of confidence in the commander in chief. Wallison sent a memo to the president suggesting he write a clarifying letter. That memo was on the president's desk the evening of February 19.

The next morning, we received on yellow-lined legal paper a black-ink draft in Reagan's handwriting. It read as follows:

> Dear John,
> This really should be addressed to all three of you. I realize that my efforts to recall the events of last August having to do with the arms shipments by the Israelis to Iran have caused some confusion. I'm trying to recall events that happened eighteen months ago, and I am afraid that I let myself be influenced by other recollections, not my own. I have no personal notes or records to help my recollections on this matter. The only answer is to state that, try as I might, I cannot recall anything whatsoever about whether I approved an Israeli sale in advance or whether I approved replenishment of Israeli stocks last August. My answer therefore and the simple truth is, 'I don't remember—period.' I'm sorry to have made things more difficult for you and thanks for what you are doing.

Alone, I went back into the Oval Office to see the president with the original and a copy that had been typed by his secretary. There were two unresolved questions. First, to whose "recollections" was he referring? On the original yellow draft, there was a reference to McFarlane crossed through.

I looked Reagan in the eye and said, "You mentioned you'd been influenced by the recollections of others. Whose, Mr. President, if I may ask?" I thought he was going to say by Bud McFarlane's recent testimony. Sitting back in his chair, Reagan replied firmly, "Don Regan's."

"Mr. President, your draft letter referred to 'last August' rather than August, 1985," I observed. "You obviously inadvertently made it the wrong year."

"Should we retype it, or should I just do an ink correction?" Reagan asked.

A sixth sense told me not to take that paper back to the president's secretary to be retyped. My instinct was correct. At that moment, Don Regan was hovering by the secretary's desk outside the Oval Office, waiting for me to come out. He knew something was up.

"Ink," I urged. This he did. I then took the original sheet of yellow tablet paper and the typed letter signed by the president with the ink correction and headed for the door of the Oval Office. Opening it, I saw Don Regan staring at me. "Hi, Don," I said as I breezed by.

Out of the White House's iron gates, I headed across Lafayette Square to Tower's office in the New Executive Office Building. The board was in session, but its dapper chair hustled out of the meeting to greet me. Handing him the typed letter on presidential stationery and the original tablet sheet, I said, "John, perhaps you would like to see the president's own handwriting." John read it. He was obviously impressed. He asked if he could keep the original. "That would be helpful, very helpful," he muttered. I gave him the original after he had a photocopy made. I detoured through Lafayette Square on my way back to the White House and with relief circled the equestrian statue of my fellow Tennessean Andrew Jackson. Nancy Reagan was waiting, probably breathlessly, to learn of the outcome. I walked to the residence to see and update her.

I think it is now appropriate to take time out from our story to examine the president's health at this low point in the Reagan presidency. He was a seventy-five-year-old president who had suffered from a gunshot wound, an earlier surgery, and a more recent operation, not five weeks before the Tower Board appearance. Medical doctors say that the impact of general anesthesia on the brain can extend beyond five weeks and that recovery time can increase with age. No doubt these conditions can explain his public fumbling and his mistake of reading the Wallison memo in front of the board. However, such a temporary lapse, although dramatic, does not justify Howard Baker's advance man, James Cannon, in concluding that the president's inattentiveness and inability merited application of the Twenty-fifth Amendment to transfer governing power to the vice president. To the contrary, Reagan was not incapacitated. During my three-month White House tenure, Reagan was acutely focused in each of our dozen private meetings. Indeed, he would go forward to lead the nation and the alliance toward the ending of the Cold War.

Transformational leaders often lack attention to detail. A longtime Reagan observer has written that, about the time Reagan turned fifty-one, he had to testify about happenings when he was president of the Screen Actors' Guild in 1952. Reagan remembered "almost nothing about it."[15] In retrospect, I believe it was unfortunate that a close associate like Ed Meese was not the leader in this preparation, and I understand Nancy Reagan's tears about the consequence of overtutoring were correct.

On the larger issue of physical condition, Reagan was not the first to face serious health challenges while in the nation's highest office. Franklin Roosevelt and John Kennedy not only continued as president but also provided extraordinary leadership in spite of the handicaps of disease and disability.

CHAPTER 14

Tower Board Report

On February 25, my fifty-second day, with thirty-eight to go, the Tower Board report was printed. Chairman Tower called me, a Texan talking to a Tennessean, as he put it again. Still unnerved by and angry at the suspicions of staff manipulation, Tower said that he and other board members did not want Regan's staff first reviewing their report, giving the president a bunch of notes, and telling him what to say. This was the president's board, and the members wanted to hand him the report and do the briefing. Tower stressed that a presidential press conference or public statement was not needed immediately. After all, it would naturally take several days for the president to read and digest the report. Then the president could respond publicly. I listened carefully and replied, "I appreciate what you are saying, John."

I reached Don Regan by phone and relayed Tower's message. Regan snapped back: "That procedure is totally unacceptable. This whole thing is completely out of line. No report goes to the president without being staffed. Make this clear to Tower." Regan did not ask for my view. He was acting like the "chief," but I let it pass.

The next morning, I phoned Tower to report Regan's comment.

Tower came back strong. "Of course the president can order us to give him the report in advance if that's the way he truly feels. But let it be known that this is *not* the way the president's board wants it. And it will take a direct order from the president to do it." I said, "John, on this one, I am backing your board, not Don Regan."[1]

It was not until that evening, from my kitchen in Old Town in Alexandria, that I reached Regan again through the White House switchboard. "Don, I told Tower your position, and he responded that it would take a direct order from the president for the board to follow your procedure. I do not believe this is worth a showdown with all the controversy we have already had in the press. I want you to know that I'm supporting the position of the board."

The chief of staff exploded. He shot back: "You're personally too close to all this to have an objective judgment. And you've been too far away to know how the White House operates. Don't you understand that a head of government or a Cabinet member has never met with this president without prior staffing?" Regan shouted.

"Don, this situation is quite different. We have a crisis of presidential survival." With my own voice rising, I added, "Don, you are your own worst enemy!" (I never said, as his book alleges, that prior review would have given the president "undue advantage."[2])

At this stormy moment, my wife, Carolyn, entered our kitchen. Feeling that I was being terribly impolite to someone, she whispered, "Who're you talking to in such a rude tone of voice?"

"The White House chief of staff," I muttered, motioning to her to keep quiet.

Regan concluded, "All right, it's your show. You take the consequences."

He knew he had to retreat. But I was fearful that he would still try to prep the president for what he thought might be in the report and, particularly, to fend off any criticism of himself. Therefore I had to make a final point: "Don, I want to be the last person with the president and alone with him the fifteen minutes before he meets with the board."

He re-erupted: "I'll bet you're going to tell the president that this is a good board and good report."

"You've got it exactly right," I retorted angrily.

The next morning, February 26, at the eight o'clock White House chief-of-staff meeting, we all sat around the large mahogany table in the Roosevelt Room. Don Regan had either regained his composure or, as one might better say, tamed his wrath. My turn came. In a matter-of-fact voice, I described the events that would emerge later that day at the board meeting with the president. I pointedly noted that the president would be receiving the report for the first time. At the strong request of the board, it would not be vetted or debriefed beforehand by the White House staff. This was not an adversarial board set up by the Congress but the president's own board reporting to him.

There would be ample time for briefing in the next few days before the president had to make any public statement. Don Regan added in a composed way, "That's right." On the surface, no one would have known there was a dispute, but I suspect some did.

At 9:40 A.M., I was hovering outside the Oval Office. Then, in my ensuing fifteen-minute meeting, I told the president, "You should know that I had a serious difference of opinion with Don. You should know that I supported the board's way of handling the report. Their way is that they hand you the report and that they, not your staff, brief you on its contents. Whether or not we agree with every criticism in the board report, and, I have said before, when Don and I met, it is absolutely essential to support the board in its investigation, which you, Mr. President, authorized." President Reagan immediately understood what I was saying. There was no equivocation.

"Yes, I fully agree. I'm with you." That made two of us, and that was all that counted, assuming no one, especially Don, persuaded the president to change his mind.

Promptly at 10 A.M., the president and I left the Oval Office and walked together to the Cabinet Room, which never failed to impress me. Its spacious French windows looked out over the new wintry rose garden. Inside, imposing marble busts of Washington and Franklin rested in the niches flanking the mantle above which hung Armand-Dumaresq's painting titled *Declaration of Independence by the United States, Philadelphia, 4 July 1776*. Portraits of Washington, Jefferson, Lincoln, and Theodore Roosevelt looked down from the walls to where a fellow president's legacy would be weighed in the balance. This was indeed one of those historic occasions and a turning point for a presidency in trouble. As we entered, John Tower, Brent Scowcroft, and Ed Muskie, members of what was officially called "the president's special review board," respectfully stood by their appointed seats next to the president's. Regan; Wallison; Carlucci; Tower's staff director, Rhett Dawson; and his counsel, Clark McFadden, stood around the oblong table.

After informal greetings, we took our seats. Chair John Tower officially presented the president with an inch-thick document. A presidential seal adorned its glossy blue cover.

This meeting was quite different from the prior one. This time the president never fumbled, and he gave the board members his unwavering attention. Tower commenced—his Texas voice resonating a bit as if he were still chairing a session of the Senate Armed Services Committee—with a brief outline of the report and recommendations. He stressed that the board had made a straightforward, honest effort and come to a unanimous view representing the collective understandings, evaluations, and judgments of all three members. He said that they had never had significant disagreements. Next, he noted that the report was divided into five parts: Following the introduction, a section appeared on the arms transfer to Iran; then, one on the diversion and support for the contras; then a narrative of the affair; next, a section on what went wrong; and finally, the board's recommendations and conclusions. The board noted that the National Security Council system had served the executive well for more than forty years, and, had it been used in this case, it could have "help[ed] prevent bad ideas from becoming presidential policy," as the report made clear. Tower stressed that the board unanimously agreed that attempts were made to trade arms for hostages and that there was evidence of a diversion of funds, with unaccounted money. The board concluded that North and Poindexter were responsible.[3]

At this point, the president came to life, asking where the money had gone and bringing up the bank account in Switzerland. Reagan referred to it as a "bridge loan," a favorite expression he had used with me before. A speculative discussion followed concerning the money trail—what went to the wealthy Saudi middleman Adnan Khashoggi; to the Pentagon for reimbursement for arms; and to the contras. There was as yet no clear answer in the investigations, and the trails had to be left to the other investigating groups such as the Congress and the independent counsel.

Moving from the speculative to the known, Tower then stressed that, while the original intent may have been a strategic opening with Iran, it very quickly deteriorated into arms for hostages. The president objected to this characterization and emphasized that no one in his government was dealing with the captors and he had no intention of swapping arms for hostages. General Scowcroft intervened. He explained in some detail McFarlane's and North's May, 1986, trip to Tehran. He also explained that General Secord's plane was on a foreign runway loaded with arms, waiting to take off once confirmation was received that hostages had been released. This was clearly arms for hostages. As Scowcroft went on, the president came to life again and exclaimed, "No question, it became arms for hostages."[4] He had finally and clearly said what I had not been able to have him conclude in our private meetings or the group meetings with Regan, Bush, and others.

The president inquired when the policy to explore a strategic opening to Iran had deteriorated into arms for hostages. Tower replied that the board did not have a precise opinion. He then reiterated that the board felt it was appropriate to investigate openings to Iran, but he noted it became clear that there were no moderates in Iran, only radicals. Furthermore, the board found that North had certainly misrepresented his access to the president and distorted the president's policies. The fundamental lesson, Tower stressed, was that the NSC should not have been circumvented and Congress should not have been held at bay. Later in the discussion, Tower emphasized that Casey should have made certain that all covert operations remained within the Central Intelligence Agency. He considered what had transpired as "amateurish." Muskie said that the NSC should not be involved in "operations." The NSC's directives were not followed, covert operations were not scrutinized, and careful records were not kept.

The vice president intervened to ask whether board members thought there would be new facts and revelation when Poindexter and North testified. Both Tower and Scowcroft responded that they felt it unlikely because the paper trail had already been identified. Muskie further added that the paper trail of the diversion of funds was a problem, however.

The discussion touched on Congress's request for timely notification and issues related to dealing with various congressional committees, each with different configurations, on covert and highly sensitive information. The board pointed out that the Iranian hostage-rescue attempt during the Carter administration had been a short operation, unlike the ongoing Iranian arms operations. I noted that there had been a few proposals for joint committees, like the precedent-setting Joint Atomic Energy Committee, which was known for never having leaks. If such a structure were created, the executive branch might feel more comfortable about providing it with sensitive information. The president related his experience on the Rockefeller Commission in the wake of the Church Committee investigation, which had leaked information to the public.

The president then expressed confusion over Poindexter's and North's refusals to volunteer testimony. Tower immediately referred the question to his counsel, Clark McFadden, who said that, because of the Boland Amendment's structure, he had so far not found criminal liability. This judgment applied to the arms sales alone, not to the diversion of funds.

Wallison intervened, asking about what the board had found on the "cover-up"; a recent *Newsweek* article alleged that Regan had led an effort in the White House to conceal the truth. Although he did not mention the article, Wallison asked "whether there had been a cover-up, and, if so, who was responsible for it?" Tower responded that the board had not used that term. He added that, in the aftermath, the NSC staff had "distorted the facts" but that the chief of staff had to bear the responsibility for their actions and for the full disclosure of the facts after the affair became public. Twice in these discussions Muskie stressed that inadequate record keeping had left the president exposed, thus creating chaos. He then implied that the chief of staff had a responsibility, if not on NSC policies, then on the NSC process: "The chief of staff should ensure that the system, the total operation, is serving the president," Muskie said.

The good news, as Tower explained, was that the report exonerated the president personally from any attempt at a cover-up. The board was convinced that the president wanted the full story to be told. On the other hand, the report highlighted the misleading statements of North, McFarlane, Poindexter, and Regan in their attempt to "distance" or protect Reagan from the scandal. The board complained that it had found notes of key meetings missing, and General Scowcroft added, "It may be that some went into the shredder, but we can't prove it." When considering Reagan's conflicting statements on January 26 and February 11 about the approval of the sales to Iran in August of 1985, the board leaned toward McFarlane's version of prior approval. Tower stressed, "We found Bud McFarlane very forthcoming, a very credible witness." I glanced at Don Regan because I knew he would not be happy with that.

Frank Carlucci asked whether the board recommended that the NSC advisor report to the president through the chief of staff. Tower answered, "No, leave it as it is."[5]

As the meeting progressed, I thought John Tower, Brent Scowcroft, and Ed Muskie had made an excellent decision to present their report face to face to the president. They had indeed explained it to him before the White House staff developed cue cards. The president remained fully engaged and extremely alert throughout the meeting and was not distracted by staff briefing cards. Most importantly, he finally recognized and accepted on the record the fact that arms had been exchanged for hostages. Moreover, he accepted the full report as I had hoped he would.

Overall, it was an extremely good meeting, lasting only thirty minutes. It was the best in my fifty-one days in the White House. On the way out of the meeting, Brent Scowcroft shuffled by Don Regan. Brent, trying to be both genial and kind, holding up his thumb and forefinger with just a little light between them said, "Don, there are just a few lines in there about you."

The few lines, however, turned out to be devastating. They read as follows: "More than almost any chief of staff in recent memory, he asserted personal control over the White House staff and sought to extend his control to the national security adviser. He was personally active in national security affairs and attended almost all of the relevant meetings regarding the Iran initiative. He, as much as anyone, should have insisted that an orderly process be observed. In addition, he especially should have ensured that plans were made for handling any public disclosure of the initiative. He must bear the prime responsibility for the chaos that descended upon the White House when such disclosure did occur."[6]

Don Regan was not the only one miffed. The report held the two competing Cabinet secretaries accountable: "Given the importance of the initiative and the sharp policy divergences involved, however, Secretary Shultz and Secretary Weinberger, while indicating their opposition, distanced themselves from the march of events." As for the terminally ill director of Central Intelligence, Bill Casey, the report says, "There is no evidence, however, that Director Casey made clear to the president that Lt. Col. North, rather than the CIA, was running the operation. The president does not recall ever being informed of this fact. Indeed, Director Casey should have gone further and pressed for operational responsibility to be transferred to the CIA."[7]

If the report exonerated the president from complicity in attempting to cover up, it still was highly critical of the National Security Council system. "The NSC system will not work unless the President makes it work. . . . The President did not force his policy to undergo the most critical review of which the NSC participants and the process were capable."[8]

After the Oval Office meeting, a somber president walked with members of the Tower Board to the Old Executive Office Building. In a packed auditorium, the president grimly greeted the press and introduced and thanked the board members for their work. Referring to the report in his hand, he said, "I intend to read and digest it first, think carefully about its findings, and promptly act on its recommendations." The president then turned the meeting over to Chairman Tower and quickly returned to the White House, brushing aside reporters' questions about Don Regan's future. The president canceled his trip to Camp David in order to study the report in the family quarters during the weekend.

Chairman Tower, speaking to the press assemblage, debriefed the report, and former senator and secretary of state Muskie offered a unanimously adopted summary. It was cutting: "The Iran initiative was handled almost casually and through informal channels. . . . It was subject neither to the general procedures for interagency consideration and review of policy nor the procedures for covert operations. . . . Intelligence analyses could also have provided independent evaluation of the Israeli proposals. . . . Concern for preserving the secrecy of the initiative provided an excuse for abandoning sound process. . . . The informality of the initiative meant that it lacked a formal institutional record and informed analysis. . . . The NSC system will not work unless the president makes it work. . . . No NSC officials deserve high marks."[9] The best news of the report was carried in these lines: "[T]he president said he had no knowledge of the diversion prior to his conversation with Attorney General Meese on November 25, 1986. No evidence has come to light to suggest otherwise. Contemporaneous Justice Department staff notes of Lt. Col. North's interview with Attorney General Meese on November 23, 1986, show North telling the Attorney General that only he, Mr. McFarlane, and VADM Poindexter were aware of the diversion." Plainly, there was no smoking gun in the president's hand.[10]

Following the Tower Board meeting, Reagan broke out of his isolation most notably on February 27, during a meeting in the White House with key Republican members of Congress such as Senators Dole and Simpson and Representatives Michel and Cheney. White House congressional liaison Will Ball, Don Regan, and I sat in. Senate minority leader Dole bluntly asked the chief of staff when he was going to resign. Regan replied only that he was thinking about it.

Sen. Al Simpson was equally direct, reflecting on parts of the report: "Very frankly, Mr. President, you should kick ass and take names. You've got to get Cap and George operating in step. It is a disgrace the way they currently operate." I was pleased at the comment but disappointed when Frank Carlucci agreed with the president that the press exaggerated the conflicts. This clash between secretaries remained his single biggest national security problem, but the president still would not face it, and Carlucci was not able to solve it either. Ironically, it was only solved months later when Weinberger resigned and Carlucci took his place as secretary of defense.

It is appropriate to pause in this narrative to analyze the process that led to the report and to the substance of the report itself. Remarkably, the report investigations were executed without subpoena power; without an interview of Bill Casey, who was incapacitated; and without an opportunity to question Poindexter and North or Gen. Richard Secord, a key intermediary. A number of principal players in the crisis were not available, especially those involved in the diversion of funds. Yet, the appendices of the report alone number more than five hundred pages.

As one whose staff reviewed and interpreted a mass of documentation in about three month's time, I very much sympathized with the board's enormous workload. In an even shorter period of time, an expert group that had to be quickly put together, the Tower Board had had to perform under extreme pressure and deadline. To add to the board's challenge, the most revealing evidence in the PROFS notes was discovered toward the end of the investigations. This entire endeavor, directed by attorney Rhett Dawson, included a staff of twenty-three who took testimony from fifty-six witnesses, developed a chronology, and produced the final document, which was well written by another attorney, Stephen Hadley, with W. Clark McFadden as the general counsel. Amazingly enough, absolutely no leaks occurred in leaky-prone Washington, D.C.

As for the three diverse board members, one was a former air force lieutenant general and a former advisor for the National Security

Council. The other two were senators who had had partisan political careers—one of whom, Muskie, had been a presidential candidate and a former secretary of state—and all had mellowed over time. As board members, they had differences along the way but worked as a team.

The thorniest issue for them was the vice president's position: Was he "distancing himself" from the president and the affair as did the secretary of state and defense? The vice president had at one point said he was "out of the loop," but this was a statement subject to interpretation. However, the board reasoned that Shultz and Weinberger had the option of resigning. Muskie would have remembered that his predecessor as secretary of state, Cyrus Vance, resigned from the Carter administration because he was not consulted and thus not "in the loop" about the 1980 hostage-rescue attempt in Iran. While resignation may have been an option for Shultz and Weinberger, that alternative was hardly available to an elected vice president. This was a sensitive challenge for the panel because the vice president would be a presidential candidate. The board solved its problem by not holding the vice president responsible as it did Shultz and Weinberger.[11]

In all of these deliberations, however, Muskie was certainly no patsy and, as the sole Democrat, reportedly was often outspoken during board discussions. At the press conference, he produced an outstanding summary of the report. Perhaps it was unfortunate that he was not called upon to provide his detailed review of the main findings during the closed meeting with the president as Wallison later noted.

Theodore Draper, in his exhaustive book on Iran-contra, articulates another criticism with the report and its release:

> President Reagan clearly set the main policy but refused to take responsibility for it. When the storm broke, he behaved as if he could get off scot-free by denying that he had known what had been going on. In the case of the diversion of funds from the Iran arms sales to the Nicaraguan contras, he chose to defend himself on the ground that he had not taken care, as if ignorance made him innocent.
>
> Reagan was not unsuccessful in this ploy. The Tower Report is at its worst in its verdict on what was wrong with President Reagan's handling of these affairs. The emphasis

is put on his "management style" instead of on his political decision. Most [of the] blame is put on Chief of Staff Regan, who is said to bear "primary responsibility for the chaos that descended upon the White House when such disclosure did occur." In fact, the disclosure was primarily handled by Attorney General Meese, and Regan, whatever his shortcomings, was not responsible for National Security Advisers McFarlane and Poindexter. Reagan's "management style" undoubtedly left much to be desired, but in these affairs it was distinctly secondary to the basic direction of his policy.[12]

I would disagree with the overall thrust of his critique. While the Tower Report exonerates the president of any cover-up and criticizes his management style, it is also a devastating analysis of his presidential leadership and policy during this period. As Senator Muskie said at the press conference, "The policy was a wrong policy, and it was the president's policy." The report held the president fully responsible for seeing that the successful processes of the National Security Council were effectively utilized.

Ultimately, Iran-contra's notorious failure was indeed the fault of the president, made possible by his evasion of the National Security Council process. This lasting lesson for the future raises an all-important question: When will presidents fully learn from history? The National Security Council had been avoided before, most notably by President Johnson during the critical decision-making period between October, 1964, and February, 1965, when U.S. participation in the Vietnam War escalated with ground troops.[13] President Kennedy also terminated the processes of the NSC, previously used by Eisenhower, which resulted in the disastrous Bay of Pigs affair. In December, 2002, before the second Iraq war, the NSC process was again aborted and the State Department excluded; preparation and execution of both the fighting and reconstruction were turned over to the Defense Department.

The National Security Act of 1947 was inspired by the wise men who had crafted the winning strategies of World War II. These men knew that all elements of national power, departments, and agencies had to be coordinated to achieve success. Organizing these constituents creates checks and balances by bringing different points of view to bear on key policy discussions. The Tower Board had emphasized this important fundamental lesson, one that Gen. Brent Scowcroft understood during the first Bush administration and the Gulf War, when he was the National Security Advisor. The result was the successful use of the NSC process during that conflict, which still serves as a model of coordinated strategies and diplomatic action.

I do fault the board for not fully examining the existing machinery that should have been used to review the quality of intelligence. Earlier in this book I discussed the role of the President's Foreign Intelligence Advisory Board (PFIAB), established by President Eisenhower, to review the quality of intelligence and to act, in effect, as a permanent team "B" to the central intelligence products. The Iranian initiative was based on two deeply flawed intelligence assumptions: first, that there were Iranian moderates with whom we could do business, and, second, that those moderates had absolute influence with the hostage holders in Lebanon to gain the release of the captives for arms trade. Both were proven unmistakably wrong; the quality of intelligence provided by the Israelis and Ghorbanifar was extremely faulty and, one might say, lousy. The director of the Central Intelligence Agency avoided his duty to disclose this entire activity to the PFIAB and, in fact, totally bypassed it.[14]

Finally, I fault those of us in the White House for our poor management of the Tower Board interface. We on the White House staff mistakenly allowed the president to present differing accounts of his approval of the arms transfer plan at the first and second Tower Board meetings. The president did approve of the arms transfer, and this essential fact was more important than the issue of when he granted approval. However, we allowed the disputed testimony between McFarlane and Regan needlessly to become a major public issue. I fault myself for returning to Brussels at the time of the first Tower Board meeting and thus not witnessing the president's good first performance. Attempts to stretch the president's memory beyond its bounds in the subsequent briefing sessions turned out to be a mistake, particularly because Reagan had not found any related diary notes to add to his memory. The president's final letter to Tower makes this clear: "I allowed myself to be influenced by the recollections of others." If only at the second board meeting Reagan had said, "I don't remember—period." Nancy Reagan had warned against this overbriefing and overquestioning during our private meetings. We all should have listened to her.

In hindsight, however, any flaws of the Tower Board report or of our staff failure are minor compared to the board's landmark achievement. After many months of serious presidential crises during a critical phase of the Cold War, the Tower Board produced a credible and broadly accepted document that created the foundation for restoring the Reagan presidency. Tower, Muskie, and Scowcroft—with their honesty, efficiency, and thoroughness—should join the list of those who helped save the Reagan presidency.

CHAPTER 15

The Departure of Don Regan

Three days earlier, on February 23, the president had finally but very gently suggested to Don Regan that it might be good for him to resign before the Tower Board report was released. "You can't do that to me, Mr. President," Regan responded. "If I go before that report is out, you throw me to the wolves. I deserve better treatment than that."[1] In a nonconfrontational mood, Reagan was embarrassed and backed down. He asked Regan when he wanted to leave. "The first part of next week" was the response.

When she heard about this conversation, Nancy Reagan phoned me. She was concerned that Regan was again attempting to tough it out and said that she hoped I would talk to the president to stiffen his position. She also asked if I knew whether George Bush had talked with Regan about departing. She feared that it would be a real mistake still to have Regan around when the president was addressing how he was going to implement the recommendations of the Tower panel.

On Thursday afternoon, February 26, Vice Pres. George Bush met with Don Regan and, on behalf of the president, again brought up the subject of resignation. Don exploded. Later an irate Regan phoned Bush and said that his resignation would be on Reagan's desk Monday morning.

But who could replace Regan and do it quickly? Reagan immediately thought of his longtime friend Sen. Paul Laxalt, but, when approached, Laxalt demurred. He said former senate majority leader Howard Baker was the man for the job.

Baker, like Laxalt, had been mentioned in the news for a possible run at the Republican presidential nomination. Reagan replied to Laxalt's suggestion, "Well, hell, he's going to run for president."[2]

Laxalt said he was not sure about Baker's intentions and this might be a graceful way for him to exit that race. Laxalt was right.

Then things moved fast. Reagan phoned Baker, who flew to Washington for an undisclosed meeting with the president and accepted the offer. Confidential though it was, that same Friday afternoon at 4 P.M. the secret was on CNN before Regan had written his resignation letter. Frank Carlucci heard the television report and dashed to Regan's office to warn him. The news made Regan furious, and he charged Nancy with leaking the news. He sent for Fitzwater.

Fitzwater describes his entry to Regan's office: "I opened the door slowly. The inhabitants of the room [Dennis Thomas and Tom Dawson] froze in place. . . . They were like bronze statues."[3] Behind the desk was the chief of staff, crying. Regan handed Fitzwater a one-line letter. "Issue it," he ordered.

> *Dear Mr. President:*
> *I hereby resign as chief of staff to the President of the United States.*
> *Respectfully yours, Donald T. Regan*

"Has the president seen it?" Fitzwater asked. "Issue it!" Regan screamed.

A bewildered Fitzwater retreated to his office and phoned the president. At that moment Mrs. Reagan was welcoming me into the family quarters. I had a meeting scheduled with the president at which Mrs. Reagan had urged me to discuss the president's Saturday radio address. I hoped to persuade him to move ahead of the Tower Board release and publicly admit that his policy had deteriorated into one of trading arms for hostages. This long-sought-after admission would help remove that issue from the table and from the news when the report came out.

I said to Mrs. Reagan, "Shouldn't you also be in the room with me to help persuade the president?"

"No, Dave, that would be counterproductive. But we've just heard that Howard Baker's appointment was reported on CNN. Ronnie's on the phone, but walk on into his study. You can be of help." I did so, but as I slipped into a chair, I was surprised by what I heard. "Well, that's too bad," grumped the president. Fitzwater was apparently reading Regan's one-liner over the phone.

The president hung up the phone and then told me that Fitzwater was suggesting that the White House release a statement accepting Regan's resignation and officially announcing Baker's appointment. Between his calls, I tried, without much success, to engage the president in a discussion about his Saturday radio speech. By then the president was too preoccupied for that discussion.

In a minute or two, Fitzwater was back on the phone to read the draft. "It is with deep regret that I accept the resignation of Chief of Staff Donald T. Regan."

I heard the president say, "Take out that word 'deep.'" Finally, he was truly angry.

During Bush's encounter with Regan on February 26, the vice president had commented that the president hoped the departure of the chief of staff would go smoothly. Regan shot back: "I don't see how it is going to go smoothly. I've been hacked to pieces in the press by these people, and now, after two years as the President's Chief of Staff and four years as his Secretary of the Treasury, I'm being fired like a shoe clerk."[4]

This was sad because Donald Regan, son of a policeman, was a self-made man, a fine wartime marine, at the top of the Wall Street culture, and an able secretary of the treasury. If only as chief of staff in crisis he had followed Lord Carrington's example, he could have departed as a sacrificial hero and not, as he termed it, "a shoe clerk."

Early the next week, I passed Don going in the opposite direction in the parking lot. We spoke politely. In the press of following up on the Tower Board report, I didn't get by to see him in his temporary office in the OEOB before his departure. I have always regretted that fact. I could never dislike him, and he had many qualities I admired.

What is the overall assessment of Don Regan's tenure during the Iran-contra months in the White House? Why should he have had the wisdom to resign much earlier? First, he had portrayed himself as "Mr. Prime Minister," as the press called him, for his boast that he controlled Reagan's agenda.[5] Other stories depicted him as the "deputy president" or as "the chief," as he often referred to himself, because of his efforts to control the president and policy.[6]

He did not control the operation of the NSC staff, but every morning at the chief of staff's White House staff meeting, the NSC advisor sat at the other end of the table and reported when his turn came.

Regan sat in on all briefings given to the president by the national security adviser. Knowing him from his Wall Street days, when he needed to constantly appraise risks, I cannot understand why from the beginning he did not align his position with Weinberger and Shultz. He was often suspicious of the NSC, and certainly he often did not trust Bud McFarlane's judgment. Unlike Shultz and Weinberger, Regan supported the Iranian arms-for-hostages policy that went wrong. Thus he bears a major burden in the Iran-contra matter.

Once President Reagan had made a decision, it was Regan's duty as chief of staff to carry it out. However, he had plenty of opportunities to dissent or offer caution, and if he had joined with Weinberger and Shultz, I believe the operation might have been turned off.

Second, as Regan loyalist Peter Wallison himself notes, Regan went to the opposite extreme of the first Reagan administration, which had a chief, a deputy chief of staff, and a counselor. "Regan never took the step of formally authorizing a deputy. Nor did he bring into the White House until the arrival of David Abshire during the Iran-Contra crisis any senior respected 'wise man' who could have served as an eyes and ears for the President and himself."[7] Howard Baker, upon his arrival, immediately appointed and empowered Ken Duberstein as deputy chief of staff.

Third, the White House by Regan's own admission was involved in a destructive conflict—Nancy Reagan vs. Don Regan. In his book *For the Record*, Regan lays much blame on Nancy Reagan and her consultation with her astrologer before major scheduling decisions were made, even the date of Reagan's July, 1985, intestinal surgery. In fact, Regan opens his book with this dramatic revelation: "Virtually every major move and decision the Reagans made during my time as White House chief of staff was cleared in advance with a woman in San Francisco who drew up horoscopes to make certain that the planets were in a favorable alignment for the enterprise."[8] If Don Regan had truly felt so victimized by the first lady in his work as chief of staff, he should certainly have stepped out before the time that he and the first lady were hanging up on each other.[9]

Fourth, Chiefs of Staff Jim Baker and Howard Baker and Baker's deputy, Ken Duberstein, had Nancy Reagan's total confidence and did not encounter insurmountable obstacles in scheduling. It does not seem so strange to conclude that one requirement of the White House chief of staff is to be able to get along with the first lady. It is hard to imagine a chief of staff who could not get along with Hillary Clinton or Barbara Bush or Betty Ford or Rosalynn Carter but still tried to stay in that position.

Fifth, Regan's judgment became impaired. This was certainly true in my shouting-match phone call with him on the eve of the Tower Board report release. If his advice had been followed, there would have been headlines all across the nation: "Reagan and the Tower Board locked in conflict." Our whole plan of presidential recovery would have been sabotaged. Certainly during my tenure, Nancy Reagan's instincts on political issues were superior to Don's.

Lastly, with all the negatives, there is a plus for Don Regan. When the diversion scandal became known through Meese's investigation, Regan was in the forefront in wanting to appoint an independent investigation board, foreswearing executive privilege, and having a special counselor in the White House. These moves were all key to the president's political recovery. If protracting his stay as chief of staff in the winter of 1986 1987 helped drag the presidency down, Regan's wise advice in December contributed to eventually saving the Reagan administration. Thus, he joins the list of those who helped restore the Reagan presidency.[10]

CHAPTER 16

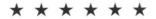

Howard Baker Arrives

When President Reagan tried to phone Howard Baker, who was vacationing in Florida, to ask him to be his new chief of staff, he reached Baker's wife, Joy. She explained that Howard was at the zoo with his grandchildren. "Well, tell him I need him because we've got a zoo up here," quipped the president. Baker later accepted, and, on a plane to Washington, he had a rather uninhibited conversation with a member of the press, not about his new job—which he avoided disclosing—but about the famed Don Regan–Nancy Reagan fights. Baker commented that "when she gets her hackles up, she can be a dragon."[1]

If Baker had momentarily let his guard down, it was back up when he arrived in Washington. It was agreed that he would take over as chief of staff on Monday morning, March 2, 1987. Baker immediately summoned his longtime confidant and one-time senate employee, James Cannon, along with another of his senate staffers, Tom Griscom, to go to the White House to query the incumbent staff and size things up. Reporting to Baker, Cannon called the White House atmosphere "chaos" and the president "inattentive . . . inept, and . . . lazy."[2] After he had picked up more gossip about the president and his competence, Cannon wrote the following in a memo to Baker: "Consider the possibility that section four of the 25th amendment might be applied." This meant involuntary retirement of the president if a majority of the Cabinet declares the president unable to continue in office.

This shocking assessment was incorrect. In my first conversation with Baker as the new chief of staff, I certainly disputed it, and Baker himself agreed after he met with and sized up Reagan. Referring to Cannon's report, Baker said, "Well, it doesn't sound like the Ronald

Reagan I just saw." It may well be that, in a bit of self-justification, some of the outgoing Regan aides were hyping the presidential negatives to Cannon to show the problem they had with such a detached president.[3]

If one had to invent the perfect model of the chief of staff at this moment in presidential history, Howard Baker Jr. would fit. In sharp contrast to the brisk and authoritative style of Don Regan, the easygoing but shrewd Baker with a Tennessee accent brought a modest and homespun manner to the office of chief of staff.

Baker's hometown is Huntsville, Tennessee, high on the beautiful Cumberland Plateau. This once-frontier community never lost its independent pioneering spirit and seceded from the state of Tennessee when it sceded from the Union. The Bakers were devoted to the historic Republican Party of Abraham Lincoln and to their First Presbyterian Church, where Howard Baker Jr. remained a deacon throughout his political life. Like Lincoln as a young lawyer, Baker had a knack for success in civil suits through his courtesy for all involved. This quality bode well for his later natural prominence in his conduct during the Watergate hearings.

Young Howard was born into politics, for his father, Howard Baker Sr., had run unsuccessfully for governor and senator and from 1950 to his death in 1964 had served in the House of Representatives. In 1966, young Howard was elected to the U.S. Senate despite the Goldwater debacle of 1964. Across the flatlands of middle Tennessee and the hills of the east, he organized the state's college youth and even made a broad appeal to the African American vote. Baker's biographer wrote the following about his stunning victory: "Here was the whig coalition he assembled in elephant's garb."[4]

Baker's father-in-law had been a wonderful political mentor. In 1951, Baker had married the daughter of the Republican icon, Illinois senator Everett Dirksen, the minority leader and a renowned public reader of Lincoln's addresses. Baker was impressed with the contrast between Dirksen and his predecessor as senate minority leader, William Knowland, who had sharp political edges. There were no edges to Dirksen or to his understudy son-in-law.

In 1970, when I was assistant secretary of state dealing with Congress, my confidant, Sen. John Sherman Cooper, took me aside: "Watch young Howard Baker. He should be the next Republican leader."[5] Cooper's prediction came true in 1976, after Baker achieved national prominence as vice chair of the committee investigating Watergate. With the 1980 Reagan sweep, Baker became the senate majority leader.

Baker's goal as majority leader was to "make things work" in true Dirksen style. His biographer wrote that he had never had—or even aspired to have—the transformational brand of leadership of a Roosevelt but instead sought the transactional kind—seeking practical compromises, as did the senate Whig leader, Henry Clay. Baker never looked for credit, and he left his ego behind. He built up his committee chairmen. When he dramatically moved from a senate career to be White House chief of staff, he was well equipped to see Pennsylvania Avenue as a two-way street and understand the political complexities in the wake of the Iran-contra affair.

This then was the short, somewhat stocky Tennessean who arrived at the White House gate as the new chief of staff on March 2. He was sitting up front in the official car with his driver. He joked that we spoke the same language without an accent (Tennessee English). At 8 A.M. he presided over his first White House staff meeting. This was followed by a 10 A.M. meeting in the Oval Office with the president, speechwriter Landon Parvin, and me to work on the draft for the president's forthcoming address to the nation. Then, at 11 A.M., a full Cabinet meeting followed. I noticed in Baker's dealings with the president that he made it very clear that Reagan, not he, was president. He openly deferred to the "president's more superior judgment" on a number of matters. The press immediately wanted to transfer the chief of staff's label from "prime minister" to "the regency"; Baker sunk the attempt by building up his president as the one clearly crowned king.

Howard's second day in office ended with a real shocker. Senators David Boren and William Cohen, the chair and ranking member of the Senate Intelligence Committee, urgently came to the White House to meet with Baker and me. They told a devastating story, reportedly from a retired navy captain who was the chief of staff of the previous Senate Intelligence Committee and was supposedly a good friend of John Poindexter. When drinking with friends, he blabbed that Poindexter was going to testify that he had briefed the president on the diversion of funds. Senator Boren warned that there was a chance that a journalist had the story. Any such story in the press, even if not true, would challenge the credibility of the Tower Board.

Baker turned to me in the style of a trial lawyer, which he once was, and said, "Have you ever seen any evidence to support this story?"

"Absolutely not," I firmly responded. After some talk, the senators departed. We worried for a day or two, but the story was never printed, and ultimately Poindexter did not so testify.[6] But it was a moment of great worry.

The task ahead was the president's critical comeback speech scheduled for the following day, March 4. A number of us had submitted background memos for the speech, and drafting had begun well before Baker's arrival. Nancy Reagan told me she wanted the drafter to be Landon Parvin, an outside consultant and speechwriter who had a knack for capturing Reagan's own style and thought process with lucid pen and words precisely on target. I had never met this diminutive gentleman before but knew of his considerable reputation.

When Mrs. Reagan and Parvin talked, Parvin asked whom in the White House he could trust. She replied, "Abshire."[7] Thus Parvin met with me, as the trustworthy guy, and then started broader rounds to include Fitzwater, Powell, Jim Baker, and of course the president himself. Eventually it was Parvin who crafted the key words that Reagan, Baker, and I reviewed on Monday morning, March 2. The draft read as follows: "A few months ago I told the American people I did not trade arms for hostages. My heart and my best intentions still tell me that's true, but the fact and the evidence tell me it is not. As the Tower Board reported, what began as a strategic opening to Iran deteriorated, in its implementation, into trading arms for hostages. This runs counter to my own beliefs, to administration policy, and to the original strategy we had in mind. There are reasons why it happened, but no excuses. It was a mistake."

Our happiness over the draft soon turned to alarm. Secretary of Defense Weinberger had written a proposed insert for the president's speech that would give Weinberger and Shultz absolution for what went wrong in the Iran-contra affair. It clearly contradicted the language of the Tower Board report, which reads as follows: "Given the importance of the initiative, Secretary Shultz and Secretary Weinberger, while indicating their opposition, distanced themselves from the march of events." Parvin's draft for the president reads, "I've studied the Board's report. Its findings are honest, convincing and highly critical; and I accept them."

As a Cabinet meeting was breaking up, the president sent Parvin to talk to the defense secretary about some compromise language. As a result of his negotiations, Parvin later commented to Howard Baker about Weinberger: "He's the most stubborn man I ever met." Baker responded, "You should try to deal with him on appropriations."[8]

I told the president he could not give in despite the fact that these two Cabinet members had courageously opposed the Iranian initiative. Howard Baker also stood firm and called in Stu Spencer and Richard Wirthlin as reinforcements. Reagan finally agreed to call Weinberger to give him the bad news that the insert would not be made.[9]

But what was even more fundamental in this address was the language Reagan would use to accept full responsibility for Iran-contra. That did not come easy for a man who really thought he had not traded arms for hostages and thought that doing so was in principle a great evil. As early as January, we had studied what President Kennedy had said publicly after the Bay of Pigs disaster: "It was all my fault." In my January phone calls and visits, not just Democrats but all the Republicans said that Reagan should be just as blunt. For many weeks now, we knew that Reagan would ultimately have to say no less.

Reagan delivered his prime-time speech from the Oval Office. The key lines were these: "I've studied the board's report. Its findings are honest, convincing, and highly critical, and I accept them." He said that, over the past three months, while he had been silent, the public must have been thinking, "Well, why doesn't he just speak to us as he has in the past when we've faced troubles or tragedies?" But he said that the public deserved the truth, not "sketchy reports, or possibly even erroneous statements. . . . There's been enough of that." He went on to say, "I've paid a price for my silence in terms of your trust and confidence. But I had to wait, as have you, for the complete story. That is why I appointed Ambassador David Abshire as my special counselor to help get out thousands of documents to various investigations. And I appointed a special review board, the Tower Board, which took on the chore of pulling the truth together for me and getting to the bottom of things." He went on to say that he was relieved to read this sentence from the report: "The Board is convinced that the president does indeed want the full story to be told." He said that this would continue "to be my pledge to you as the other investigations go forward."

He announced that he took full responsibility "for my own actions and those of my administration. As angry as I may be about activities undertaken without my knowledge, I am still accountable for those activities. . . . This happened on my watch," as they say in the navy.

What was particularly important were the next lines: "Let's start with the part that is most controversial. A few days ago, I told the American people I did not trade arms for hostages. My heart and my best intentions tell me that was true, but the facts and the evidence tell me it is not." He said he did not know about the diversion of funds to the contras, "but as president, I cannot escape responsibility." He criticized his own management style and said that he had met with the entire National Security Council staff. "And I told them that there'll be no more freelancing by individuals when it comes to our national security." The president said it still bothered him that "no one kept proper records of meetings or decisions," a point I had drummed into him. As for his new appointments, he announced that he had nominated Judge William Webster, "a man of sterling reputation" who understood the meaning of the "rule of law," to be the next director of the Central Intelligence Agency. With regard to the NSC, he had created the post of NSC legal adviser "to assume a greater sensitivity to matters of law." Toward the end he said, "Now what should happen when you make a mistake is this, 'You take your knocks, you learn your lessons and then you move on.'"

I thought the speech was just right. The press did, too. Veteran *New York Times* journalist R. W. (Johnny) Apple Jr. wrote that "President Reagan spoke to the American people tonight in a spirit of contrition that has not been heard from the White House in a quarter century; . . . not since John F. Kennedy took the blame for the catastrophic Bay of Pigs invasion in 1961 has any president so openly confessed error."[10] The Kennedy speech had been our model. First, credit again goes to Nancy Reagan for telling us to bring in Landon Parvin for his way of capturing Reagan's language and portraying his soul. Second, credit goes to the Tower Board report, a credible document that helped pull us out of our hole and save a presidency. Third, credit goes to Charles Brower and all his departmental and agency general counsels who had processed and delivered thousands of documents and convened investigations of an open, honest process. As a result, we moved into the president's speech with integrity restored to the White House and with a new chief of staff.

The president had an immediate approval-rating jump of nine points in the CBS news polls. Respondents approved of his job performance by a 51–42 margin. This was also accompanied by widespread favorable editorial comment. Reagan had his shortcomings and his failures, but he was still the leader.

CHAPTER 17

The Gipper on Top

Now, for the first time, I felt I was free to speak publicly because at last we no longer stood on shifting sands but on the firm ground of the Tower Board report. I came out of the closet and accepted all invitations to talk shows—*Good Morning America, Face the Nation*, CNN, and others. I proudly defended the president, his speech, and our process. Of course, there was still controversy.

I had this exchange with Lesley Stahl on *Face the Nation*:

STAHL: With us now, David Abshire, outgoing ambassador to NATO, now serving as special counselor to President Reagan during the Iran investigation.

Ambassador Abshire, the president and, I believe, you have said that Mr. Reagan knew nothing about the diversion of profits from the sale of arms to Iran going to the Contras, but this morning, in the *Washington Post*, there's a story saying that John Poindexter, the former national security advisor, is planning a defense in which he will say that he told the president twice that those arms sales to Iran generated money for the Contras.

ABSHIRE: Well, Lesley, I would not think of commenting on rumors about John Poindexter's defense. There's one thing I know from my experiences over the last two months of dealing, often directly, with the president of the United States, alone. There is one Ronald Reagan, he's deeply honest, he's deeply dedicated, and he tells the truth. And when he says he has no knowledge, he has no knowledge.

STAHL: With all due respect, he also told the American people there was no foundation to the story about us sending arms to Iran or McFarlane going to Teheran.

ABSHIRE: Indeed he did in those early days, and he was very poorly served by his staff, which did not get him the facts.

STAHL: Well, he knew Mr. McFarlane was in Teheran.

ABSHIRE: Oh, sure, he did, but the other side of that, there were certain diplomatic reasons because of concern about the hostages, the hope of still getting the hostages out, that he felt it was inappropriate at that point to make all of this clear. But it was for the—it was as a result of this experience that he set up this two-track system—and I'm the second track; the first track is the agenda of the nation, but to facilitate these investigations by credible, independent bodies so you get the truth and you get a comprehensive picture, as well as justice being done by the independent counsel, Judge Walsh.

STAHL: All right, then, let me ask you a question about the president's memory. He seems to have forgotten when he approved the arms sale to Iran. Is it possible that he forgot that he was told about the diversion of money?

ABSHIRE: No, it is not, because the Boland Amendment he was very aware of—that was discussed. But, Lesley, I've got to go back to that presidential memory. I don't think the president of the United States should be a note taker in meetings—I think that's ridiculous. And, of course, secrecy was carried to the point that a record was not kept. That first decision on the sale of arms or replenishment should have been done on paper and not handled the way that it was. And, if you ask me, in early August of 1985, that NATO in a given meeting with Peter Carrington, what happened—I don't have perfect recall on it. That's staff work that's needed.

STAHL: This was a crucial decision in his presidency to send weapons to the ayatollah of Iran.

ABSHIRE: Indeed it was an important decision, and he knows that he approved it, and it's a question of when.

STAHL: But what about the possibility that he may have forgotten that he was told about the diversion. That is a possibility, is it not?

ABSHIRE: Not in my judgment because that is too clear an area, and the president is strong on aiding the Contras, but to do it through anything that was a violation of the law is totally opposite Ronald Reagan.

Another issue then raised controversy in the interview. Somebody new in the White House had loosely talked to the crack *Washington Post* investigative team of Bob Woodward and David Hoffman. This produced a *Post* banner headline article, "Baker Orders Preparation of Iran-Contra Defense." The article says that, according to informed sources, the new chief of staff, who was "appalled" by the absence of serious legal efforts inside the White House to protect President Reagan and prepare for the investigations into the Iran-contra affair, had ordered a detailed internal effort to gather all the facts. This, of course, made it appear that the new team thought the president might be guilty, despite the investigation and report of the Tower Board to the contrary.

Lesley Stahl pounced on this story in our interview:

STAHL: This morning we are told in the *Washington Post* again that Howard Baker is appalled at how this process has gone, that he wants a legal counsel to come in to get all the facts organized. Is this an implicit criticism of you?
ABSHIRE: That's totally wrong. I talked to Howard Baker just before coming on this program; I've dealt with him on a daily basis. And he doesn't know where that story came from. Howard Baker very much wants to stick to the two-track approach. There is no legal defense of the president necessary, the president's got nothing to hide, the president wants the information out. And I am a facilitator, coordinator. When I was called to duty to take this job, I asked for a charter—by the way, I'm not a lawyer, so I wanted to bring in a senior lawyer, Judge Brower—but we have serviced the committees, we have serviced the special counselor, we have serviced the Tower Board. There have been no confrontations, things have worked well, so somebody now wants to turn this around and say why have we been so forthcoming. That's not Howard Baker.

STAHL: But what about the possibility that all these investigations do start focusing in on what the president knew and the president's involvement? Won't he need some legal defense?

ABSHIRE: There is a counsel to the president—that's Peter Wallison. There will be a new counsel to the president. And the new counsel to the president, a very able person, will have an enormous amount of work to do to get up to speed—and, by the way, I have suggested certain things to Howard Baker on preserving that institutional memory because Peter Wallison and his staff have been there over the last couple of years. By the way, could I just say I think the way this story probably got started is because the work that the new team has got to do to get on top of things— you know, we've moved three thousand documents, there's a lot of information there.

STAHL: But the story said that a lot of documents went out without anybody looking at them, without—

ABSHIRE: Silly, absolutely silly.

STAHL: Did you copy them?

ABSHIRE: Absolutely. There were no originals that have been given to the Hill—that is an absolutely silly story because, number one, the lawyers have to go over the documents to see if they are relevant, and their security status.

STAHL: And all that was done?

ABSHIRE: That was done.

White House press spokesperson Marlin Fitzwater was even quoted the next day in *USA Today,* saying that the story that the White House was preparing a legal defense of the president likely came from "a wino on Pennsylvania Avenue." This turned out not to be entirely so.

To follow up on the televised speech, we scheduled a presidential press conference for March 19, 1987, at 8:00 P.M. It would be the first press conference since the president's disastrous performance the previous November.[1]

In the press conference preparatory meeting on March 16, with Howard Baker and the president, I brought up again how poorly served the president had been by his staff in inaccurate public statements he had made on November 6, 13, and 19. The press had not forgotten these statements. The next day, I sent him a follow-up memo and outlined four egregious examples: First, on November 6, the president had said that there was no foundation to stories emanating from the Middle East. That was flatly wrong. Second, in his November 13 address, when asked about reports of Danish ships carrying American arms, he responded, "not one of them is true." That was wrong. (Former members of his staff had chartered a Danish vessel to transport arms from Israel to Iran.) Third, further to his November 13 address, he had said that the shipment of defensive weapons and spare parts to Iran "taken together, could easily fit into a single cargo plane." This was wrong. Fourth, in the November 13 address, he said that "[t]he actions I authorized were and continue to be in full compliance with federal law."

The Tower Board stated that the legal issues were never adequately addressed. With all these past errors, I said, it was important not to defend the past but to stress that initiating the Tower Board inquiry was to give the president as well as the public an accurate database of what had really happened. The president agreed.

As is done for all presidential press conferences, there was a prebriefing in the family theater of the White House. White House staff members fired questions at the president as if they were the reporters. The president enjoyed these sessions because he was doing what he liked to do and was trained to do—perform on a stage.

At some point, someone asked the larger question: "The Iran-contra affair and all the things you do now know about have undermined your credibility with the American people and world leaders. How are you gonna go about rebuilding the Reagan presidency when this is all over?" With a mischievous smile, Reagan quipped, "Who the hell wants to rebuild when I'm quitting in two years anyway?" We all broke into laughter, the president in the lead.

Nancy Reagan phoned me after the prebriefing, at 4:45 P.M. How had he done? The memories of the last press conference in November were still with her, along with the fear that the reporters would try to relive those mistakes that I had pointed out. She was also afraid he would be overly briefed to the point of confusion.

I said that the president had regained much confidence and that she would be very proud. I added that we had urged him not to be trapped in excessive details, and we really felt that he was on his game.

Later in the evening, I was with the first lady and the president when Press Secretary Marlin Fitzwater briefed the president about the East Room seating chart. We indicated where the press sharks looking for blood were to be seated—where Sam Donaldson would be and what he might fire off, or assertive Helen Thomas, or Dan Hoffman of the *Washington Post,* who knew the facts on Iran-contra far better than the president. As Marlin briefed, I eyed the president; he was steady and collected, with his usual quips. Despite what I had said to Mrs. Reagan earlier, I was nervous. So was Fitzwater.

As I had seen before, an aide brought the president a clear glass of something. I figured it had to be water, not vodka. The president, as I had noted before, picked it up but set it down quickly. This time I asked, "Mr. President, is that too cold?" "Oh no," he replied, "too hot." Nancy added that in Hollywood they frequently drank warm Coca-Cola. The heat opens up the throat and avoids hoarseness when one is speaking a lot. Ronald Reagan's voice was a precious commodity.

At precisely 8:00 P.M., the president left us to enter the Blue Room through the side door. He strode majestically down the red-carpeted hall as cameras rolled. Fifty million people were watching on TV. Marlin Fitzwater was later to write, "He was the best walker in the business. He strode with purpose, straight and erect, well tailored and ready for any script. You could not look at Ronald Reagan without feeling good about America." Fitzwater added, "But I was sweating."[2]

The president started with what he called a short statement on bringing government spending under control and said that "we've been able to bring taxes down and subdue the monster of inflation." Then he quipped, "Do you have other questions on your mind?" When the laughter ceased, he said that he had felt it important for the Tower Board report to be completed before he had another press conference, "and that now has happened."

Terry Anderson of Associated Press fired off the first question. There were still eight Americans held hostage: Had the scandal complicated their release? The president said we had gotten some hostages out, and if there had not been the leak, maybe he would have gotten more. Sharp-tongued Helen Thomas asked about reports that the president had been told at least twice that the contras were benefiting from the Iranian arms sales. The president responded that that was not true at all. She asked whether the two military officers (Poindexter and North) thought "they were doing your bidding."

"Helen, I don't know. I only know that that's why I have said repeatedly that I want to find out."

He was asked whether—if his memory was faulty on the August, 1985, date—it could be faulty on being told of the diversion.

The president replied, "Oh, no. You would have heard me without opening the door if I had been told that." This was the same expression he had used with me.

As to the issue of when he had approved the first arms sale, he said he knew he had approved the sale, but he simply could not remember whether the approval was before or after early August, 1985.

Bill Plante of CBS asked, "Do you still believe it was not arms for hostages?"

The president responded that the policy was flawed and had deteriorated into arms for hostages. The questions rattled on, but the president stayed in command. When he concluded and turned to depart by the long hallway, we knew his comeback was a formidable success. Sam Donaldson himself was to say, "Ronald Reagan is back from the standpoint of style, if that is what you are looking for. He was number one tonight. Fifty years in Hollywood came right through."[3]

The Gipper was on top! Not quite where he was before, however, because Iran-contra would forever leave a wound, and within weeks the public would be watching a television soap opera of congressional hearings. John Wayne had traded arms for hostages. But he was forgiven and out of personal danger. Don Regan, the prime minister, was gone. The flawed process of November and December had moved to due process, and bipartisanship had held. Now it was up to Howard Baker to rebuild the vigor of the administration's domestic agenda. In the final phase of the Cold War, the president could resume his leadership of the grand alliance. For me, this was day seventy-four, but what a joyous one, with only sixteen more to go.

After the arrival of Howard Baker, the Reagan address to the nation, and the comeback press conference, much of the drama of my White House tenure vanished. We all settled into the routine of more normal business. The review and transmission of documents, however, was vastly increasing. Brower and I had many meetings with Judge Walsh and his staff and with members of Congress involved in the investigation, with the new counsel to the president (who had replaced Peter Wallison) A. B. Culvahouse. I talked frequently with a much happier Nancy Reagan. I was free to contact members of the press, and I even had the time to play NATO ambassador and accept the invitation of the Senate Armed Services Committee and later the House Appropriations Subcommittee to testify on the status of the North Atlantic Alliance. At this point in the Cold War, I could say with pride that we had a reborn leader of that alliance.

Domestically, the Howard Baker team came up with a creative idea: an economic bill of rights, written in the style of the original Bill of Rights. It was the brainchild of Tommy Griscom. He repackaged some old ideas and wrote in the style of the Bill of Rights with the assertion that every American was entitled to basic freedoms: to work, to enjoy the fruits of their labors, to own property, and to participate in a free market. These freedoms demanded a truth-in-spending plan in which Congress would have to see how much each governmental program would cost and how it would be financed. A three-fifths majority vote in Congress would be necessary for a tax increase. The Gipper was building a new agenda with a new staff.[4]

On March 28, I sat on the dais at the Gridiron Club. This was the annual command performance of an exclusive 102-year-old journalists' club given to a white-tie roast of high and mighty governmental leaders and to be roasted in return. Gridiron president, James C. Cartney of Knight Ridder, called it an incredible assemblage of privilege and power. Outspoken Maureen Reagan was there as a guest and was parodied on stage by Helen Thomas, singing "My heart belongs to daddy." I was neither high nor mighty, but Bob Novak quipped that I had solved the Iran-contra mystery without leaving the basement of the White House. All along, I thought I was on the top floor of the Old Executive Office Building.

It was Ronald Reagan who stole the show, over George Bush, the journalists' parodies, and everybody else. As for the Iran-contra affair, he announced that the missing money went to the Southern Methodist University football team. (There had been a scandal there, which was being investigated by something like the Tower Commission.) He said he was correct in seeking ties with the moderates—moderates in the media, that is. Forcefully he announced that "since I came to the White House I got two hearing aids, a colon operation, skin cancer, a prostate operation, and I was shot. The damn thing is I've never felt better in my life."

David Broder later wrote the following: "Not all presidents have understood the value of a laugh. Lyndon Johnson, Richard Nixon, and Jimmy Carter couldn't forget, even for a few hours, that they really despised the journalists in the room. . . . But Reagan grasped from the first that this was a made-to-order occasion for celebrating the healthiness of the critical relationship that inevitably exists between the press and the government—and laughing away its ugly overtones of personal antagonism."[5]

Reagan's ironic humor and self-deprecation—a man comfortable with himself—was part of his leadership, and its display was essential to his comeback.

On April 1, Lord Carrington paid the president another visit, and there was a meeting in the Cabinet Room that included National Security Adviser Frank Carlucci, Senators Nunn and Warner (the chair and ranking minority member of the Senate Armed Services Committee), and me. It will be recalled that Carrington had previously been worried about the "breakdown" at Reykjavik and what he considered to be the provocative nature of SDI. However, a dramatic breakthrough had occurred on February 28, 1987, when Gorbachev announced that the Soviets would drop their previous conditions, which tied general progress in arms control to our concessions on SDI. This was a dramatic vindication of the president's position at Reykjavik. The Soviets were now willing to move forward toward an agreement to eliminate all intermediate-range nuclear missiles.

Four trends were converging rather dramatically: Gorbachev's conclusion that his counterpart Reagan had reemerged from Iran-contra and was strategically on the move again. Second, Reagan's ace in the hole, SDI, regardless of when or whether such a system worked, was the embodiment of the American information-technology revolution with which the Soviets simply could not compete. Third, Gorbachev was concluding that he needed to undertake radical reform measures at home and had to cut back military expenditures. Fourth, if anything, Reagan was ahead of his advisers in sensing that real change was possible, and he spoke of a major breakthrough and "a moment of hope." In line with these four factors, by late spring Gorbachev had even announced a new "defensive" military doctrine and had moved toward acceptance of the so-called zero option to remove all intermediate-range missiles on both sides.[6] On Reagan's June trip to Europe, he gave the most memorable speech of his presidency standing before the Brandenburg Gate in Berlin: "General Secretary Gorbachev, if you seek peace, if you seek prosperity for the Soviet Union and Eastern Europe, if you seek liberalization, come here to this gate! Mr. Gorbachev, open this gate! Mr. Gorbachev, tear down this wall."

The Cold War was winding down.

CHAPTER 18

My Departure

March 31, the eighty-sixth day of my tenure dawned clear but, for springtime, exceptionally cold. At 1:30 I took my staff of fourteen to the Oval Office for a farewell party with President Reagan. For most, it was the first time they had been in this historic room. After introducing each by name, on behalf of us all I thanked the president for the honor of serving him.

The president began to laugh even before we did as he quipped, "I'm the one to give the thanks. You didn't find me guilty!"

Of course it was not our job to find him guilty or innocent. He found himself not guilty when without fear he instructed us to "get everything out." There was no smoking gun in what we had sent to investigators.

After small talk, we bade farewell. The staff was amazed at the president's geniality. Then we trooped over to the finely paneled Anderson Room on the second floor of the Metropolitan Club, a block from the Old Executive Office Building. There we raised our champagne glasses especially to Elise Callaghan, first to arrive when we set up office, the one who had held off the likes of Brendan Sullivan and who had remained calm and flawless when others of us flapped. Our job was done. We could begin to pack up our OEOB suite and quietly steal away. It was nearly the end of ninety days, most of them perilous ones in the life of a presidency. On the senate floor, Bob Dole was paying an excessively generous tribute: "It would be hard to imagine a 'hot seat' any hotter than the one that Dave Abshire took over. And it would be hard to imagine anyone who did a better job—for the president and for the country—than Dave has done."[1]

Dole had been a special friend when I was at NATO and while at the White House, always with wise advice from his perch as senate leader. Also, I was touched when biographer-in-residence Edmund Morris slipped into my office to present his wonderful work, *The Rise of Theodore Roosevelt*. There was a generous inscription: "Ambassador, historian, and a true servant of Presidents. With thanks and best wishes." Indeed, I looked forward to what I thought would surely be a magnificent, definitive biography of Ronald Reagan, for Morris had unparalleled access to history in the making, and he certainly had unusual literary skills. I was to be disappointed.[2]

The other important farewell was with the first lady. If, with the departure of Don Regan, an East Wing–West Wing civil war had come to an end, a press war over Nancy Reagan and Don Regan was yet again heating. Since Abigail Adams, many first ladies had been accused of manipulating their husbands, but Nancy Reagan was about to receive an overdose. Just after Regan's departure, formidable, conservative *New York Times* columnist Bill Safire launched a sixteen-inch shell at Nancy in a column titled "The First Lady Stages a Coup: She Can't Be Fired or Impeached." In it Safire said, "At the time he most needs to appear strong, President Reagan is being weakened and made to appear wimpish and helpless by the political interference of his wife." Safire continued, "Nancy Reagan's campaign to force her husband to fire White House chief of staff Don Regan has been crowned with success. With extraordinary vindictiveness, the First Lady issued a gleeful victory statement when her target was brought down." (Mrs. Reagan later sent Regan a note saying that CNN had called her press secretary asking for a comment on Regan's replacement by Baker, and, assuming the story was out, Mrs. Reagan authorized a statement wishing Don "good luck" and welcoming Howard Baker.[3])

One of Safire's biggest complaints was that "she objected to the idea of having her husband, at 76, and recently hospitalized, stand up without a script and subject himself to hostile questions after the issuance of the embarrassing Tower Commission report." Safire argued that such a performance would "be a test of the President's grasp of the crisis." Of course, such an exposure before the president had even studied the report and spoken to the nation in a well-crafted speech would have been a disaster. But Safire went on: "This is not Rosalynn Carter, the Steel Magnolia, stiffening her husband's spine; this is an incipient Edith Wilson, not elected and unaccountable, presuming to control the actions and appointments of the executive branch."[4]

Nancy Reagan deeply felt the blow from the former Nixon speechwriter. Three days later, as tension increased, Ronald Reagan uncharacteristically exploded before reporters. While he posed for photographs in the Oval Office with the new director of Central Intelligence, Judge William Webster, Reagan vehemently decried as "despicable fictions" reports that his wife played a major role in the dismissal of Regan and that she was involved in key governmental decision making. She was no dragon lady, the president angrily declared.

A reporter quickly shot back, "Howard Baker used the phrase," as the room erupted in laughter. Sitting uncomfortably on a nearby couch, an embarrassed but smiling Baker blurted out, "No, no, I didn't say that," and the president muttered, "No, no, he didn't."[5] It was the worst public anger the president ever displayed, and it was not a coincidence that it came on the Reagans' thirty-fifth wedding anniversary.

In his column, Safire had referred to a "coterie of media biggies in whom Mrs. Reagan regularly confides." Taking up the battle on Mrs. Reagan's behalf, the longtime, equally formidable *Washington Post* columnist George Will referred to the "rubbish" that had been said about Nancy Reagan: "It has been feverishly reported she issued a statement she did not issue, attended a meeting she did not attend . . . and espouses views she does not hold. . . . The suggestions that Mrs. Reagan is a Catherine de Médici [sic] are issuing from the same press corps that six years ago believed with equal certitude that she was Valley Girl emeritus, interested in clothes and china."[6]

At least in my judgment, George Will had by far the best of both the exchange and the argument. But the time had come for my farewell with the first lady. On the second floor of the mansion, against the backdrop of that now-so-familiar fan window, a vivacious Nancy Reagan and I reminisced. Years later, in the Century City office of the retired president, we reminisced even more. She read me what she had written in her diary on April 11:

> At our meeting, David Abshire said to me, "I'm not saying
> this to flatter you but I've known a lot of First Ladies in my
> time but I've never known one like you—no one understands
> what you did for your husband and for the country. You saved
> it because you knew he was being cut off and shielded and

wasn't getting opinions from other people because of Don Regan—You've taken a bum rap—most first ladies, if their husbands were in trouble, would have played to their ego and said 'you're right, dear' and crawled into a corner but you hung in there and fought—not only for his physical good but for the presidency. People here tried to compare you with Edith Wilson—there's no comparison—first of all she did exactly the opposite. She tried to shield him from people—you did the opposite.[7] I admire you." What a nice thing for him to say—it meant a lot.

Nancy Reagan was driven by her vision of Ronald Reagan's legacy—his place in history. She quickly saw that the entire Iran-contra scandal threatened just that. At worst, it could produce impeachment. At best, it would tarnish him and his "shining city on a hill." She was distraught as the scandal deepened and the investigation quickened. She believed that so many of the players, beginning with the chief of staff, were looking after themselves and their own reputations—and not the president's. We noted earlier what her husband had indeed said in December, when quarreling with those who would fire Don Regan: "I'll be goddamned if I'll throw somebody else out to save my own ass."[8] She felt it was not a reciprocal sentiment, that those below were bent on saving their own asses. If this perception was at times overdone in her own mind, Don Regan confirmed it by clinging to his position in the face of overwhelming advice.

She feared that Reagan's place in history was being destroyed bit by bit. She immediately saw what "Ronnie" did not see: Plain and simple, he had traded arms for hostages. "Ronnie" himself had said that would be immoral, so he could not conceive that he had done just that. Trading arms for hostages in itself was not illegal, but it violated presidential declarations. Thus it undermined the moral authority of the president and the moral image of him in history.

The polls showed that this issue was more important to the public than an arcane something called the Boland Amendment violation or even the illegal fund transfers. Nancy Reagan knew that he should confess and say it was not his intention but that he had slipped into it nevertheless; he should then clean house of all the crowd that had helped make this grave moral error possible. Then, with a new team, he could restore the presidency. It was a grievous error that, if not corrected, would exact an even greater price in history. Toward this end she pushed the president and her other allies, including me.

Contrary to Bill Safire's portrayal of her total power creating the image of a "wimpish" president, she had to make allies to try to move a stubborn president. But she was, throughout it all, conscious of the limits of her own position. Nancy Reagan did not attempt to make policy as did Hillary Clinton on health care.

A splendid tribute comes to Nancy Reagan from an unsuspected source: Richard Neustadt, Douglas Dillon Professor Emeritus at Harvard University, the dean of presidential scholars who was an adviser on presidential organization to Democratic presidents beginning with Truman. In 1991, he provided future presidents, Republican and Democratic, with a rule of thumb: "[N]ever let your Nancy be immobilized."[9] His point was that, in President Reagan's case, Nancy was the disinterested party, committed and dedicated only to the president. FDR kept abreast of dangers and vulnerabilities because he "read five daily newspapers, gossiped incessantly with contacts across the country, saw reporters twice a week, congressmen almost daily, and constituent groups in droves. He also had a famous nose for trouble. Mrs. Reagan may have been a substitute for much of that."[10] So says Neustadt.

Nancy Reagan was a bit like FDR in habits: She read not just publications like *Vanity Fair* and *Women's Wear Daily* but also the *Washington Post*, the *New York Times*, the *Wall Street Journal*, and *USA Today*. Her circle of telephone pals included diverse people such as George Will, William F. Buckley, *Washington Post* publisher Katherine Graham, and, as we have already seen, Bob Strauss and Charlie Wick as well as Mike Deaver, Paul Laxalt, and former CIA director Dick Helms and his wife, Cynthia.[11]

No wonder Ronald Reagan called Nancy his "extra set of eyes and ears." Reagan once said, "She'd be the first to tell you I can be a stubborn fellow when I don't agree with her."[12]

If she was so good in this role of his eyes and ears, however, why then did she not "spot and spare" her husband on Iran-contra? Secrecy. She was cut out. Their usual radar was down, and "his Nancy" was thus immobilized. When Nancy was brought in after the scandal broke, she was key in the turnaround, bringing in outside advisers, protecting the president from foolish moves on premature public appearances, and—looking long term—bringing in a new chief of staff. Truly, it can be said that Nancy Davis Reagan played the crucial role in saving the Reagan presidency and has thereby achieved a special place in the history of first ladies.

By the time she left the White House, her public image received a 72 percent approval rating. Perhaps she deserved even more.

CHAPTER 19

The Continuing Curse of Iran-Contra

Despite the bipartisan welcome with which the new Baker White House staff was received on the Hill and in the media, the curse of the Iran-contra scandal would not be lifted. There remained the ongoing investigations, ensuring that no new cover-up occurred in the executive branch and attempting to maintain bipartisan support in the Congress. But the bipartisanship would break down once the televised congressional hearings began. Although the danger of impeachment was past, the curse of the scandal was later to jeopardize the careers of two Cabinet members and, much later, President Bush's reelection. At the time, however, no one foresaw in their wildest imaginations what would happen over the next six years.

As my tenure was coming to a close in the White House, so was our two-track approach that had avoided further cover-ups following the notorious ones executed by Poindexter and especially North. Furthermore, the integrity of those two tracks, with an independent special counsel to the president, had been a means of maintaining bipartisanship on Capitol Hill.

On March 3, I had written a memorandum to Baker, urging that the two tracks be continued. The memo was titled "The Future of the Office of the Special Counselor." I noted my commitment to return to CSIS in early April and that my agreement was to serve for three months only. I also wrote the following: "Furthermore, I feel that by then, I effectively will have made my contribution in establishing good liaison arrangements with the Tower Board, Independent Counsel, and the Committees on the Hill: we have avoided all confrontations, while producing for them more than 3,000 documents. In addition, I have given the president and others the benefit of my ideas of 'Post-Tower Board strategy' of presidential leadership for restarting the presidency."

Then I went on to emphasize that an important function of my office remained. During the several ongoing investigations, a separation between any needed defense of the president afforded by his legal counsel and the independent had to be maintained. I noted the availability of my deputy, Judge Charles Brower, to take my place and reiterated his background and fine legal credentials. I recommended that the second track be continued with Judge Brower or someone else of independent stature. I commented that my team of fourteen people had "become a sort of referee for conflicts between the investigating bodies on the one hand—and the administration on the other." I explained that "a serious threat of the independent counsel to subpoena the allegedly uncooperative CIA was averted by a last minute 'peace treaty.'" I warned that the public-hearing phase of the congressional investigations would be burdensome and that Judge Brower could certainly stay through this. I also urged that our two key lawyers, two associate counsels to the president, Dean McGrath and Jay Stevens, along with Alan C. Raul, should be kept focused on this endeavor. I stressed that Congress and the independent counsel had to be assured of the continued, totally open process separate from any legal defense of the president. Furthermore, a separate, independent White House office had to be maintained to ensure against future cover-ups that in some unforeseen way might come about and get us into trouble yet.[1]

Howard Baker did not accept this recommendation for several reasons. First, Brower was not really a Baker man, and Howard understandably desired to surround himself with his own team of close associates from his Capitol Hill days. The new legal counsel to the president, A. B. Culvahouse, had previously been Baker's staff associate on Capitol Hill. Second, there was some talk about the advantages of wrapping up my second-track operation as a success and, symbolizing that the crisis was over, declaring victory. Special procedures were not needed any longer. Finally, to the new chief of staff it seemed to make sense to return to the organization that existed before I arrived, wherein the legal counsel to the president handled the investigative interface as well as any defense of the president. After all, Howard Baker had no conflict of interest and therefore needed no Mr. Clean to be a check for this highly respected and nationally known figure.

I had made my strong case and I lost. Despite my disagreement, I chose not to lobby the case with Mrs. Reagan behind Howard Baker's back or with the president himself. Baker, the new chief of staff, was my friend. I trusted his extensive political experience, which was much greater compared to mine. After I left my office, Baker consolidated all operations under the legal counsel to the president.

Unfortunately, Baker's plan to declare victory on the Iran-contra affair was stillborn. The magnitude of the investigations and the multiplicity of issues swamped the new Baker team. Indeed, attorneys Baker and Culvahouse, unfamiliar with what had gone on in the previous months, soon became fearful about the outright defense of the president during this morass of forthcoming hearings and the movement of thousands of documents. Perhaps it was inevitable. People began circling the wagons in preparation for the chief's defense. Was it possible after all that he was guilty? Was he vulnerable legally? After all, could he have known of the diversion?

My outgoing team felt the answer to the famous Baker Watergate questions about Nixon—"What did the president know, and when did he know it?"—was about Reagan: "Not much!" But the new team worried.

Over the coming weeks, a vastly enlarged legal team was formed and reoriented toward the legal defense of the president. To defend the president thoroughly, the new lawyers felt they had to reinvestigate the issue, including the president himself.[2] Bob Woodward's book *Shadow: Five Presidents and the Legacy of Watergate* claims that during the Iran-contra affair "the closest to a real investigation of presidential involvement in Iran-Contra was conducted not by Independent Counsel Walsh, the Tower Board or Congress, but by Reagan's White House lawyers."[3] He was referring to the assignment of William B. Lytton III, a tough former federal prosecutor, to the White House as a deputy counsel authorized to set up a massive legal task force of just under seventy people—more than five times the total number of staffers that I had.

The president was put through thirteen new interrogations on top of all those from January through May for fear that Poindexter might yet testify that Reagan knew of the diversion. What happened in the White House legal personnel turnover was similar to what happened in Judge Walsh's several legal turnovers: an aggressive new team, reviewing old stuff with greater tenacity and searching for new clues.

All the old clues were again reviewed. But confusion developed in the new team over some sensitive documents that had been examined and carefully dealt with during the previous winter.[4]

Their third degree did not help the president's memory; it added to his confusion. This is what Nancy Reagan always feared in the overbriefings of her husband. The overbriefings and quizzing had added to his previous confusion before the Tower Board. In May, 1987, the same thing happened when Reagan made a blanket public denial that he knew anything about contra resupply efforts from third countries. Yet the third-party operations had been in the papers and were known in the Congress, and investigators had a document showing that Reagan knew. A new credibility crisis was created.[5]

In retrospect, it appears the extensive and dramatic Lytton investigation produced nothing except such confusion. By May, it should have been clear that Poindexter would not testify that he had briefed the president on the diversion because he had already taken the Fifth Amendment five times before the Senate Committee on Foreign Relations.

The Iran-contra drama soon moved to the nationally televised hearings. It was a credit to the committee leadership—Inouye, Rudman, Hamilton, and Cheney—that for the first time the House and Senate agreed to joint hearings and common ground rules. The joint House-Senate Iran-Contra Committee heard thirty-two witnesses from May 5 to August 6, 1987, with Maj. Gen. Richard Secord as the first public witness. More than 250 hours of testimony followed. The committee eventually received more than three hundred thousand documents totaling more than one million pages.

The handsome retired major general was selected largely because he willingly, without a grant of immunity, relinquished his Fifth Amendment privilege against self-incrimination. The committee made its first terrible mistake by publicly interrogating witnesses before setting the broader context of the hearings. Senators Cohen and Mitchell later wrote, "Lacking adequate background to place the testimony in context, the viewing public responded by focusing on the personalities of the witnesses, the counsels, and members of the committee, instead of the substance of what had been done."[6]

Secord, with the help of his fine military bearing, won the television ratings that his inquisitor, the brilliant Arthur Liman, lost. Two sympathetic committee senators wrote that, on television, Liman "has dark, penetrating eyes and a habit of tucking his chin to his chest as he lowers his head with visible scorn for a witness."[7] His spaghetti hair, New York accent and culture, and abrasive, aggressive manner produced within days thousands of adverse telegrams and telephone calls to members' offices. The network coverage of testimony taken from the several dramatic military witnesses ran for twelve weeks. It was high soap-opera drama at its best. Ironically, it was President Ronald Reagan, after the dark Vietnam period, who had taught the military once again to hold their heads high and the public to admire them as heroes. The public did just that, and the military won hands down.

Witness Vice Adm. John Poindexter, the impassive former national security advisor, was very different from the dashing Secord. Dressed in civilian clothes, wearing rimless glasses, pipe clinched between his teeth whenever possible, he testified without emotion, apparently at peace with himself. Cynics said he took the rap for the president. He was the one who had briefed the president every morning. Beyond question, he had had full responsibility. He showed a remarkable stoicism and selflessness. He was dispensable in the service of his commander in chief. His wife, an Episcopalian priest, sat behind him in clerical collar.

Yes, he confessed, once the Iran-contra affair became known, he himself had torn up a presidential finding, signed by the president in early December, 1985, and authorizing weapons sales to Iran in exchange for hostage relief. However, Poindexter categorically denied North's assertion that Poindexter had directed him at different times to write five memoranda intended for the president about the diversion and that went to the president. "False," said Poindexter. Ronald Reagan had not been told. (So much for all the speculation of Baker's lawyers and Hill staff and some Democratic members of the Congress that Poindexter would testify the opposite.)

Following Poindexter, Bud McFarlane testified for five straight days, as he later wrote, without a grant of immunity, "as openly and honestly as I could and wholly prepared to bear whatever consequences would result." He had no access to his White House records to jog his memory. It showed. There were many embarrassments, such as the September, 1985, letters from him to Lee Hamilton and others that he could state "with deep personal conviction" that there had been no violation of the letter of the law of the Boland Amendment. If Poindexter's religious faith helped lead him to total self-containment, McFarlane's led him to a total confessional.[8]

Poindexter's stoicism and civilian clothes were a letdown for the show watchers, but the real superstar, exceeding even Secord, was charismatic Lt. Col. Oliver North. He was a straight arrow in Marine Corps uniform, covered with decorations, proud, patriotic, and appealing. He was front and center from July 7 to July 14. After all, following his resignation, the commander in chief himself had called Lieutenant Colonel North a hero for his distinguished military career.

The soap operas were literally preempted. Steven Spielberg later commented on the Hollywood-like setting. In the marble caucus room, North and his lawyer were at a simple table, with two rows of eleven senators and fifteen house members plus aides elevated on a two-tiered platform: North, in the pit, looked up at his older judges as in a Spanish Inquisition scene. In what ensued, Spielberg noted that North was televised at the hero's angle, as it is called in Hollywood, and the judges were televised at the villain's angle. The principal inquisitors completed the scene: If Arthur Liman had been diminished by his "spaghetti" hair, John Nields had something worse, the long hair of a Vietnam War protester. Thus the public cast Liman and Nields as antimilitary, and Hollywood could not have created a more sinister scene for what looked to be an ambush of a uniformed war hero.[9]

North's attorney, Brendan Sullivan, informed the committee chair that he was "no potted plant" and proudly stated that he would sound off when he felt his man was wrongly treated. Despite Judge Walsh's strenuous opposition, Sullivan had gained from the committee "use immunity" for his client, a legal guarantee that nothing said by him could be used against him in any criminal proceedings that might follow. The aggressive and shrewd Sullivan obtained other concessions: that North would not be deposed before his testimony, that the testimony duration would be limited with no allowance for him to be recalled, and that relevant documents would be turned over only three days in advance. Sullivan also instructed his client, "Above all, don't perjure yourself."[10]

North's mix of charisma, patriotism, medals, and earnestness made him almost overnight a popular national hero. Following Sullivan's instructions, North proudly admitted lying to Congress, falsifying evidence, and shredding documents—all under this noble call of patriotism—hostages returned, freedom fighters sustained. North readily admitted that he, along with Iranian expatriate Albert Hakim, had established the enterprise to do what the CIA was not permitted to do, with Richard Secord as its head. It was to take monies raised from foreign countries and later from arms sales to Iran and funnel these to the contras. Casey had been the one who suggested the diversion in the first place. According to North, "The president surely knew."[11]

McFarlane was infuriated by North's testimony and courageously returned to the witness stand. McFarlane later wrote, "North's testimony revealed, first of all, that he had lied to me, all through 1984 and 1985. When he had flat-out denied raising money for the contras, he had lied. . . . He had not only raised money for them, he had set up, without my approval or my knowledge, an off-the-shelf enterprise with Dick Secord to funnel funds and weapons to the Contras." But now North was claiming he had done all of this with McFarlane's approval.[12]

The drama of the preceding witnesses was brought back to sobriety with the plainspoken testimony and radiating honesty of Secretary of State George Shultz. I was delighted that in his testimony he also quoted Bryce Harlow's mantra, "Trust is the coin of the realm." He, too, had been a marine long ago, but now he had neither uniform to wear nor medals to display. Nevertheless, Senators Cohen and Mitchell were later to write that "Shultz's appearance before the Committee was as welcome as that of a Saint Bernard at the site of an avalanche. He sat at the witness table alone and spoke with fervor about the need for, and the ability of, public officials to serve their president with candor and respect." Shultz noted that he was a very strong supporter of helping the contras in their fight for freedom. "But our major concern should be to conduct ourselves so that we maximize the chance of persuading Congress to come back on board and give support." Under questioning, he argued that the president's "judgment is excellent when given the right information, and he was not being given the right information." He criticized CIA director Casey for becoming so involved in policy and saw him as driving much of the Iran-contra policy. This also produced a distortion of intelligence, including that being given to the president.

Shultz was also grilled by Rep. Henry Hyde and others as to why he had not done more to prevent the flawed initiative. Shultz said that for eighteen months he tried to block the initiative. No, he didn't give himself an A+, but the more he found out, the more he had come to see how much the National Security Council staff had deceived him. Hyde still responded, "I wish you had gone to the brink." As Shultz later wrote, he was caught between the Republican right, who—with Olliemania—were upset because Shultz had taken issue "with the glorification of North's testimony," and those on the left, who did not like his defense of Ronald Reagan.[13]

Next came Ed Meese, who defended his initial investigation, and Don Regan, who stressed how little he knew about the Iran-contra affair. Then came the critic of the Iran initiative, Cap Weinberger, who was especially devastating in terms of the off-the-shelf radical procedures followed by the two previous national security advisors, along with Bill Casey and Lieutenant Colonel North. Weinberger said he and Shultz had been taken off the intelligence distribution list, that the Joint Chiefs of Staff had never been consulted on what impact the arms sale would have on the Iran-Iraq War, and furthermore that there were no moderates left in Iran to negotiate with. In response to one question he gave a memorable answer: "We can't fight with an enemy, whoever that may be, and we can't fight with Congress at the same time. We need to have the United States government unified if any kind of activity is going to succeed over the long run." Weinberger, like Shultz, denied that he had distanced himself intentionally from these operations, or that, acting together, they could have stopped them, or that they should have resigned in protest.

It was not the two secretaries and their wise words that had public impact. "Olliemania" carried the ratings, and it had a real influence on the development of a committee minority report.

It was in November, 1987, as a presidential election year neared, that the joint report of the congressional investigating committees was published. The nonpartisanship I had known in my three months was missing, especially in the House. The majority report, signed by all select committee senate and house Democrats and by Republican senators Warren Rudman, William Cohen, and Paul Trible, addressed who was responsible: at the operational level, Lieutenant Colonel North, coordinator of all activities, with the approval of National Security

Advisor Admiral Poindexter, and before him, Robert McFarlane, who gave tacit support. William Casey "encouraged North, gave him direction and promoted the concept of an extra-legal covert organization." Further, it was Casey who brought Richard Secord, who, with Albert Harkim, organized the enterprise. These facts provide strong reasons to believe that Casey was involved both with the diversion and with the plans for an "off-the-shelf covert capacity." The report says "there is no evidence that the Vice President was aware of the diversion."

What was the role of the president? The report reads as follows: "On this critical point, the shredding of documents by Poindexter, North, and others, and the death of Casey, leave the record incomplete." However, it adds, "the ultimate responsibility for the events in the Iran-Contra Affair must rest with the President. If the President did not know what his National Security Advisors were doing, he should have. . . . The Constitution requires the President to 'take care that the laws be faithfully executed.'" The report continues: "Members of the NSC staff appeared to believe that their actions were consistent with the President's desires." The president had created or at least tolerated this environment.[14]

The minority report led by house Republicans is of special interest to this story of partisanship on the Republican side. The political climate had changed since Congressman Henry Hyde, a signatory of this report, had told me over the phone and stated to the press that President Reagan should publicly apologize to the nation. The minority report reads thus: "The bottom line, however, is that the mistakes of the Iran-Contra Affair were just that—mistakes in judgment, and nothing more." While the minority report admits that in November, 1986, Poindexter and North "did falsify the documentary record in a way we find deplorable," it goes on to say there was no constitutional crisis, no systematic disrespect for the "rule of law, no grand conspiracy, and no administration-wide dishonesty or cover up." Having offered this exoneration, it goes on to make some strong contradictions to its earlier summary: "[T]he Administration decided to work within the letter of the law covertly, instead of forcing a public and principled confrontation that would have been healthier in the long run. . . . No President can ignore Congress and be successful over the long term." These are wise words, where both the majority and minority reports agree. The minority report then argues that the president should have "vetoed the strict Boland Amendment in mid-October 1984. . . . Once the President decided against the veto, it was self-defeating to think a program this important could be sustained by deceiving Congress."

In criticism of the majority report, the minority report addresses the controversial "diversion" of funds: "The [Majority] Report does grudgingly acknowledge that it cannot refute the President's repeated assertion that he knew nothing about the diversion. . . . Instead of moving forward from this to more meaningful policy questions, however, the Report seeks, without any support, to plant doubts. 'We will never know what was in the documents shredded by Lt. Col. Oliver L. North in his last days on the NSC staff,' the [Majority] Report says."

The minority report addresses the "legal arguments on both sides of the question of whether the proceeds of the arms sales belong to the U.S. government or to Secord and Hakim." It concludes that "the ownership seems unclear under current law." However, the report admits "that Secord and Hakim were acting as the moral equivalents of U.S. agents, even if they were not U.S. agents in law." This means, in sum, that both the majority and minority reports conclude the diversion was wrong. The minority report adds that "we can find nothing to justify or mitigate its having occurred." In other words, the minority report begins by saying that the Iran-contra affair involved "mistakes in judgment, and nothing more" and concludes with something quite different.

The minority report argues that the $35 million raised from Third World countries from mid-1984 to mid-1986, plus the unauthorized diversion that actually reached the contras, saved the contras from annihilation. Of course, the relatively small $3.8 million that the contras actually received from North's diversion of funds was not decisive in their survival, although it was helpful.

It is amazing that the minority report also concludes that the president made a mistake "when he acceded too readily and too completely to waive executive privilege for our committee's investigation."[15] One can only conclude that those who drafted this report did not know Ronald Reagan and the strength of his character and leadership: He was in a leadership crisis and wanted all the facts out, for he had nothing to hide despite wide speculation in the press, the polls, and Congress to the contrary. This was his single greatest act in this entire story, and the drafters missed it.

If the congressional climate had polarized and politicized since early 1987, so did the work of the independent counsel. The trials of the principals in the Iran-contra drama played out slowly, initially in the U.S. District Court under Judge Gerhard Gesell, a former partner of Dean Acheson in the esteemed firm of Covington and Burling and who had also been through the Watergate experience.

On April 7, 1990, Admiral Poindexter was convicted of five felony charges related to obstruction of Congress and perjury, and he was sentenced to a six-month prison term. On November 15, 1991, an appeals court overturned the charges on the basis that North's immunized congressional testimony might have tainted the Poindexter trial; that is, some witnesses might have seen some of the televised hearings or read about them in the newspaper and been influenced. Poindexter, the stoic, disappeared from public sight but maintained his dignity and reemerged for a period in 1992 at the Pentagon.

Oliver North was convicted of destroying NSC documents, aiding and abetting in the preparation of false chronologies for congressional testimony, and accepting an illegal gratuity. The obstruction charge was reversed by an appellate court. North was sentenced by Judge Gesell on July 5, 1989, to a concurrent one-, two-, and three-year suspended prison term, two years of probation, $150,000 in fines, and twelve hundred hours of community service. The appeals court, as in the Poindexter case, overturned the convictions on the basis that North's immunized congressional testimony had been used against him because witnesses were called who had heard that previous testimony. Charges regarding the diversion had to be dropped as a result of the defense attorney's request for hundreds of classified documents that the administration (by then the Bush administration) was unwilling to declassify for security reasons. Colonel North later wrote the following about the reversal: "Brendan had insisted that my compelled testimony to Congress made it impossible for the prosecution to proceed. And now, five years after it all began, Walsh finally admitted that Brendan was right."[16] A reinvigorated North went on to write his autobiography, run for the U.S. Senate, and become a television commentator.

Robert C. McFarlane, on March 11, 1988, pleaded guilty to four misdemeanor counts related to withholding information from Congress and was sentenced to two years probation, a $20,000 fine, and two hundred hours of community service. Heroically, he had not sought immunity during his congressional testimony, and he paid the price. He served his sentence and applied himself wholeheartedly and creatively to his community service. He worked with Democratic senators Nunn and Kennedy and Democratic representative McCurdy to develop a pilot program in which young people volunteering for public service (under the National Service Act) would assist people with disabilities in their homes.

Despite his public acceptance of responsibility, Bud McFarlane developed a bitterness toward his commander in chief, whom he had so admired. This antipathy was shared by most of the Iran-contra co-defendants. "Iran-Contra," McFarlane later wrote, "was at the heart a political disagreement. We should have expected that the Congress would be angry and disagree with our actions. But since those actions had been taken in good faith and with the President's approval, they should never have led to criminal prosecution." He went on to write, "But Ronald Reagan lacked the moral conviction and the intellectual courage to stand up in our defense and in defense of his policy."[17] This was a very damning statement by a sincere, deeply wounded individual.

The curse of Iran-contra played on through its mixture of patriotism, passion, and deceit. The morality play had many facets. Bud McFarlane was in on the very inception of trading arms for hostages, the violation of congressional restrictions, and the misleading of Congress; he tried to stop the operation when he realized it was failing: He was lied to by Oliver North, and, of course, he never knew of the diversion. He took responsibility for his acts and paid a price that the other two Annapolis graduates never did. He had a conscience and carried guilt. He wore it on his sleeve and in his heart, which at the lowest point drove him to attempt suicide. When the nightmare ended, he established a new and successful career for himself in international consulting and policy advice. At his fiftieth birthday party at Wolf Trap in Virginia, a wide range of friends rallied round, including George H. W. Bush, Brent Scowcroft, Paul Nitze, Zbig Brzezinski, Mac Baldrige, and CNO Adm. James Watkins, in addition to about ninety others.[18]

Even more ironic was what happened between the independent counsel and the two eminent Cabinet secretaries who so vehemently opposed the entire Iranian initiative: George Shultz and Cap Weinberger.

Shortly after I left the White House, the house select committee requested that the Defense Department produce all documents related to the Iranian initiative, including diaries, appointment books, records of meetings, and handwritten notes. On June 17, 1987, members of the select committee staff took the deposition testimony of Secretary Weinberger, under oath. He was asked whether he had made notes at the time of or after key meetings in the White House and elsewhere, to which he replied, "Yes, occasionally, but comparatively rarely. I don't know we kept these in any formal way."[19] It turned out that there were massive notes that were withheld and discovered well into the Bush administration in the Library of Congress in an unclassified file. Walsh asserted that these extensive notes were critical to his investigation, and, for this, the man who opposed the Iran-contra initiative was indicted.

In addition to Weinberger, Shultz, on returning to the State Department after key White House meetings on Iran-contra issues, had dictated to his assistant accounts of these meetings. As in the Weinberger case, Walsh asserted that these notes were evidence that the president and secretaries of state and defense had far greater knowledge of these events than indicated and that the lateness of these revelations had obstructed his investigation. Judge Walsh decided to seek an indictment against Weinberger but not Shultz.

No one anticipated the tenacity and determination of the highly frustrated and increasingly angry independent counsel. As time went on, Walsh became more and more determined to bring down some high officials, including Presidents Reagan and Bush. Walsh believed he had been lied to and that if he had received the Weinberger and Shultz documents earlier he would have been able to finger Reagan and Bush, the grand prizes.

These two secretaries' notes were indeed embarrassing, and Walsh had a right to be angry, anger that was then increased by the belated discovery of a Bush diary. However, even if these important and revealing Weinberger and Shultz notes had become available earlier, Walsh still would not have had credible cases against Presidents Reagan and Bush. There was embarrassing evidence that Reagan, Bush, Shultz, and Weinberger had more knowledge than generalized statements about being "out of the loop" indicated. None, however, were in North's loop of the telltale diversion or many of his other operations. Two White House national security advisors had organized their activities precisely to keep the principals out of the loop.

Could the continuation of a second track have prevented all this belated controversy regarding cover-ups? One can easily paint a scenario different from that which occurred: The counselor for the second track would seek to impress upon the Cabinet members the need to comply with the request for diaries and notes so that evidence was not withheld. Even more important were the weekly meetings with the general counsels of the departments—including State and Defense. In this investigation, what the White House had to fear was not the revelation of documents and notes but backing into a cover-up. One can speculate that the mistakes and oversights of Shultz and Weinberger (which Walsh called their lies) would not have occurred if the two-track system had stayed in place. This of course is speculation, but it may offer a lesson for future presidential crisis management.

To Judge Walsh, all of these subsequent notes and diaries, which were not turned over until discovered by Walsh's staff, remained part of a huge cover-up. This was to him the "firewall" around the president, as he titled his book *Firewall*. On the other hand, to the Bush and Reagan people, the Walsh exercise was what they called "the criminalization of policy differences." Accurate or misleading statements before the Congress were put in the context of policy differences, what had to be done by administration representatives because the Congress was blocking parts of the president's foreign-policy initiatives.

In any event, the Iran-contra investigation started in November, 1986, with a cover-up, then was put on sound ground for a few months, and then gradually deteriorated into six years of recurring charges of cover-up and eventually may have influenced a presidential election.

Cap Weinberger had been adamantly against the Iran-contra initiative. He was against trading arms for hostages. He warned the president that he (Reagan) was required to notify the intelligence committees and leadership on Capitol Hill; he had no knowledge of the diversion, which, if he had, he would certainly have opposed. He did not tell the truth about his notes, but the fact that these notes were in unclassified files at the Library of Congress implies some form of naïveté and lack of intent to lie.[20]

Now, however, we come to the final curse of Iran-contra. On October 30, 1992, five days before the presidential election, Judge Walsh issued a one-count indictment of former defense secretary Caspar Weinberger: "false statements." As one reporter explained, "Not only did Walsh indict Weinberger, but he chose—he was not required—to release at that time a piece of prosecutorial evidence that seemed to implicate President Bush in the scandal."[21]

This was front-page news. President Bush had been closing the gap with Clinton. The effect on the campaign was immediate—a drop in the polls for Bush. Mary McGrory, writing on election eve, noted that "Bush's attempts to wrest the election away from the economy and into character were succeeding. In the past few weeks Clinton underwent a sinking spell in the polls. But now the president is, as Lyndon Johnson might put it, 'being bit by his own dog.'"[22] Charles Krauthammer later quoted McGrory, "With Walsh's tomahawk between his shoulders, Bush's comeback collapsed."[23]

Boyden Gray, George Bush's White House legal adviser as vice president and then as president, later wrote the following: "Iran-Contra became the defining saga of the Reagan and Bush Administrations. Iran-Contra bracketed the Bush presidency, almost costing him the election in 1988, and finally contributing to his defeat in 1992."[24]

George Stephanopoulos, a key Clinton campaign hand, saw it somewhat differently: Iran-contra independent counsel Lawrence Walsh had just indicted former Secretary of Defense Casper Weinberger, and a note included in the indictment indicated that Bush had both known about and supported trading arms for hostages—a charge President Bush had repeatedly denied. The Weinberger note was the closest thing yet to a smoking gun. Bush's campaign was dead anyway, but this was the nail in the coffin.[25] On Christmas Eve, 1992, outgoing president Bush pardoned Caspar Weinberger, along with Elliott Abrams, Dewey Clarridge, Alan Fiers, and Robert McFarlane.

The Bush pardon of Weinberger became controversial because it was charged as being the first time a president had pardoned someone in a case in which that president had some actual or potential involvement. In quite a few press accounts, Bush was charged with pardoning himself. President Bush had a very different view. In his public statement, he noted that, since the Walsh investigation had begun, "The last American hostage has come home to freedom, worldwide terrorism has declined, the people of Nicaragua have elected a democratic government, and the Cold War has ended in victory for the American people and the cause of freedom we championed."

Bush went on to note that "it is a bitter irony that on the day the first charges against the secretary were filed, Russian president Boris Yeltsin arrived in the United States to celebrate the end of the Cold War." He appropriately praised Weinberger in contributing to this victory. He added that he was pardoning him not just out of compassion or "to spare a 75-year-old patriot the torment of lengthy and costly legal procedures, but to make it possible for him to receive the honor he deserves for his extraordinary service to his country."[26]

With this, the curse of Iran-contra had finally played out, and the curtain closed on one of the most intriguing morality plays in presidential history, matched only by the drama of Watergate and the Clinton impeachment, subjects of the next chapter. In any event, William Shakespeare lived in the wrong era.

CHAPTER 20

Watergate, the Clinton Affair, and Iran-Contra

It may be instructive to end this story of the Reagan presidential crisis with a comparison of the crises of Richard Milhouse Nixon and William Jefferson Clinton. The legendary biographer in the Roman Empire, Plutarch, notes the instructional value of studying parallel lives to better learn about the character of leaders under the stress of pressure and temptation. Three times in the latter part of the twentieth century presidencies have been placed in jeopardy by cover-ups of situations that the respective presidents either created or allowed. They each faced the stress of pressure and temptation. The ultimate test of presidential character is not in never making mistakes but in dealing with mistakes when they are made. How then did Reagan compare with the other two presidents in his character test, and how are the respective crises similar and different? My answer may be prejudiced because I worked so closely with President Reagan. But here it is.

We start with Nixon. On June 18, 1972, while vacationing at Key Biscayne and drinking a morning cup of coffee, he approvingly read the *Miami Herald* headline story, "Ground Combat Role Nears End for the U.S." This was certainly big news for his successful presidency. He was on top of the world. He then noted a small story on the middle of the page on the left-hand side that was to alter his presidency: "Miamians Held in D.C. Try to Bug Demo Headquarters." Nixon dismissed the story as a prank and never brought it up when he talked later that morning with his chief of staff, H. R. Haldeman.

Back in Washington, on June 20, Nixon learned of the burglars' connection with the Committee to Reelect the President (CRP) and the White House. By June 23, he tried to have the CIA block the FBI investigation; the obstruction of justice had begun. In three days, he had done the deed that wrecked his presidency. As the investigations closed in on the president, on April 30, 1973, more than ten months later, on national television he assured the American public that he "personally assumed the responsibility" for the investigation, that he was "determined that we should get to the bottom of the matter, and that the truth should be fully brought out—no matter who was involved."[1] Faced with lies, obstruction of justice, and impeachment, Nixon was ultimately forced to resign.

Supposedly the lessons of Watergate were learned for all time, but, as we have already recounted, on November 6, 1986, President Reagan told the public that the story about trading arms for hostages "has no foundation," and a week later he added, "We did not—repeat—did not trade weapons or anything else for hostages." The Reagan presidency was headed for deep trouble, and we have told that story.

More than ten years later and supposedly with more presidential lessons learned, President Clinton said, "I want you to listen to me. I'm going to say this again: I did not have sexual relations with that woman, Miss Lewinsky." His story and prevarication dominated the news for more than seven months and led to the first impeachment in 130 years.

Each of these three presidents was, in his own way, an extraordinary leader with multiple achievements—Nixon, opening China and re-balancing power; Reagan, the great communicator turning Gorbachev around to triumph in the Cold War; and Clinton, the best Democratic politician since FDR, stealing the vital conservative center from the Republicans in a remarkable comeback after the Republican revolution of 1994 and finally presiding over a financial surplus and booming economy.

The stories of all three are of triumph and tragedy, of brilliance and corruption, of tragic flaws in extraordinary personalities and leaders, all of which belong with the dramatists of Periclean Athens or Elizabethan England as well as to Plutarch's *Lives*. Tragic flaws came to bear in Watergate, Iran-contra, and the Clinton affairs. I discuss the many differences, some similarities, and numerous common lessons. As in the Nixon administration, small decisions made early in all three crises shook the foundations of the White House.

First, let's address alibis, lies, and whitewashes.

Perhaps not surprisingly, a body of literature has developed in each case that attempts to exonerate each president from strict accountability. This is done under the guise of current atmosphere: that the president and his men, under test of character, were merely the product of their times and acting accordingly. In the Nixon case, it would come as no surprise that from the right would emerge Victor Lasky's book *It Didn't Start with Watergate*, which offset Bob Woodward and Carl Bernstein's *All the President's Men*. However, some sympathetic scholarly writings from the left, most notably, Joan Hoff and her *Nixon Reconsidered*, come as a surprise. Her appropriate admiration for Nixon's domestic record is not a part of our story here, but she notes that Nixon's name "continues to dominate public awareness as few presidencies in this century have. It is possible that historians in the next century will refer to the age of Nixon as they do now to the age of Jackson." She asks, "What is this Nixon phenomenon? First, there is longevity. . . . Second, Nixon's long public career and truncated presidency represent both the best and the worst of the post–World War II political system in the United States—nothing more and nothing less. This is something that 'Nixon haters' have always simply refused to accept."[2]

She sees Nixon as a transitional president "who faced the forces of the past and the requirements of the future in an exceptionally difficult period of U.S. history." Someone might write these very words about Clinton, who, by the way, as president became Nixon's admirer and friend. Hoff believes that Nixon was fighting a war and, like other war leaders in American history, he violated constitutional rights; hence, he carried out illegal actions. Her answer to this war problem would have been to end the fighting much sooner.

Likewise, following the Reagan Iran-contra scandals, hearings, convictions, and overturning of convictions, there grew a body of literature primarily from the conservative side that says, basically, that these affairs represent the attempt by those who opposed the foreign policies of the Reagan administration to make his foreign policy criminal, especially with regard to Central America. This has been part of the thrust of books written by Bud McFarlane, Oliver North, Elliott Abrams, and other participants in the crises. They criticize their commander in chief because he did not stand up to the Congress and defend and immediately pardon them when, as they saw it, they were essentially carrying out his policies, which were the right ones in the first place.

The argument also runs that many presidents have lied to Congress—Roosevelt did so dramatically about his undeclared shooting war in the Atlantic—and likewise presidents lied to their subordinates. A notorious case is Robert McNamara and Lyndon Johnson regarding the progress of the war in Vietnam.[3]

From Robert Dallek to James Pfiffner, presidential historians have studied presidential lies. Pfiffner categorizes lies as follows: lies to protect national security; trivial lies to prevent embarrassment and preserve political viability; lies to cover up important facts; and lies of policy deceptions.[4] Dallek, Lyndon Johnson's biographer, says of his subject, "When he is pulling on his ear lobes and stroking his chin, he's telling the truth. When he is moving his lips, he was lying."[5] Kennedy had Adlai Stevenson lie at the UN about our involvement in the Bay of Pigs. Eisenhower let his aides describe Gary Powers's U-2 as a weather plane. But, as Michael Beschloss observes, "there are lots of examples of lack of candor and forthrightness, but most presidents take care not to lie directly, because they know the bond between them and the American people will snap."[6] This is what so worried Reagan.

President Eisenhower later explained why he had worried about his "plausible denial" of the U-2 mission over the Soviet Union. When a president has lost his credibility, "he has lost his greatest strength."[7] Liberal law professor Jamie Raskin, however, further refines the problem: "In our everyday life, people distinguish between lies all the time. But we don't excuse lies under oath, especially from the president. That is where it gains a much more complicated resonance."[8]

Those defenders who are tolerant in regard to Iran-contra do not extend this same tolerant logic to the Bill Clinton affair. During the 1999 Serbian Kosovo War, Oliver North became a television cohost for an interview program on MSNBC, where he would righteously tear apart President Clinton for his lies as if he himself had not had problems with veracity. Moving from the political right to the political left, the eminent historian Arthur Schlesinger Jr. rounded up historians to minimize Bill Clinton's acts and point to other examples in American history of hanky-panky. It was an embarrassing sexual affair, but "everybody lies about adultery." To criminalize such consensual sex into impeachment and conviction is preposterous, disproportionate, and even threatening to our constitutional government, for the president's opponents are using these incidents to try to reverse Clinton's election.

If the preceding arguments are all accepted (and they all have *some* truth), there are no ethical lessons for future presidents to learn. People who are willing to tolerate these situations argue that the problems in Watergate, Iran-contra, and the Clinton affairs were caused by intrusive media and special or independent counsels who went too far. Presidents should make sure that they do not get caught. That is the ugly bottom line of this logic.

Bill Clinton declared at his impeachment that he was proud to have the opportunity to uphold the Constitution. Nixon said about Watergate only that "mistakes were made." And Reagan remained detached, saying that he did not trade arms for hostages. But make no mistake about it: Each president and the country were profoundly injured. One resigned, one was tarnished, and a third was impeached and tried. The tragic results cannot be explained away. There is no redeeming factor in these three episodes if future presidents do not learn from them.

In what follows I take more of a consistent and strict constructionist view, whether dealing with Republicans or Democrats. In my first chapter, I quote Hubert Humphrey relating to me the conundrum that, in executive-legislative politics, too frequently "where a man sits will determine where a man stands." That is certainly true of those who excused those whom I have mentioned, but in this chapter we stand on the law. We look at full accountability as the standard for the past and for the future, notwithstanding mitigating circumstances, and we seek to develop observations and lessons of relevance to the presidency in the twenty-first century.

Each scandal existed in an immediate climate conducive to triggering the public embarrassment. Nixon was a wartime president. There was a counterculture in America, with dissident activists and sometimes violence, and it was believed that the administration's enemies had to be spied upon. Indeed, there were wiretaps, "plumbers," and break-ins prior to the Watergate burglary. Nixon had called the heads of intelligence agencies together in the White House to discuss what became the Houston plan (named after a White House aide), which dealt with domestic unrest, including countermeasures such as campus informants, mail openings, burglaries, and electronic surveillance. Sometime later, Nixon told his legal aide that, if there was a newspaper story saying "The president authorized a super-duper activity in 1970" involving "burglary, etc. and wiretapping," Americans would understand the plan was to control riots by pro-testors of the Vietnam War.[9] Nixon stressed that he was a wartime commander in chief.

The flash point was when, in June, 1971, Daniel Ellsberg leaked to the press the so-called Pentagon papers. This was a four-thousand-page confidential critical history of the Vietnam War that the earlier secretary of defense, Robert McNamara, had prepared. I remember sitting in Secretary of State Bill Rogers's morning staff meeting as he talked of every legal measure to block publication. The White House was in a frenzy. The publication was embarrassing, but it was all about events that had occurred during the Johnson administration. I could not understand why the administration wanted to mount this particular battle, which, of course, would not only associate the Nixon administration with a Johnson administration document but also further dramatize its importance.

What I did not know was that, by the time the Pentagon papers were released, the so-called plumbers—the group designed to plug the security leaks—were in operation. On September 3, 1971, the plumb-ers burglarized the offices of psychiatrist Lewis Fielding to obtain Daniel Ellsberg's confidential files. In this first illegal black-bag job, the precedent was set for the Watergate break-in.

James Pfiffner observes, "what eventually brought down President Nixon was his involvement with the cover up of the crimes. Nixon never seemed seriously to consider the possibility of denouncing the break-in and promising that the White House would not conduct any such activities in the future." He quotes Nixon's lawyer: "The tran-sition from bungled break-in to cover-up took place automatically, without discussion, debate, or even the whisper of gears shifting."[10]

Much has already been written in this book about the climate of the Reagan administration that led to Iran-contra. Ronald Reagan pursued all means to get the hostages back and the contras supplied. After all, he had told McFarlane to keep the contras together "body and soul." In his detachment and North's duplicity, Reagan did not know or understand the details of what was going on. But there was never a question of whether the Iran-contra scandal would break into the open. The question was only when. There were too many hair-raising schemes for it to be otherwise. In this regard, it resembled Watergate.

Of course, there is another similarity between the policies behind Watergate and Iran-contra. Nixon saw himself besieged by the liberal press, the establishment, the antiwar protesters, and indeed the bureaucracy. His exaggerated demons were a phobia because he had actually won reelection by a landslide. The leaks of the Pentagon papers did not truly jeopardize his presidency. The Nixon measures taken against them truly did.

Reagan's personality was much different from Nixon's; each had very different motives. Bill Casey excited Reagan about seven hostages. To free them, a wild effort was set in motion. There was no public groundswell about the seven hostages as there had been during the Carter administration, when, in November, 1979, fifty-two Americans, mostly staff members at the U.S. Embassy, were seized.[11] At the time, there were massive issues to be faced elsewhere in the Cold War that could affect the lives of millions of Americans. The freedom of these seven hostages was important, but not of such importance as to place at risk the credibility of the presidency. Despite this mind-boggling misbalance, an ad hoc, super-secret effort was launched lacking both oversight and clear accountability.[12]

Now we move to the heart of the three presidents' tests of character. Nixon and Clinton reacted far differently than Reagan when their respective crises broke. Very quickly, both Nixon and Clinton were in total charge of their cover-ups. Both were skilled in the management of crises. They were smart, cunning, agile, and, in the last analysis, notoriously foolish.

In the Nixon case, H. R. Haldeman suggested that Nixon use the CIA to thwart the FBI's investigation of Watergate—a clear obstruction of justice. The Nixon tapes revealed the president himself pushing this obstruction of justice, and the tape of June 23 furnished the smoking gun. This dramatic revelation produced the collapse of Republican senate support, and Nixon's resignation followed because it was clear that after impeachment he would face conviction.

Such a smoking gun did not exist in the Reagan or Clinton crises. There was no proof that Reagan knew of the diversion. In Clinton's case, although the stained dress indicated perjury, the majority of the public and two-thirds of the Senate did not consider this an adequate cause for removal from office.

But the Reagan story is different. The reaction of the Reagan administration to the disclosure of trading arms for hostages and the diversion of funds to the contras produced the November, 1986, cover-ups led by Poindexter, North, and McFarlane. The president was involved at least to the extent of false public denials.

By late December, Reagan had fired Poindexter and North, created the bipartisan Tower Board and an independent special counselor instructed to "get it all out," and waived executive privilege. The Reagan response, after the initial cover-up, was not only exemplary but also a model for future presidents. Clinton did not follow the model.

The Clinton administration's reaction was dominated by the fact that the president alone knew all the facts. David Broder wrote on August 19, 1998, that "in one respect what Clinton has done is every bit as bad as what Richard Nixon did. Like Nixon, who knew [almost] from the moment the Watergate break-in occurred what had really happened, Clinton knew from the first moment he was questioned about the White House intern what was going on between them." In the beginning of the crisis, Clinton confided in no one, not even—or perhaps most of all—his wife. He deliberately misled his own staff into making false statements and, much later, offered ambiguous and probably untruthful testimony before a grand jury.

On July 29, 1998, a lead editorial in the *New York Times* titled "Bill Clinton's 29 Months" spoke of the "aura of loneliness" surrounding the president. "In other days in the capital, presidents could summon, from the legal or diplomatic worlds or from Congress, wise and disinterested elders, who as the saying goes, had heard the owl and seen the elephant. This President seems surrounded by staff people who are passing through."

If Clinton had decided to get everything out and called in an outsider, one can imagine perhaps only a footnote to history about the Monica affair. If Bill Clinton had called in seasoned Washington attorney Lloyd Cutler, confessed completely that he had done things inconceivably embarrassing, and asked what he should do, we can be assured of what Cutler would have told him: "Tell all." In January, former White House chief of staff Leon Panetta and former counselor

George Stephanopoulos used the press to advise the president to tell all. They became persona non grata.[13] The only outside advice Clinton ever sought was from Richard Morris, who had also been discredited in a sex scandal.

The original motives of these three presidents serve to explain their initial actions. Richard Nixon, who saw demons all around him, aspired to be the great peacemaker, conclude the Vietnam War while sustaining the South Vietnamese government, and develop a new world order with China and a détente with the Soviet Union. He also wanted to be reelected. Reagan was passionately concerned about both the hostages in Lebanon and the contras fighting the Communists in Nicaragua, and he wanted to end the Cold War. Clinton, who also saw "enemies," set a devastating example in attempting to subvert the rule of law when in trouble over the Monica affair. He wanted to spare his wife, daughter, and the increasingly prosperous nation from his disgrace. The problem was that the chief law enforcer spoke under oath. However, the Monica affair did not threaten to subvert the Constitution, whereas the conspiracy following Watergate and that among Reagan's subordinates clearly did. This point was made over and over in the impeachment proceedings and the trial, and it carried the vote for acquittal.[14]

There were some good presidential intentions mixed up in all three stories, each of which forms a morality play. Intent carries some weight in a court of law. But the intentions of these presidents were misplaced and misapplied and produced national tragedy.

Let us briefly compare the congressional investigations. We have already covered the Iran-contra story on Capitol Hill. The Watergate saga was on a long fuse from the revelations of the break-in on June 18, 1972, to the hearings and smoking-gun revelation and the House Judiciary Committee beginning its impeachment hearings in April, 1974. The committee reached its impeachment resolutions on July 27. The smoking-gun tape was released on August 5, 1974; then it was obvious that Nixon would be not only impeached but also convicted by the Senate. Nixon resigned on August 9. As the evidence piled up, the Nixon congressional hearings were, overall, characterized by a high degree of bipartisanship.

It was exactly the reverse in the Clinton case, where the House was divided along partisan lines. At the beginning of President

Clinton's house impeachment process, Rep. Henry Hyde had said that impeachment must enjoy bipartisan support to succeed. There, of course, was an option to obtain a high degree of bipartisanship in both the House and Senate through a censure resolution, but a vote on a house resolution was blocked by the Republican leadership.

As for the Senate, 29 out of 45 Democratic senators signed Sen. Dianne Feinstein's proposal stating that President Clinton "gave false or misleading testimony and his actions have had the effect of impeding discovery of evidence in Judicial Proceedings." If Republicans had joined in, this would have meant 79 senators behind such a telling statement. The Republican refusal of the bipartisan consensus proposal led to a simple acquittal of the president.[15]

We next turn to the comparative roles of the special and independent counsels. The Watergate experience of the special prosecutor clearly had an impact on the handling of the independent counsel in the Clinton affair. As to special prosecutors—later called independent counsels—in May, 1973, the Watergate scandal had reached the point that the new attorney general, Elliott Richardson, appointed Harvard Law School professor Archibald Cox to be the special Watergate prosecutor. With the revelation of the White House tapes, Cox went to the courts to enforce subpoenas. By late October, Nixon ordered Richardson to fire Cox, resulting in the resignations of Richardson and his deputy, with Solicitor General Robert Bork taking over as acting attorney general and firing Cox. Texas lawyer Leon Jaworski was appointed to replace Cox, but to Nixon's chagrin he followed in Cox's prosecutorial direction.

The Clinton administration, with its intense disdain for independent counsel Kenneth Starr, nevertheless remained determined not to repeat the Watergate-type firing and to avoid asserting executive privilege, which had been given a bad name by Watergate.

Although Cox and Jaworski were certainly part of the Nixon controversy, they never became negative figures with the mass of the public, the press, or the Congress. During the Reagan crisis, Judge Walsh was initially not a point of controversy, but, as the years went on and the inquiries stretched out, Walsh became a major target of Republican attacks. On the other hand, Judge Starr was controversial early on, and this was best summed up in a *New York Times* op-ed piece by conservative David Brooks, senior editor of the *Weekly Standard*, on January 22, 1999: "Remember, the supposed lesson of

Watergate was that stonewalling never works. The cover-up is always worse than the crime. But Mr. Clinton did stonewall and effectively." However, Brooks asserts, Starr made this possible. "On February 1 [1998], Ms. Lewinsky wrote out a proffer detailing the testimony she would give in exchange for immunity. Starr ended up rejecting this offer. In retrospect, that was a fatal mistake. He noted that it was another six months until what was close to the smoking gun, the telltale DNA-stained dress, emerged, "exposing the President's lies." The delay gave the White House time to conduct an election-like media campaign. Brooks writes that Starr spent those months "staggering from one publicity blunder after another." Hillary moved into the right-wing conspiracy idea; Starr was tarred as being a part of the tobacco lobby. By the time the Starr report was released, he was looked upon as an out-of-control independent counsel, and the president "looked reasonably even tempered" when his grand-jury testimony was broadcast.

Ironically, if the ultimate impact of Judge Walsh was the Weinberger indictment (which arguably contributed to the defeat of George Bush and the election of Bill Clinton), the ultimate impact of Judge Starr may have been the survival of Bill Clinton. This, however, according to the polls, the majority of the public favored.

Now let's turn to the aftermath—the postpresidential periods of these presidents. During the decades following Watergate, Richard Nixon began a rather successful campaign of rehabilitation. Joan Hoff points out that his thirty-nine-minute resignation speech was carefully done, with memorable phrases such as one can "know how magnificent it is to be on the highest mountain [only] after being in the deepest valley" and that if you hate those who hate you, "then you destroy yourself."[16] Nixon later produced well-written and well-received books, especially about foreign policy.

He also reminisced about Watergate in his writings and interviews. Hoff notes that his rationalizations about Watergate "grew rather than diminished." In his March, 1977, interview by David Frost, he even concluded that the president could not break the law. This doctrine would, of course, make the president an absolute monarch, like Louis XIV: "L'état, c'est moi."

Sun King or not, this remarkable man—Richard Nixon—was ever so concerned with his role in history. I recall my meeting with him on a cold January day in 1973. Adm. Arleigh Burke had given me an ultimatum to get out of government to return to CSIS so that he could retire. Secretary of State Rogers had talked to me about other supposedly more attractive positions in government, and I had then been sent to the president for one last attempt at persuasions. I explained to him that my problem was not with the job, but with the Burke summons. Nixon respected this legendary admiral and immediately conceded.

Then he looked at me and asked, "Dave, what's your doctorate?"

"History, Mr. President."

"Ah, that's my first love. That's what I read. I've taken all this criticism over our so-called Christmas bombing of North Vietnam because they've gone back on negotiations. I don't care what the public or the press says about me now. I care about what is said 50 or 100 years from now."

As we all know now, everyone in the Oval Office was being taped. Nixon was taping conversations so that he could later write his great opus. Ironically, he was taping his downfall. Tragic though his mistakes were at the time, how much more tragic that this man—who survived so long and wrote so brilliantly after his presidency—could not enhance his place in history by a heroic analysis of what he had really done wrong.

By contrast, Ronald Reagan's autobiography is far more honest, if far less brilliant, than Nixon's. "Yes, I believed in helping the Contras," he wrote, "but no one, including presidents, is above the law."[17] Thus, he regretted the doctrine of some of his subordinates—that violations of law were justifiable on behalf of their noble and patriotic ends.

He, of course, continued to have great problems with the issue of trading arms for hostages even after admitting it at the Tower Board meeting and in his March comeback speech. Nancy Reagan called me some weeks after I had left government. "Ronnie has reverted to his original story. Come talk to him."

Reagan simply would not lower the standard. He believed that trading arms for hostages was immoral, and he therefore had a difficult time accepting that, on some level, he had failed to live up to this moral standard. His struggle was not to rationalize his own actions in the scandal—as Nixon and Clinton did—but to accept that in the Iran-contra matter, through his publicly admitted failings, he had compromised his firm moral belief.

While still in office, Clinton's remorse tended to vary. As the House Judiciary Committee was voting its first article of impeachment, Clinton emerged from the White House to give reporters a further act of contrition. He used the phrases "profoundly sorry" and "the shame of wrongful conduct" and said that it was hard to hear that he had been called deceitful and manipulative. The *Washington Post* editorialized, "What would be right is for him to admit finally the now obvious facts that he lied under oath and encouraged others to do so."[18]

It is significant, however, that he said, "Should Congress and the American people determine that my errors of word and deed require their rebuke and censure, I am ready to accept that."[19]

After the senate trial, Clinton declared that he did not regard the historic impeachment vote in the House as a "badge of shame": "I do not because I do not believe it was warranted and I just don't believe it was right." He went on to say, "I am honored that something indispensable was pursued and that I had the opportunity to defend the Constitution."[20] The noble, self-critical lines had vanished.

What Clinton continued to achieve was an ability to compartmentalize bad news and drive forward on new endeavors since he closely studied the lives of other presidents. He often spoke of his presidential legacies. One of his evident abilities, even in his Renaissance weekends before becoming president, was to look ahead at looming issues: One of those great issues was the entitlement problem and aging effects on Medicare and retirement. Dealing with this through "triangulation" from the political center was one of his great aims. Emerging from the Monica affair wounded him, and, more dependent on the Democratic left, he went against the Social Security reform plans offered by Democratic Leadership Council senators Moynihan, Breaux, and Kerry. On Medicare he went against Senator Breaux, who had chaired the commission Clinton had created. In foreign policy, he was clearly weakened in managing his "constructive engagement" policy on China, and his Middle East policy stalled. With the Serbian ethnic cleansing in Kosovo, however, he was a leader in building a remarkable alliance unity in NATO's first war. But the president who had come to Washington to set a new moral tone did the opposite. People enormously benefited from the Clinton economy, responded to his warm personality, and admired his communication ability, leading George Stephanopoulos in his memoir to conclude hauntingly,

"Wondering what might have been—if only this good president had been a better man."[21]

To return to Ronald Reagan, he dealt with Iran-contra at a distance. He earlier had denied arms for hostages, but then, in his March, 1987, comeback speech, he said "mistakes were made." He finally admitted "arms for hostages." It took a long time. What he did promptly, however, was to ensure an honest investigation. Here he clearly stands ahead of Nixon and Clinton.

CHAPTER 21

The Reagan Presidency in History

What then is Ronald Reagan's place in the long history of the American presidency? Reagan's own assessment is interesting and revealing: "I never thought of myself as a great man, just a man committed to great ideas."[1] Preeminent presidential scholars have given us their thoughts, but I add mine as one who saw him close up and often alone. I saw him at the time of his most severe leadership crisis, which ultimately led to what in my view was his greatest triumph, his comeback.

Ronald Reagan left office with the highest approval ratings of any president since FDR: 63 percent in the Gallup poll and 68 percent in the *New York Times*–CBS poll. The damage of Iran-contra, however, left Reagan's reputation vulnerable. This has invited critics to make retrospective generalizations about our oldest serving president that call into question his prize roles in restoring the presidency and in building a successful strategy to end the Cold War.

Critics have used Iran-contra not only to claim flawed judgment and cover-up but also to assert that, throughout his presidency, an inept Reagan was merely a figurehead—an actor and communicator with flair, but in effect operating from his cue cards. As for ending the Cold War, critics argue that Reagan lucked out by having a canny Gorbachev, whom they credit as responsible for that achievement. These assertions are typified by one mocking title about Reagan's comportment, *Sleepwalking through History*,[2] and another, more recent, book on his SDI (Strategic Defense Initiative) strategy, *Way Out There in the Blue: Reagan, Star Wars, and the End of the Cold War.*[3]

These negative assessments of Reagan—one by a Pulitzer Prize winner—come at a time when other prominent and exacting historians and journalists, who had for the most part been early Reagan critics, offer a far more favorable assessment.[4] The most notable in this group is Harvard scholar Richard Neustadt, a great admirer of Roosevelt. In the 1990 update of his classic work, *Presidential Power and the Modern Presidents,* he writes that Reagan "was the last Roosevelt Democrat we shall see as President." Neustadt notes that Reagan voted four times for Roosevelt and once for Truman and that Reagan's "[p]residency restored the public image of the office to a fair (if perhaps rickety) approximation of its Roosevelt mold: a place of popularity, influence, and initiative . . . like or hate his politics—a presence many of us loved to see as Chief of State." He notes that the image of the office Reagan sought to live by was "implanted there by FDR while Reagan was a youthful, ardent Democrat"[5] and that Reagan's "incuriosity and delegation on the one hand, and commitments and convictions on the other—at once framed Reagan's operating style and seemingly accounted for his impacts on the course of public policy."[6]

In his acclaimed book *The Politics Presidents Make,* Yale's Stephen Skowronek, winner of the Neustadt Prize, analyzes Reagan, along with Jefferson, Jackson, and Roosevelt, as one of the major presidential "reconstructive leaders." Skowronek says Reagan was "the most masterful politician in the presidency since Franklin Roosevelt."[7]

On the foreign-policy front, Princeton's Fred Greenstein, Eisenhower's biographer, in his latest work comments on the great paradox of Reagan's sentinel foreign-policy achievement: "Reagan formed a personal bond with Gorbachev and supported those of his own aides who were prepared to find an accommodation with the Soviet Union, contributing to the end of the cold war simply by being who he was. Like Richard Nixon, he was too well known as an anticommunist to be vulnerable to attack from the right. In short, he was capable of a paradoxical moderation that would have been less feasible if he had been a moderate."[8] Yale's John Lewis Gaddis, in his towering history of the Cold War, commends Reagan for "bringing about the most significant improvement in Soviet-American relations since the end of World War II."[9]

It is not that these historians, who are often of a liberal persuasion, have suddenly failed to see Reagan's unevenness, frequent disengagement, lack of attention to detail, and often excessive delegation of authority to his subordinates. Rather, they see the larger picture that relates to the difficult art of presidential leadership and that Reagan, with all of his blemishes, had mastered that rare art and led with ideas and an overarching philosophy that enabled him to communicate nationally and affect attitudes.[10]

As for the critical side, if Neustadt compares Roosevelt and Reagan as great leaders, one might also compare them as poor managers. Roosevelt's veteran secretary of war, Henry L. Stimson, once referred to the president's "grasshopper mind—a mind that does not follow easily on conclusive chain of thought, but . . . hops from suggestion to suggestion."[11] A biographer refers to Roosevelt's "disorderly, even chaos-engendering ways of administration."[12] This is why the Roosevelt and Reagan presidencies are such tantalizing studies in presidential leadership.

Like Stimson with Roosevelt, I witnessed all sides of Reagan's mystifying unevenness. As I noted before, I was with Ronald Reagan at his absolute best at NATO in 1985, when a majestic Reagan, appearing before fifteen heads of government, had just turned this first U.S.-Soviet summit in almost seven years into a personal triumph, one that led Gorbachev to tell his staff, "Don't say anything bad about that man again."[13]

I was also with Ronald Reagan at his absolute worst at the second Tower Board meeting in 1987. A fumbling, faltering Reagan went to his desk, rummaged through papers, and read directly from Peter Wallison's aide-mémoire, "You might want to say . . ." The board members thought the presidency had collapsed, as Sen. John Tower indicated to me later. This blunder marked the low tide of the events that had entangled this tall-standing leader in devious covert policies that were totally out of character and utterly contrary to his openness, upon which his extraordinary trust with the American public had been built. This quality, then at risk, afforded him the very basis for his leadership with ideas and its credible communication to the American public.

Having witnessed the best and the worst, how then can one measure this president and his standing in the history of the presidencies? I draw on historian James MacGregor Burns's division of presidential leadership into two types: (1) transactional leadership—managing the duties and challenges of the presidency, and (2) transformational leadership—changing the culture, economy, or politics of the country.

Although Lincoln possessed both types of leadership, finding both equally mixed in a single person is rare. In Ronald Reagan, perhaps, the United States has never had a president with such great talent for transformational and so little interest in transactional leadership.

Reagan could often be distant and inert at managing his administration, especially when let down by subordinates, upon whom he was dependent. He lacked daily knowledge of detail, often of his own proposals. He failed to deal with quarreling aides and, in the national security process, allowed too much hostility between his secretaries of state and defense. Iran-contra was his biggest failure because it destroyed the Cabinet checks and balances that structured the NSC process. As a transactional president, he was dependent on the success of his delegation to the right people.

He delegated brilliantly in the beginning with a team of the right people, who included Baker, Meese, Deaver, and Gergen. His first hundred days, when he and his team set aside all other issues and drove his economic program through Congress, can be matched only by Roosevelt's second hundred days following his reelection or Johnson's hundred days following his 1964 election.[14] Reagan, like Carter and Clinton, ran against Washington, but, unlike them, Reagan put experienced Washington hands in charge of his first term. Perhaps because of his able staff, his first term is something to be studied and admired at both the transactional and the transformational levels. House Speaker Tip O'Neill reflectively wrote, "All in all, the Reagan team of 1981 was probably the best-run political operating unit I've ever seen."[15]

However, Reagan's personal transactional focus deteriorated markedly in his second term, when he traded the stimulating team of Baker, Meese, and Deaver for the monolithic control of Don Regan. The operational rigidity and rote ceremonial performance in office became stultifying. Long gone was the Reagan who engaged in details of presidential policies and who wrote his own speeches, radio scripts, and columns.

In the 1970s, Governor Reagan served on the Rockefeller Commission on intelligence reform. Toward the concluding session, there was an impasse, and Reagan skillfully scratched out summary language that led the group to a unified conclusion.[16] It has recently come to light, through the research of Kiron Skinner that, of the more than one thousand daily radio broadcasts he gave from 1975 to 1979, two-thirds were written in his own hand. George Shultz, analyzing this, wrote, "Reagan was acting as a one-man think tank."[17] This was not quite the Reagan I dealt with in 1987, but the Eisenhower of 1959 and 1960 was also not the Eisenhower of his first term.

Despite the clear effects of aging and illness, Ronald Reagan was truly a transformational leader who accomplished his transformational objectives: He changed people's views of the presidency and the role of government; he electrified the Republican Party and moved it toward a majority party; he restored national optimism and pride damaged by the Vietnam War; he turned the tide in the Cold War; and then, with that war nearly won, he pursued peace and freedom, even with Russia. Throughout all of this, it should be admitted, as Peter Wallison later wrote, that "Reagan reigned rather than ruled," but he accomplished this through the force of his few large ideas.[18]

Of course, it is important to recognize that transformational leadership is made possible only when the right person faces times of either crisis or special opportunity. Lincoln's greatness reflects our most severe national crisis. Theodore Roosevelt sensed the right moment and seized upon the great Progressive Movement. Franklin Roosevelt, Reagan's hero, faced not only the Great Depression but also the greatest war in history. These players on the historical stage, if elected twenty years earlier or later, would not have had the opportunity for such a transformational role.[19] So it was with Reagan.

Let's look at additional criteria to measure transformational leadership. First, as I have noted, a transformational president must have ideas, a vision, and a sense of strategic direction. It was Ted Kennedy, speaking at Yale, who said this about Reagan: "It would be foolish to deny that his success was fundamentally rooted in a command of public ideas. Ronald Reagan may have forgotten names, but never his goals. He was a great communicator, not simply because of his personality or his Teleprompter, but mostly because he had something to communicate.[20]

Further, in 1999, columnist David Broder wrote the following: "Reagan was a political natural and a gifted leader—one who had clear goals, strong principles and a great gift for translating abstract issues into compelling narratives conveying lessons anyone could grasp."[21] Kennedy and Broder are not conservative commentators.

Second, a transformational leader must also be able to make hard, at times unpopular, decisions. Greatness is not obtained by following polls. Reagan, like Truman and Eisenhower, mostly did not follow the polls. It must be recalled that I learned this characteristic dramatically during my first visit with a frail, just-returned-from-the-hospital President Reagan, when I shoved a devastating poll onto his desk. It showed that the vast majority of the public rejected his statement that he had not traded arms for hostages and many thought he was simply lying. The reader will recall his statement to me: "I don't care if I'm the only man in America that believes the way I do." In this case, his stubbornness and defiance of public opinion was not just wrong headed but also politically harmful and came close to wrecking his presidency. Still, that very stubbornness in not giving up SDI and increasing defense spending and speaking up on human rights were all key factors in winning the Cold War. Recall William Manchester's lines in his magisterial biography of Winston Churchill, in which he notes how young Winston's obnoxious stubbornness so injured his early career but later saved Britain.

Third—while this may seem to contradict number two—in transformational leadership, ideology and ideas must be separated. Ideology can become a rigid mindset to predetermine conclusions and actions; the Communists, for example, used it when they tried to impose Marxism on the realities of human nature and ended up imposing totalitarianism.

Some think classical conservatism is defined in terms of a fixed, dogmatic ideology from which leaders derive all of their actions. But a truly classical conservative has a general, yet consistent, philosophy founded on realism about the human condition, a way of thinking that also includes a vision of hope and progress. As Russell Kirk has written in *The Conservative Mind*, "Conservatism is not a fixed and immutable body of dogma, and conservatives inherit from [Edmund] Burke a talent for re-expressing their conviction to fit the time."[22] Burke rallied against the French revolutionary proponents of the blind ideology of "abstract rights" and believed that means must be determined by circumstance and that governing involves "changing, reforming, balancing, and adjusting."[23]

I did not know Ronald Reagan well before his election, but I knew William French Smith, the Los Angeles attorney who was his confidant, quite well. "You know," Smith said to me in late 1979,

"Ronald Reagan isn't deeply ideological like some make out. He knows where he wants to go, but he can often be shrewd and practical getting there."

A transformational president—liberal or conservative—must be able to project a consistent political philosophy and at the same time know how to deal with constantly changing circumstances. James David Barber, in his work on presidential character, notes the dangers of what he calls presidential rigidity. He cites Woodrow Wilson in dealing with the ratification of the covenant establishing the League of Nations, Herbert Hoover in not dealing with the deepening depression, and Lyndon Johnson in dealing with the Vietnam War.[24]

We all know the classic example of President Lincoln in managing change. Initially, he clearly stated that the Civil War was being fought to preserve the Union. Then, in altered circumstances, he moved on to emancipation to aid his military effort, inspire a holy crusade, and finally once and for all free the slaves and thus complete the American Revolution. Franklin Roosevelt was a master at communicating an overall strategic direction, but he also knew how to alter course with both the New Deal and, later, with war policy. Ronald Reagan displayed the ability to change thinking and positions in ending the Cold War.

Early on, Reagan moved Cold War strategy from the containment policy that ran through all postwar presidencies—from Truman to Carter. He did not buy the status quo of the Cold War. He shifted to an offensive of ideas, promoting the market economy and mounting a military and high-tech buildup to tip the balance of power in our favor. As early as January, 1984, however, fifteen months before Gorbachev's rise to power, Ronald Reagan made a speech calling for cooperation and dialogue with the Soviet Union. He was generally careful to reach out while building superior strength and alliance unity. When Gorbachev began to make his U-turns, Reagan met him to forge agreements for the first time in the Cold War, eliminating not just the growth of nuclear weapons but also an entire class of weapons. These transformational sweeps are stunning.[25]

Finally, Ronald Reagan's transformational leadership cannot be understood without realizing that this one-time actor was a romantic. Who else would have declared as early as 1982 to the British House of Commons that democracy "will leave Marxism-Leninism on the ash heap of history"? Whether or not he ever read much of the nineteenth-century American romantic novelists, poets, and philosophers, he had their romantic themes: Intuition often overrides reason; individualism is at the center of life and, certainly, of American exceptionalism; a Divine Providence guides the American people and the nation; and any ought-to-be that can be dreamed can be made into reality. Yes, he dreamed of a strategic defense initiative—not a star wars but a star peace—as a way out of the mutual assured apocalyptic strategy of the Cold War. Of course there were flaws. His lack of transactional abilities hurt the cause of his strategic initiative because, in his naïveté, he created an image in the mind of the public of an absolute, impenetrable shield instead of employing the U.S. high-tech revolution to seek defensive offsets and deterrence in place of a precarious nuclear-destruction strategy.

Furthermore, if details still matter in great visions, romanticism can never substitute for character—the glue of trust that must hold the presidency together, especially in crises. Nothing so tests presidential character—the ability to take setbacks, be knocked down, accept rather than cover up mistakes, and get up and go forward.

Several years ago, I developed a talk for young college students about George Washington, the man who took setbacks, learned, and developed character for his bigger leadership challenges. I spoke of the young, headstrong, overly ambitious Lieutenant Colonel Washington who constantly argued with Governor Dinwiddie over pay, who went over the mountains and camped in a vulnerable site, only to be overrun and forced to surrender to the French and Indians, and who was written up in the London newspapers as a disgrace. Such setbacks molded the character of Washington, who later lost more battles in the Revolutionary War than he won. But he won the war and brought success to the Constitutional Convention and the nation's first presidency.[26]

Reagan had his own setbacks, although they were quite different from Washington's. Reagan's included a failed first marriage to Jane Wyman, who had outstripped his acting career and left him, some wags said publicly to his humiliation, because she found him boring and too talkative. Reagan also eventually lost his movie contracts and had to go to television with *General Electric Theater*, another contract he eventually lost.

Remembering these experiences have helped me understand how this depressed individual managed that whole winter of 1987.[27] This seventy-six-year-old man had previously been wounded in an assassination attempt, endured three operations, and was nearly deaf in one ear. To add to his personal drama, he was humiliated by the trade of arms for hostages, for not heeding the advice of his secretaries of state and defense, and finally for allowing a rogue operation by a lieutenant colonel to be run out of the executive offices of the president. As noted earlier, Ronald Reagan's magic flame barely flickered during those weeks and months. As Pat Buchanan has said, "The music stopped playing."[28]

Peter Wallison later wrote, "During the four months that it [the Iran-Contra crisis] continued, the administration was brought to a standstill. Ronald Reagan, who just prior to its onset enjoyed the highest approval ratings of his presidency, watched these ratings plummet to levels he had not seen since the severe recession of 1981–1982."[29] Yet Reagan's character would not let him collapse. After the initial November speech and press conference that covered things up, he totally turned around and ordered, "Get it all out. No executive privilege." In March, I stood with him in the waiting room before his press conference with the hungry reporters, who crowded into the East Room. There was no tremor in his hand, no crack in his voice—except a cracked joke or two.

Peggy Noonan, in her *When Character Was King*, concludes that "Iran-Contra . . . contained no hidden gifts, no lucky loss, was bad from beginning to end."[30] For once, I disagree with this perceptive exposition of Reagan. Character above all was king in the way Reagan came back from his crisis, in a way so lacking in the Nixon and Clinton cases. Reagan had dug himself a hole but then climbed out, while the other two besieged presidents dug theirs deeper.

Upon his death on June 5, 2004, this conservative icon had become a national one. He was mourned and saluted by Republicans and Democrats alike across the political spectrum as millions watched in person or on TV the horse-drawn hearse on Pennsylvania Avenue, the service in the National Cathedral, or the final rites at Simi Valley.

This unified spirit of Americans, somewhat similar following 9/11, came at a time when the nation was more politically divided down the middle than in recent memory. Maybe it was a hidden desire to memorialize the longing for a lost unity of the leader who won all but one state. But he played the part of a father figure in the

American psyche, I believe, through a characteristic called civility, defined as respect, listening, and dialogue, which often allowed him to gain a higher ground of creativity. Barry Goldwater, who many saw starting the conservative movement, lost about as many states in 1964 as Reagan won in 1980 because he frightened people with his "extremism in defense of liberty is no vice" and his hard demeanor. His style changed later during his tenure as a senator, when I worked with him on bipartisan security issues. On the other hand, Reagan always had the soft touch, a style of civility that drew people to him and made him a uniter. This culture of inclusion seemed to have been lost on Washington at the time of Reagan's death, the style of a uniter and not a divider. This style was not simply an act to be played on a stage; it was also genuine because the first element of his civility was respect for the individual, an ability to disagree without being disagreeable and to differ without being mean, and without ever a touch of arrogance.

Granted, Reagan had helped turn the tide of history, but he had done it with a particular style that built affection and great successes.

Furthermore, even though Reagan entered the presidency with roots in the Republican right, he was an inclusive president in governing the executive branch. His first chief of staff was James Baker, campaign manager for George Bush. He asked former senate majority leader Mike Mansfield to remain as ambassador to Japan. His arms-control negotiators were Hubert Humphrey democrat Max Kampelman and Kennedy democrat Paul Nitze.

These same Reagan characteristics of inclusiveness and civility, which won the affection of the American people, as demonstrated during his funeral, equipped him to bring the Cold War to an end. Ambassador Jack Matlock, a career foreign-service officer who observed him firsthand with Gorbachev, has written this about Reagan: "He believed in his ability to persuade, but he was not an arrogant know-it-all. He welcomed opportunities to learn more, not only about the issues but also, and particularly, about the nature and philosophy of the people he dealt with. He dealt with others, whether friends, adversaries, or subordinates, openly and without guile."[31]

There was a genuine lack of malice in Ronald Reagan, perhaps because he was comfortable with his own persona. His muscular Christianity did not take him to church as often as George Bush or Bill

Clinton, but when he was shot, from the hospital bed, he prayed for his assailant that he might be changed.[32] Often distant and aloof from those who worked immediately around him, and even his children, he often related better, oddly enough, to those at a distance—his would-be assassin, the hostages, the average American on Main Street.

This, however, does not mean that he had empathy for the underdog as did his icons, the two Roosevelts. Speaker of the House Tip O'Neill, who became Reagan's Irish-ancestry liberal pal, declared Reagan "as beloved a leader as the nation has ever seen" and talked about how their modest backgrounds and admiration for the New Deal president were in common. Yet O'Neill was a major critic of Reagan's conservative domestic policy and wrote, "In view of the many parallels in our lives, I've often wondered how we came to have such different visions of America. Maybe it all boils down to the fact that one of us lost track of his roots while the other guy didn't."[33] But the periods that O'Neill so admired—TR's Progressive Movement and FDR's New Deal—required much greater centralization, an increased federal government role, and federal regulation. The Reagan period—of the information revolution and opportunities for more creative market approaches—called for moving in the opposite direction toward decentralization. Even President Carter previously had recognized this need in his deregulation policies. Reagan personified and dramatized this new direction, and Clinton continued it.

Ronald Reagan propagated the idea of smaller government, which George H. W. Bush and Bill Clinton followed. However, Reagan lacked that suspicion and hostility toward people in government, that thing called "bureaucracy" that Richard Nixon so loathed and often imagined as the enemy, suspect enough to be wiretapped. As for members of Congress, I recall that before Reagan's first election, at George Will's dinner party, Reagan told me we might "just lock 'em up." But, as president, he personally got along famously with them. Indeed, at the end of the day, he had Speaker of the House Tip O'Neill and others around for drinks and jokes.

Ronald Reagan simply did not hate people; he hated only "the evil empire," an evil system. But when he came to know Gorbachev in Geneva, he liked their give-and-take and saw a man caught in an evil system; hence, "trust but verify." Reagan was fascinated by his Communist counterpart's presumed atheism, which was so often belied by his conversational references to the Deity. He wondered whether his intransigence on accepting SDI—mutual assured security in place of mutual assured destruction, as Reagan put it—reflected Gorbachev's lack of economic strength and maneuver room at home. Reagan became the man around whom Gorbachev pivoted 180 degrees. Gorbachev, Reagan saw, had changed; indeed Reagan's Cold War strategy helped force that change. Reagan himself changed to deal with the new Gorbachev.

Reagan's good will toward men and women—the frequent desire to believe the best and avoid confrontation—of course had its downside. Casey, North, and Poindexter all played upon his compassion for the hostages. Reagan blanked out things, just as he had done as a boy dealing with his drunken father. He was unwilling to face the highly destructive rivalry between Weinberger and Shultz. He could neither face the Don Regan situation nor seem to get as angry as I did that his national security advisers left him without records of events and decisions.

Reagan wrote in his memoir that, in retrospect, he regretted that, when he fired Admiral Poindexter, he did not demand an explanation face to face. Who was Reagan kidding in that memoir? He would never have set up such a confrontation.[34]

A poor manager indeed, but what America needed at this time in history was not a good manager to effectively maintain the status quo. Still scarred by Vietnam, frustrated by an inflationary economy, and waging an old and unending Cold War, America needed a leader who could see beyond the murky present to bold, new visions. It needed a leader with transforming ideas and the ability to communicate them, a leader with the good will and incredible optimism to attract others to accept his visions of the future. It also needed a leader with character to stand up after a fall, to restore the integrity of the presidency, and to gracefully leave office with the end of the Cold War in sight. America needed Ronald Reagan.

APPENDIX A

Comparative Charges

Watergate, Iran-Contra, Clinton Impeachment

As to the legal charges against Nixon in the articles of impeachment, Article I states that Nixon had "prevented, obstructed, and impeded the administration of justice"; Article II, that he had "repeatedly engaged in conduct violating the constitutional rights of citizens, impairing the due and proper administration of justice and the conduct of lawful inquiries or contravening the laws of government agencies of the executive branch and the purposes of these agencies"; and Article III, that "he has failed with lawful cause or excuse to produce papers and things as directed by duly authorized subpoenas."

In the case of Iran-contra, no legal charges were made against the president whatsoever. The legal issues involved first the Boland Amendment. On the one side—the Republican side—it was argued that the Boland Amendment contained no civil or criminal penalties, and, hence, its violation was not significant. On the other side, it was argued that there are many laws that do not contain specific penalty but that this does not exempt violators from prosecution. It is true that, reflecting ambiguity, there were several successive Boland amendments and an Intelligence Authorization Act of 1985, which contained a provision in the classified annex that allowed some forms of military intelligence aid. Of course, there is also that constitutional provision about the laws being faithfully executed.

In Clinton's situation, the articles of impeachment were simply stated in the House of Representatives: "William Jefferson Clinton has undermined the integrity of his office, has brought disrepute on the presidency, has betrayed his trust as president, and has acted in a manner subversive to the rule of law and justice, to the manifest injury of the people of the United States." There were four articles: He committed perjury before the federal grand jury on August 17, 1998; lied on two occasions related to the Paula Jones case; obstructed justice in a number of situations; and responded falsely to some of the questions in writing from the Senate Judiciary Committee. In the Senate, Clinton was acquitted. However, on April 12, 1999, federal Judge Susan Webber Wright of Arkansas held the president in contempt of court for giving "intentionally false" testimony about his relationship with Monica Lewinsky in the Paula Jones civil lawsuit. This was a dramatic and damaging end to a battle that had been mounted in both houses of Congress but ended up with a legal judgment.

★ ★ ★ ★ ★ ★

David M. Abshire, "The Tower Report and Due Process," *Wall Street Journal*, February 26, 1987

The Tower Special Review Board report commissioned by President Reagan will be presented to him at 10 this morning. While neither the president nor I will have seen the report before then, it promises to be one of the most extraordinary reports to have emerged from either the executive branch or Congress.

There are several reasons for this. First, the wealth of documents and testimony amassed by the board, coupled with intense public interest, ensures that the report will be exceptionally thorough and critical. Second, the board membership of just three—John Tower, Edmund Muskie, and Brent Scowcroft—uniquely combining extensive congressional, diplomatic and military experience, has made for an unusually expeditious and expert report. Finally, the report fills an immediate need, for the president must now proceed to fix whatever led him astray on Iran. The last point is critical, for a dramatically flawed process underlay the entire Iran affair.

When the story of the Iran arms transfers first broke in the press, the president, with the instinctive honesty that has characterized my private meetings with him, said: "Let's get it all out. I will talk to the public." Initially, however, this was more easily said than done. In preparation for his Nov. 13 speech and Nov. 19 press conference last year, he was not given all of the facts by his own staff. In fact, he was misinformed. Sharply disappointed, he charged Attorney General

Edwin Meese to investigate, and it was soon learned, as announced by the president himself on Nov. 25, that in the alleged diversion of funds to the contras some laws might have been broken. Following this revelation, any thought of the executive branch investigating itself was jettisoned.

Upon my arrival at the White House last month, the president underscored his determination to eschew anything that could be taken as a self-serving executive-branch investigation and instead to encourage wholly independent investigations by others, which might take longer but would discover the facts, make them available in a credible way, and suggest the remedies.

The president's appointment of the Tower Board had been the first step. It was followed by the appointment, at administration request, of an eminent independent counsel, Judge Lawrence Walsh. Finally, the president encouraged Congress to make a unified effort to examine all relevant issues. Happily, while Congress did not find it feasible to establish a single select investigating committee, the two committees it did form have responded by organizing themselves in an extremely orderly fashion, even arranging to alternate hearings and perhaps hold some jointly. They have the advantage, too, of every fine preliminary account of the Iran affair prepared by the Senate Intelligence Committee.

And what has been my role in all of this? As special counselor to the president, my job is to implement his commitment to "get out all the facts." The media and others still sometimes wonder why my team did not do this by starting its own investigation and quickly publishing our version of "the facts." Indeed, that would have furnished drama and controversy, but it would have been contrary to the independent, credible "due process" wisely chosen by the president. My task instead is to support that due process.

By Feb. 6 roughly 3,000 documents, most of them classified, had been made available to the house and senate investigating committees, even before they had secure storage facilities of their own or staffs dared to review them. My staff worked into the late hours of last Saturday to satisfy additional requests of the Tower Board before it completed its report.

The work of the independent counsel also has been facilitated by our intercessions. My deputy, Judge Charles N. Brower, chairs weekly meetings of all general counsels or their equivalents from the relevant executive-branch departments; their purpose is to ensure maximum disclosure while taking care that intelligence sources and methods are not compromised.

In my personal dealings with the Tower Board, the independent counsel and the congressional committee's bipartisan leadership, I find something quite remarkable and truly admirable. It is the sense of deep concern that all of these investigations be carried out in a deliberate, organized and responsible way. As a result, the two congressional committees, even at the risk of being unfairly criticized for foot-dragging, are pledged not to rush into public hearings before preliminary questioning of witnesses is completed and their inquiry thoroughly prepared.

This responsible approach could be expected from the people involved in the process. Sen. David Boren (D., Okla.), chairman of the Select Intelligence Committee that issued the first official report, has publicly stressed the importance of bipartisanship in this process. In Chairman Daniel Inouye (D., Hawaii) and Lee Hamilton (D., Ind.) of the senate and house committees and their Republican counterparts, Warren Rudman (R., N.H.) and Richard Cheney (R., Wyo.), I find two deep concerns: first, that the investigations be carried out in a way that leaves no haunting questions for the future; and second, that our ongoing foreign policy and even the strength of the presidency not be denigrated just as we are within sight of completing the first two-term presidency since Eisenhower.

Not long after my arrival in Washington from NATO, I said, concerning the ongoing investigations, "Let the chips fall where they may." It is not news to the White House that the Tower Board report will be critical; the president set up the board to be critical. It is a measure of the president's commitment to the truth. It is also a measure of his resolve and belief in moving forward. The report, I believe, will give the president a sound framework for this.

Notes

Introduction

1. David Abshire, "Genesis of the Iran Policy" (personal files), p. 3.

Chapter 1

1. The committee would meet once a week and include members from all key legislative areas. Since we were soon in a major national security debate over the "missile gap," I was also able to organize a major study of some twenty Republican professors such as William Yandell Eliot of Harvard and other experts under the chairmanship of the emerging young Republican leader, Gerald Ford. We also organized a series of speeches by innovative members such as Rep. Tom Curtis on a wide range of economic and social issues that were then published in pamphlets.
2. I soon persuaded him to swap the word "association" in his operative title for "institution."
3. David M. Abshire, *The South Rejects a Prophet: The Life of Senator D. M. Key, 1824–1900* (New York: Praeger, 1967).
4. William P. Rogers was secretary of state and carried the public lead on Capitol Hill.
5. Robert Dallek, *Flawed Giant: Lyndon Johnson and His Times, 1961–1973* (New York: Oxford University Press, 1998), pp. 143–56.
6. See Dean Acheson, "Chief Lobbyist for State," in *Present at the Creation* (New York: Norton, 1969), chap. 12.
7. To take an example, in 1970, Democratic senator Frank Church from Idaho and liberal Republican senator John Sherman Cooper from Kentucky crafted an amendment to restrict our Cambodian operations, including those in the air, in a way that would unwittingly endanger our troops. In secret but separate conversations with me, they agreed to an alteration of language if each could brandish a clarifying letter of intention from the secretary of state on the floor of the Senate. I

obtained the letters, and, with their altered amendment, major legislation was unblocked and moved forward over the opposition. Our objective was to avoid stopping the war by amendment, especially while Secretary of State Henry Kissinger in secret negotiations sought to end it by treaty.

8. While enrolled at Sewanee in the early 1940s (while my uncle was the vice chancellor), Bolling had visited the little resort town of Monteagle, where there was a Communist cell. Bolling, a strong New Deal liberal, was infuriated at their attempt to take him in and in Congress became a liberal anticommunist in the school of Sen. Scoop Jackson.

9. Bolling, who retired in 1982, represented the Fifth Congressional District of Missouri for thirty-five years after chairing the Rules Committee. He was described as "one of the truly creative critics and effective leaders of the House. As the initiator of reforms including the election of committee chairmen and the congressional budget process, he is probably more responsible than anyone else for the way the House works—and it does work—today." Michael Barone and Grant Iyifusa, eds., *The Almanac of American Politics 1986* (Washington, D.C.: 1986), p. 769. One of Bolling's books is *Power in the House* (New York: Perigee, 1974).

10. In this case, as with the end-the-war amendment, two key Democrats played the decisive role with a Republican administration.

11. David M. Abshire, *Foreign Policy Makers: President vs. Congress* (Beverly Hills: Sage, 1979).

12. Murphy was a brilliant career foreign-service officer who came to President Roosevelt's attention in 1940 and subsequently ran many special and sometimes dangerous missions for Roosevelt, Truman, and Eisenhower. He served as undersecretary of state and our first postwar ambassador to Japan. He later wrote a classic memoir, *Diplomat among Warriors* (Garden City, N.Y.: Doubleday, 1964).

13. John F. Lehman, *The Executive, Congress, and Foreign Policy: Studies of the Nixon Administration* (New York: Praeger, 1976), p. 204.

14. Stephen E. Ambrose, *Nixon: Ruin and Recovery, 1973–1990* (New York: Simon and Schuster, Touchstone Edition, 1992), p. 135.

15. Likewise, exposure to certain members of Congress dramatized for me what the executive branch could learn from wise and innovative legislators such as Senators Hubert Humphrey (D-MN), Sam Nunn (D-GA), Ted Stevens (R-AK), and John Warner (R-VA). They worked together with us in developing a major senate initiative to set aside

defense funds exclusively to support armament cooperation and better defense-investment efficiencies within NATO. For a detailed account of Abshire's work at NATO and the particular he attention gave to the Congress, see Joseph Fitchett, "U.S. Envoy to NATO Warns of Soviet Pressure on Alliance," *International Herald Tribune* (Dec. 29, 1986).

Chapter 2

1. The *Washington Post*'s Nov. 29, 1986, front-page story reads, "NATO envoy may get NSC job: Abshire emerges as congressional preference of top Reagan Aides." The article describes Secretary Shultz as a top supporter and states that Don Regan found him accountable. It notes that White House congressional liaison Will Ball had pushed for his former congressional boss, John Tower. It also notes that there was support for former CIA Deputy Director Bobby Ray Inman, but he was strongly opposed by Casey. On Nov. 30, 1986, the *Washington Post* printed an article by Judith Havemann, who noted that Abshire, as a "pragmatic conservative," was the leading choice for the position but said that he was not the favorite among some conservatives. I also had a group of younger "spies" in Washington, especially political consultant Wayne Berman and Deputy Undersecretary of Defense Dennis Kloske, both formerly with CSIS, who kept me informed as to the state of play on such contests.

2. Senator Dole also suggested the establishment of a special counselor. This is revealed in an interview of Buchanan on the television program *Evans and Novak* on Dec. 28, 1986.

3. There has never been any public mention of Buchanan's memo before, in Don Regan's memoir or elsewhere. In *For the Record* (New York: Harcourt Brace Jovanovich, 1998), Regan does say, "I had been telling the President that he must put one man in charge of the crisis" (p. 64). He claims that Nancy Reagan suggested Herbert Miller, a well-known criminal lawyer who was representing Mike Deaver, and that Reagan had raised the name himself. Regan responded that appointing a criminal-defense expert would send the wrong message, although the former White House legal counsel, Fred Fielding, would be an option. It turned out that Fielding was unavailable and that the first lady was less than enthusiastic about him. I believe that Pat Buchanan's memo, with its excellent job description, moved the White House to appoint a special counselor to serve as a coordinator, not a legal defender.

It was my Chicago friend and adviser, the late attorney Morris Leibman, who had advised the White House on this crisis in December. Somehow he was given a copy of the memo and did not rediscover it in his papers until after I had left the White House, when he gave it to me. While Buchanan's exact structure was the same as that put into effect, his memo did not focus on the aspect of the second track related to restoring the integrity of the White House through an independent counselor with the mission to "get everything out" and avoid more charges of cover-up. Regan quickly endorsed the Buchanan idea because it would aid in his own survival.

On Dec. 5, 1986, a Republican delegation at the White House had urged the president to appoint a special counselor, but the suggestion got nowhere at that time (*Washington Post*, Dec. 6, 1986, p. 1). The suggestion focused more on an independent legal investigation.

On Dec. 18, 1986, a paper circulated titled "An Organizational Concept for Handling in the Office of the President the Current Legislative Inquiry Relating to Arms Transfers." The concept envisioned a task force with a committee chair, but this was quickly trumped by the creation of a special counselor.

4. Regan, *For the Record*, p. 64.
5. An eight-point charter for the special counselor was also created. See Appendix B.
6. Author's files.
7. W. Dale Nelson, "Reagan Picks NATO Envoy as Point-Man on Iranian Inquiries," Associated Press, Dec. 26, 1986.
8. *Wall Street Journal* (June 5, 1986).
9. Richard B. Cheney and Lynne V. Cheney, *Kings of the Hill* (New York: Simon and Schuster, 1983).
10. Telephone conversations are from my telephone log and notes.
11. *Report of the President's Special Review Board: Tower Board Commission Report*, introduction by R. W. Apple Jr. (New York: Bantam Books and Times Books, 1987), p. 85.
12. Peter Wallison, conversation with David Abshire, Aug., 1999.
13. *Wall Street Journal* (Dec. 29, 1986).

Chapter 3

1. The reason that I was surprised is that, in accord with CSIS policy and practice, when CSIS reached a level of considerable bipartisan

influence in Washington, I had ended my partisan politics. Earlier, during the 1960, 1964, and 1968 Republican conventions, I had been the national security subcommittee adviser for the platform although, even then, I exempted myself from the political campaign. After 1968, I avoided even the platform committee work. I think I was the only person not involved in the campaign who was brought into the transition, and, of course, this was resented in some quarters, especially by the Hoover Institution partisans led by Glenn Campbell, who had been in the political trenches with Ronald Reagan since the 1960s.

2. The White House well remembered that the Carter administration had sought to fill a NATO tactical-deterrent gap through the deployment of the so-called neutron bomb, which was actually a weapon capable of killing enemy soldiers in their armor and tanks without destroying towns and cities. In the public debate, the Soviets and the peace movement in Europe so demonized these weapons that the Carter administration buckled under the pressure and withdrew the initiative.

3. Richard Allen, conversation with David Abshire, July 6, 2000. The Nitze philosophy was that not only were the Soviets achieving strategic superiority in some areas but also that their civil-defense measures showed that their doctrine was not based on reciprocating MAD, that is, maintaining their vulnerability. The story of Paul Nitze's role in Team B—set up as a result of concerns by PFIAB—and then as chair of policy studies for the Committee for the Present Danger is well told in Strobe Talbott, *The Master of the Game: Paul Nitze and the Nuclear Peace* (New York: Random House, 1988), pp. 142–61.

4. Martin Anderson, *Revolution: The Reagan Legacy* (Stanford: Hoover Institution Press, 1990), pp. 80–84. Reagan was further fired up on this issue by the April 26, 1986, Chernobyl nuclear disaster; when he heard that Chernobyl in Ukrainian meant "wormwood," he related it to the Book of Revelation (8:10), which he knew by heart, where the fallen star as a portent of Armageddon is called "wormwood." See Lou Cannon, *Reagan* (New York: Putnam, 1982), p. 757.

5. David Abshire, *Preventing World War III* (New York: Harper and Row, 1988), p. 96. In 1988, I wrote that "Carrington responded with an anecdote about the First World War. I think it was taken from a famous cartoon of 'Old Bill,' a British predecessor of G.I. Joe [Bill Mauldin's Willie and Joe]. Two men were in a muddy foxhole. One kept complaining and wanted to leave. His foxhole mate snapped, 'If you know

of a better 'ole, go to it!' The moral to Carrington's story for Reagan
was that a new deterrent foxhole had not yet been dug, by SDI or any
other means. But there was a problem Carrington did not identify: The
sides of the foxhole had eroded, the bottom had been filling up, and the
men were exposed to danger, whether they knew it or not." However,
the practical Carrington had a point: Don't overly debunk your existing
strategic capability before you have an assured alternative.

6. Reagan had a certain naïveté on certain operational aspects of SDI
and should never have portrayed it as a "shield" as compared with a
new kind of method for deterrence, but he was more astute than most
of his experts in seeing, like Kissinger, that the MAD strategy was
flawed and in recognizing that a defensive solution should be explored
not casually but as a priority, as was the World War II Manhattan
Project. He understood full well the advantage and superiority gained
by the United States as a result of being the world leader in technology and the upcoming information revolution. Some Reagan advisers,
such as Bud McFarlane, saw SDI as an ultimate bargaining chip; others, such as Richard Perle, saw it as a way to gain a decisive advantage
over the Kremlin. Reagan had a bolder, more idealistic, dream of the
elimination of nuclear weapons and avoidance of a potential Armageddon. Regardless of the interpretation of Reagan's motivation, his
initiative was a technological flanking maneuver in contrast with Cap
Weinberger's frontal, military buildup of new ships, aircraft, and more
nuclear capability. Ultimately, this initiative was one decisive factor
in changing Gorbachev's will, as we shall see. But before that change,
Gorbachev used every maneuver, every inducement, to get Reagan to
give up his ace—SDI. For a fuller discussion of the CSIS conference
and the issues, see Abshire, *Preventing World War III*, pp. 198–207.

7. Kenneth Adelman, *The Great Universal Embrace: Arms Summitry—
A Skeptic's Account* (New York: Simon and Schuster, 1989), p. 103.

8. When Gorbachev first came to office in March of 1985, he continued
to press the Soviet military buildup and Third World aggressive activists. By the time of the Geneva Summit, he began to recognize that his
country's deepening economic crisis demanded new thinking, and this
was revealed at the Twenty-seventh Communist Party Congress in
February, 1986.

9. Ronald Reagan, *An American Life: Ronald Reagan* (New York: Simon
and Schuster, 1990), pp. 678–79.

10. Lou Cannon, letter to David M. Abshire, May 4, 2000. Despite the

initial image of failure and the obvious fact that the conference ended abruptly, from a historical vantage point, many important products emerged: Gorbachev had to adjust to Reagan's staunch SDI stand; Gorbachev for the first time agreed to major cuts in Soviet SS-18 missiles that had driven U.S. strategic concerns; Gorbachev had shown flexibility on British and French missiles; and Gorbachev no longer insisted that SDI research be terminated but instead be confined to the laboratory. But until the final rupture, there was a chemistry change among the negotiators. Shultz's assistant commented that the Soviet negotiators became not programmed minds but individual human beings (see Don Oberdorfer, *From the Cold War to the New Era: The United States and the Soviet Union, 1983–1991* [Baltimore: Johns Hopkins University Press, 1998], pp. 198–205). Also, for a detailed description of Reykjavik and especially the aftermath in Washington, see Frances FitzGerald, *Way Out There in the Blue* (New York: Simon and Schuster, 2000), pp. 347–69.

11. Deeply angry at the time, Gorbachev later came to view Reykjavik quite differently. He wrote the following in his book *Gorbachev: On My Country and the World* (New York: Columbia University Press, 2000): "A real breakthrough occurred at the Reykjavik summit meeting with President Reagan. At that meeting we did not reach a point of joint signing of documents, but we moved a considerable way towards one another on major questions of security. Later on, after the results of this meeting had become thought over, we began to work out specific steps towards nuclear disarmament" (p. 195).

Chapter 4

1. Sept. 7, 1986.
2. Myra MacPherson, *Washington Post* (Dec. 5, 1986), p. C1; David Hoffman, *Washington Post* (Dec. 12, 1986), p. A1.
3. Lou Cannon, *Reagan* (New York: Putnam, 1982), p. 643.
4. Robert Strauss, conversations with David Abshire, Dec., 1991. Strauss later complained to me that he never got a drink, not even a glass of water, during this meeting. He said Nancy Reagan, whom he really did not know that well at the time, called him later to say that Reagan was furious over what he had told him, but Nancy could not thank him enough. See Nancy Reagan, *My Turn: The Memoirs of Nancy Reagan* (New York: Random House, 1989), p. 321.

5. Cannon, *Reagan*, p. 72. This story has been related to me several times and once by Nancy Reagan.

6. Ibid., p. 724.

7. One might wonder about the stark difference between the two, and I think it goes back to the difference between these two personalities. I knew Secretary of State Bill Rogers and worked immediately under him from 1970 through 1973, when I was his assistant secretary of state dealing with Congress. I also know Bob Strauss well.

As secretary of state during the first part of the Nixon administration, Rogers faced the problem of competition with Henry Kissinger, not only a brilliant global strategist but also a Washington strategist. Strangely enough, Bill Rogers, former head of a prestigious law firm and a multimillionaire, was no match in the contest with Kissinger. I have asked myself many times why Rogers—such a high-powered Wall Street lawyer—lacked a broader effectiveness as secretary of state and was so extremely offbeat in his colloquy with Ronald Reagan compared with Bob Strauss. Rogers was always for narrowing the issue to the very basic ingredients or facts. He would, therefore, reject the broad landscape. This is what served him well in his corporate cases in New York. What served him well in New York served him poorly in Washington and in advising President and Mrs. Reagan.

Strauss is no such literalist as a lawyer. He looks at a very broad context, he knows how these situations of human failure and partial conspiracies compound and play out, and he knew that there was deep trouble. Again, in many cases, it is wise to take a worst-case scenario in a crisis, rather than the best, most optimistic one, and Strauss had it right. Frankly, so many who were going in to see the president became "common prostitutes." To put it on a higher level, they didn't want to hurt the president's morale, and they wanted to be asked back.

8. His father was one of the police officers fired by Calvin Coolidge during the 1919 Boston police strike. Regan later wrote, "He was immensely proud of belonging to the force, and his belief in duty was very strong" (Donald T. Regan, *For the Record* [New York: Harcourt Brace Jovanovich, 1998], p. 102).

9. I first met Don Regan soon after he became head of Merrill Lynch through my close friend Ken Crosby, who represented Merrill Lynch in Washington. Crosby had attended social events during their International Monetary Fund (IMF) meetings in DC and had visited Regan several times in New York. Additionally, Merrill Lynch was a

financial supporter of CSIS. Regan helped CSIS obtain funds from the Merrill Lynch Family Trust.

10. Cannon, *Reagan*, p. 553.

11. The entire staff remained intensely loyal to their chief throughout the crisis. Mitch Daniels, the political director, is the only one who not only thought Regan should resign but told him so, citing samplings of party supporters throughout the country when asked about how the president should handle the crisis.

Chapter 5

1. Joseph E. Persico, *Casey: From the OSS to the CIA* (New York: Viking, 1990), p. 57.

2. Ibid., p. 61.

3. Dulles called this "storybook stuff" because Germany was a hostile territory. He believed in trying to develop agents in place (Peter Grose, *Gentleman Spy: The Life of Allen Dulles* [Boston: Houghton Mifflin, 1994], pp. 210–12). Young Casey got Donovan's support and was able to mount 102 missions, of which he rated 62 "a success" (Persico, *Casey*, pp. 82–83).

4. He was competing with Cherne's business. A shocked Cherne later said that Casey's setting aside a friendship in such a ruthless way was an act of betrayal. Later, however, their friendship was revived and even deepened over common interests such as the International Rescue Committee, created at the time of the Hungarian uprisings.

5. At the first organizational meeting, after getting support from the White House, Sen. Mike Mansfield (the senate majority leader who had appointed himself), and the ranking house Democrat on the commission, Foreign Affairs Committee Chair Clement Zablocki, I nominated Ambassador Murphy to be our chair, a nomination that unanimously carried. His autobiography is *Diplomat among Warriors* (New York: Doubleday, 1964). This Hoover-type commission was composed of two members from the executive branch (Bill Casey and Anne Armstrong, newly arrived counselor to President Nixon); two members appointed by the president from outside the government (former ambassador Murphy and myself); plus eight appointed by the congressional leaders, four from the Congress itself and four more from outside the government.

6. Admiral Burke, conversations with David Abshire, 1962. The unaudited growth of this operation is well described in Evan Thomas, *The*

Very Best Men (New York: Simon and Schuster, Touchstone Edition, 1995): "What had begun in the spring of 1960 as a plan to infiltrate a few dozen commandos to slip into the jungle and join the resistance had become by November a full-scale invasion. . . . The escalation had come about not because things were going well, but rather because they were going badly" (p. 241). Burke was the acting chair of the Joint Chiefs when the Bay of Pigs operation took place. Compartmentalization was so great that there was no written plan by the CIA for the operation. Also see Richard M. Bissell Jr., *Reflections of a Cold Warrior* (New Haven: Yale University Press, 1996), pp. 152–204.

7. That law explicitly stated there should be absolutely no future intelligence-agency involvement in this reconstituted operation. Indeed, Radio Free Europe and Radio Liberty, which had been previously funded covertly by the CIA, were placed under the jurisdiction of a public board confirmed by the Senate. A new transparency was now the foundation of the radios' credibility.

8. California governor Reagan served on the commission and especially impressed Rockefeller's counsel, Peter J. Wallison (memorandum to author, June, 1999):

> When it came time to draft the commission's report, most of the discussions at commission meetings were discussions among the lawyers—the commission had a staff of five or six— addressed to whether a particular activity could or could not be justified by the charter. Reagan's participation in this portion of the commission's work was extremely impressive. He has a gift for summary, and many times—while the members and the lawyers went round and round about how to describe and characterize a particular CIA activity—Reagan would come up with a solution. He did this in an unusual way. After listening to the debate for a while, he would start writing on a yellow pad. When he had two or three paragraphs done, he would ask whether he could read some suggested language, and then would proceed to read off what he had written. In most cases, his formulation was adopted without change in the language of the report.

9. *Commission on the Organization of the Government for the Conduct of Foreign Policy*, stock no. 022-000-00108-6 (Washington, D.C.: GPO,

June, 1975), p. 11. The 40 Committee was an executive branch group set up to approve covert operations.

10. William Casey, *Where and How the War Was Fought: An Armchair Tour of the American Revolution* (New York: William Morrow, 1976).

11. The prestigious board had been created by President Eisenhower to have full access to intelligence and to examine its quality. In this Eisenhower period, with members such as Emory Land of Land Camera fame, the board had pushed innovations such as the U-2 spy plane, which was key in determining whether there was actually a missile gap. Throughout its history, the board had a roster of eastern-establishment heavyweights such as former banker and high commissioner to Germany John J. McCloy, former Joint Chiefs of Staff chair Maxwell Taylor, veteran diplomat David Bruce, and Gov. Nelson Rockefeller.

12. Persico, *Casey*, p. 163. Persico also relates how Ronald Reagan later told William F. Buckley that "My problem with Bill was that I didn't understand him at meetings. . . . I didn't know what he was actually saying" (p. 571).

13. Ibid., p. 123.

14. Ibid., p. 202.

15. I served on the Naval War College Board shortly after Turner's tenure and saw his work and, hence, was surprised by his difficulties as DCI. Robert Gates was later to write the following: "In short order [Turner] cut himself off from the organization." Despite the cuts in the human-intelligence capabilities in the agency, actually beginning in the latter part of the Nixon administration with the purges of 1973 and going through Ford and into the Carter administration, the Soviet invasion of Afghanistan led to a jump in covert operations there and later in Central America under the stimulus of National Security Adviser Brzezinski. See Robert M. Gates, *From the Shadows: The Ultimate Insider's Story of Five Presidents and How They Won the Cold War* (New York: Simon and Schuster, Touchstone Edition, 1997), pp. 137–53. A critical appraisal of the Turner period is contained in Ray S. Cline, *The CIA under Reagan, Bush, and Casey: The Evolution of the Agency from Roosevelt to Reagan* (Washington, D.C.: Acropolis Books, 1981), pp. 268–74.

16. President Carter had made the mistake of abolishing the President's Foreign Intelligence Advisory Board. Reagan immediately reestablished it with Anne Armstrong as chair. In 1976, Armstrong had

served ably as ambassador to the United Kingdom after her White House role. Having indicated that I was not in a position at CSIS to go into government at that time, I was slated to be vice chair; like the chairmanship, it was a part-time assignment to a board that met every two months.

I was surprised to learn that Casey intervened with the White House to insist that I should not be vice chair and, in fact, should not even be on the board. Anne Armstrong was chair of the CSIS Board of Trustees, and this would be too much CSIS, argued Casey. He insisted that Leo Cherne be the vice chair; he argued that Cherne's experience could help guide Armstrong in her work because she did not have experience in intelligence. Surprised by the position of my good friend, I phoned Casey to clarify his opposition to me on the board. He mumbled rapidly, "I was against you as vice chair, too much CSIS, but not against you on the board. Somebody got that messed up, Dave." Casey was right about too much CSIS, but, in the corner of my mind, that one Murphy Commission argument about my not being in the OSS culture seemed to be the real reason. In addition, Cherne was probably his best friend. In any event, the following winter I was sworn in with the rest of the board.

17. Persico, *Casey*, p. 284. Casey was wrong about a strategic void in the State Department, especially in early 1986, when Secretary Shultz placed Elliott Abrams, the forthright Harvard-trained intellectual and defender of human rights, in the position of assistant secretary of state for Latin America. Abrams became an effective advocate of the Reagan Doctrine, for he had a strategy for democratic reform among the contras and was far more effective than Casey and the CIA at building coalitions on Capitol Hill.

18. The most enthusiastic book about Casey's role, which was obviously quickly written and relies largely on interviews, is Peter Schweizer's *Victory: The Reagan Administration's Secret Strategy That Hastened the Collapse of the Soviet Union* (New York: Atlantic Monthly Press, 1994). A much more carefully done work is Constantine C. Menges, *Inside the National Security Council: The True Story of the Making and Unmaking of Reagan's Foreign Policy* (New York: Simon and Schuster, 1988). It is critical of McFarlane, Poindexter, Shultz, and North and includes Menges's firsthand experiences of North's inability to tell the truth. He defends Casey from any knowledge of the diversion. The most balanced account by far is found in Gates,

From the Shadows. Bob Woodward's *Veil: The Secret Wars of the CIA, 1981–1987* (New York: Pocket Books, 1987) has special significance because of the large amount of material Casey gave the author.

19. Persico, *Casey*, p. 377; Casey's admiring special assistant, Herbert Meyer, on Oct. 1, 2001, wrote in an op-ed in the *Wall Street Journal,* "in our country's history, there have been few people who have had more contempt for Congress than Bill Casey."

20. Persico, *Casey*, p. 342.

21. Reagan wrote the following in his memoirs, *An American Life: Ronald Reagan* (New York: Simon and Schuster, 1990): "My decision not to appoint Jim Baker as national security adviser, I suppose, was a turning point for my administration, although I had no idea at the time how significant it would prove to be" (p. 448).

22. George P. Shultz, *Turmoil and Triumph: My Years as Secretary of State* (New York: Scribner's, 1993), pp. 800–802; Lou Cannon, *President Reagan: The Role of a Lifetime* (New York: Simon and Schuster, 1991), pp. 369–74.

23. "Hezbollah" means the "party of God," a term from the Koran; it was organized in 1975 during the Lebanese civil war and became more violent with the Syrian and Israeli interventions. The victory of Ayatollah Khomeini and his supporters in Shiite Iran gave much-needed outside backing. See Walter Laqueur, *The New Terrorism: Fanaticism and the Arms of Mass Destruction* (New York: Oxford University Press, 1999).

24. Da'wa was a Shiite terrorist group based inside Iraq and sponsored by Iran.

Chapter 6

1. See Robert Timberg, *The Nightingale's Song* (New York: Simon and Schuster, Touchstone Edition, 1996). *The Nightingale's Song* should be made required reading at all of our service academies because it shows how patriotic academy graduates, despite the honor-code teachings and training—the finest in the nation—still mixed up moral ends with immoral and at times illegal means. North's own story is found in Oliver L. North, with William Novak, *Under Fire: An American Story* (New York: HarperCollins, 1991), and a critical biography is Ben Bradlee Jr., *Guts and Glory: The Rise and Fall of Oliver North* (New York: Donald I. Fine, 1988).

2. Bradlee, *Guts and Glory,* pp. 108–109; Timberg, *The Nightingale's Song,* pp. 207–11. In any event, he made a remarkable comeback, psychologically and spiritually, including a reuniting with his estranged wife, Betsy. (This meltdown and healing is very openly discussed in Oliver North, *Under Fire,* pp. 130–49.)

3. Robert C. McFarlane with Zofia Smardz, *Special Trust* (New York: Caddell and Davies, 1994), pp. 123–25.

4. Ibid., p. 153.

5. Ibid., pp. 151–52.

6. Alexander Haig, *Caveat* (New York: Macmillian, 1984), p. 70.

7. Timberg, *The Nightingale's Song,* p. 362.

8. Ibid., p. 416.

9. McFarlane, *Special Trust,* p. 19. McFarlane wrote in his book that he encouraged Ledeen to conduct informal discussions, but, because Ledeen asserted that he was an official representative, Shultz heard about it and became angry at being undercut.

10. Ibid., pp. 25–26.

11. Ibid., p. 27.

12. Theodore Draper, *A Very Thin Line: The Iran-Contra Affairs* (New York: Hill and Wang, 1991), p. 128.

13. Ibid., p. 297.

14. George P. Shultz, *Turmoil and Triumph: My Years as Secretary of State* (New York: Scribner's, 1993), p. 796.

15. McFarlane, *Special Trust,* p. 34.

16. McFarlane asserts that this call is verified by the notes of Weinberger and of Shultz's assistant that were revealed in the course of the Walsh investigations.

17. *Washington Post* (Dec. 4, 1985).

18. Ibid.

19. The *New York Times* (Dec. 4, 1985) mirrors much of what the *Washington Post* reports.

20. Lou Cannon, *President Reagan: The Role of a Lifetime* (New York: Simon and Schuster, 1991), p. 623.

21. Geoffrey Smith, *Reagan and Thatcher* (New York: W. W. Norton, 1991), p. 207.

22. See chap. 6, "Terrorism Strikes NATO," in David M. Abshire, *Preventing World War III* (New York: Harper and Row, 1988), pp. 79–88.

23. Timberg, *The Nightingale's Song*, p. 104.

24. Ibid., p. 345.

25. A difficult part of the Iran-contra investigation centered on these secret Swiss bank accounts and access to the record. The Tower Board had to conclude its report without gaining access, and, after expenses, almost $20 million remained unaccounted for; the board noted that this was an NSC account. This was to remain the most difficult problem my office faced after the Tower Board report. Memorandum to A. B. Culvahuese from Charlie Brower, "Swiss Bank Records for Congressional Investigation," Mar. 16, 1987. Author's files.

26. Bob Woodward, *Veil: The Secret Wars of the CIA, 1981–1987* (New York: Pocket Books, 1987), p. 588.

27. Persico, *Casey*, pp. 558–61.

28. McFarlane, *Special Trust*, p. 54.

29. Donald T. Regan, *For the Record* (New York: Harcourt Brace Jovanovich, 1998), p. 38. See Reagan's account in *An American Life: Ronald Reagan* (New York: Simon and Schuster, 1990), p. 530. In the subsequent North trial in 1989, North's attorney, Brendan Sullivan, questioned Attorney General Meese about how seriously he had taken the possibility of impeachment, and Meese confirmed that, unless the administration got the story out first, this was his fear. Oliver North, *Under Fire*, p. 7.

30. Shultz, *Turmoil and Triumph*, p. 837.

31. Ibid., p. 857. Draper, in *A Very Thin Line*, is less critical of Casey's role. He sees that role "during these days as something of a puzzle. He was far from being the commanding figure who masterminded the abortive cover-up or manipulated North and others to do their bidding" (p. 494). Needless to say, I am inclined toward Shultz's conclusions.

32. Casey's unsteadiness before his collapse is recounted in Robert M. Gates, *From the Shadows: The Ultimate Insider's Story of Five Presidents and How They Won the Cold War* (New York: Simon and Schuster, Touchstone Edition, 1997), pp. 409–11. Also see Persico, *Casey*, pp. 544–49.

Chapter 7

1. The president had a colonoscopy to determine whether there was any recurrence of his colon cancer from eighteen months earlier, and the

next day he underwent a surgical procedure to widen his urinary tract to offset an enlarged prostate gland.

2. Peter J. Wallison, *Ronald Reagan: The Power of Conviction and the Restoration of the Presidency* (Boulder: Westview Press, 2003), p. 132.

3. Dwight D. Eisenhower, *Mandate for Change, 1953–1956* (New York: Doubleday, 1963), p. 114.

4. Eisenhower was a far better manager than was Reagan.

5. The departure of Adams can be compared to that of Regan: intense political pressure for a change in the chief of staff and a stubborn president who would not give in. Stephen E. Ambrose, *Eisenhower*, vol. 2 (Simon and Schuster: New York, 1984), pp. 480–82.

6. James P. Pfiffner, ed., *The Managerial Presidency*, 2d ed. (College Station: Texas A&M University Press, 1999), pp. 78–79, 100.

7. Marlin Fitzwater, *Call the Briefing! Bush and Reagan, Sam and Helen: A Decade with Presidents and the Press* (New York: Times Books, 1995), pp. 76–77.

8. On June 2, 1987, a member of my staff, Razvigor Bazala, presented me with a thirty-two-page document he had prepared, titled "Practical Politics and Crisis Avoidance: A History of the Special Counselor to the President." In it, he traces the history of the two-track approach from his viewpoint and the staff's perception of tension with the chief of staff.

9. Wallison, *Ronald Reagan*, pp. 187–205.

10. I made notes on all these calls in a loose-leaf notebook I maintained as an aide-mémoire for follow-up.

11. Alan Charles Raul, associate counsel to the president, memorandum for file, Feb. 2, 1987. Meeting with Brendan Sullivan. Author's files.

12. Memorandum from Roman Popadiuk to Abshire, Feb. 27, 1987.

13. There was a major partisan dispute over the disclosure of the preliminary staff findings of the outgoing Senate Select Committee on Intelligence on the Iran-contra issue. The committee voted 7 to 6 against the release of the findings. The Republicans liked the fact that the report indicated that Reagan most probably did not know about the fund diversion; the Democrats thought the report was not sufficiently critical.

14. In his next career, Boren became president of the University of Oklahoma, where I have the pleasure of serving on an advisory board for him.

15. Any additional people, even if borrowed from other departments or

agencies, had to go through the process of having their names added to the White House access list, getting short-term identification passes, having it confirmed that clearances by other agencies were acceptable to the White House security, and, in some cases, being cleared again.

16. See Razvigor Bazala, "Practical Politics and Crisis Avoidance."

17. Popadiuk later became ambassador to the Ukraine.

Chapter 8

1. *Washington Post* (Jan. 11, 1987), p. 1.

2. *New York Times* (Jan. 29, 1987).

3. "The Diplomat in the Trenches," *National Journal* (Jan. 29, 1987).

4. Much later, on Feb. 26, 1987, I supplemented this by writing an op-ed piece in the *Wall Street Journal* about the function of the office as facilitator. See Appendix C.

5. Peter J. Wallison, *Ronald Reagan: The Power of Conviction and the Restoration of the Presidency* (Boulder: Westview Press, 2003), p. 133.

6. Fred Ryan managed the schedule and also was the author of "The Private Sector Initiative." Both he and Kuhn, two very able people, were a source of support for the president at this low point.

7. William Seale, in a two-volume book titled *The President's House: A History* (Washington, D.C.: White House Historical Association with the cooperation of the National Geographic Society, 1986), notes that the Oval Office was wholly moved in 1934 from being on axis with the front door to its current southeast location (p. 947).

8. A poll in the *Los Angeles Times*, a paper Reagan often read, showed that 14 percent of the public believed Reagan had not traded arms for hostages, and the White House polls showed similar results. Donald T. Regan, *For the Record* (New York: Harcourt Brace Jovanovich, 1998), p. 32.

9. Author's files.

Chapter 9

1. Memo in Abshire papers.

2. *Washington Post* (Jan. 29, 1987), p. A1.

3. Eve Zibart, in "Low-Down, Snowbound Blues: Digging Out, Digging In, Washington Area's Got the Low-Down, Snowbound Blues" (*Washington Post*, Jan. 30, 1987), declares that "Washington's been hostage to the weather."

Chapter 10

1. *Washington Post* (Jan. 25, 1987), p. A1.
2. Donald T. Regan, *For the Record* (New York: Harcourt Brace Jovanovich, 1998), p. 76.
3. Soon after his arrival, he had turned to me for advice on public diplomacy because, in the 1970s, CSIS had sponsored the Stanton Commission, which led to the reorganization of our government's public diplomacy and the agency Wick now headed.
4. Quoted in the *Los Angeles Times* (Mar. 22, 1987).
5. Carl Sferrazza Anthony, *First Ladies,* vol. 2 (New York: William Morrow, 1991), p. 350.
6. *Los Angeles Times* (Mar. 22, 1987).
7. Jacqueline Kennedy's efforts to "restore," as she called it, the White House resulted in a one-hour national television special narrated by Charles Collingwood. Betty Boyd Caroli, *First Ladies* (New York: Oxford University Press, 1995), pp. 224–25.
8. Ibid., pp. 275–76.
9. Onto this central cross hall opened all second-floor rooms, including three bedrooms, among them the Lincoln bedroom and the president's study. Other rooms during the Reagan years were the Yellow Oval Room, dining room, Nancy Reagan's office, the Queen's Bedroom, exercise room, living room, three sitting rooms, kitchen, and bathrooms.
10. Ironically, Marlin Fitzwater, who, in February, became the new press spokesperson, later wrote a book saying that I was brought into the White House in the first place because I was a "friend of Mrs. Reagan"; see Marlin Fitzwater, *Call the Briefing! Bush and Reagan, Sam and Helen: A Decade with Presidents and the Press* (New York: Times Books, 1995), p. 113. Some others later thought that also, but, no, my friendship began midafternoon on Feb. 3.
11. I was not the only one who felt that way. "This simple-minded strategy was more revealing of the deficiencies of Regan's political judgment than were the harsh criticisms of those who were trying to force him out of the White House," biographer Lou Cannon notes in *President Reagan: The Role of a Lifetime* (New York: Simon and Schuster, 1991). "It should have been evident to Regan that Reagan was too confused and emotionally strained to launch a speaking tour or hold

another news conference, as was evident to Paul Laxalt and David Abshire." Then Cannon adds what I think is perhaps true: "But Regan's judgment was clouded by his effort to save his own job and reputation" (p. 726).

12. I realize this was and is a difficult judgment. I myself found Ronald Reagan to be stubborn on his interpretation of arms for hostages. What they could have done perhaps was to truly attempt to ally with George Bush and persuade Chief of Staff Regan to join with them in dealing with the president. After all, Reagan, as noted, implies in his memoirs that, if Jim Baker had been named national security adviser instead of Bud McFarlane, he might have been saved from the Iran-contra disaster.

13. More than ten years later, Nancy Reagan showed me her diary. For Feb. 3, she recorded the following: "Charlie Wick phoned. David Abshire wants to see me. He told me what he was doing. He had good ideas. A very impressive man. I called Kathy [Osborne] to see that his appointment with the president is longer and alone" [Nancy Reagan, interview by David Abshire, Jan. 15, 1999].

In addition to Kathy Osborne, who had been Reagan's secretary since Sacramento, he was well served during these dark times by two highly talented and sensitive assistants, Jim Kuhn, his personal assistant, and Fred Ryan, in charge of schedules and the president's private-sector initiative, an imaginative program of neighbor helping neighbor, including volunteers and charitable giving.

14. Personal phone log and calendar, author's notes.

15. Nancy Reagan, reading aloud to author from her diary (Jan. 15, 1999).

16. Bob Colacello, "Ronnie and Nancy," *Vanity Fair* (July, 1998), p. 82.

Chapter 11

1. Lawrence Walsh, *Firewall* (New York: W. W. Norton, 1997), p. 56.

2. Ibid.

3. Ibid., p. 58.

4. Ibid., p. 55.

5. Walsh has made much of his difficulties in having his office set up and his staff cleared and in place and in operation. I told him that the same was equally true of our operation, which started up eighteen days *after* Judge Walsh's.

Chapter 12

1. Author's notes.
2. Abshire's presentation outline in author's files. Even though by then the plea had been discussed by me orally, on Feb. 19, 1989, I put it in writing in a memo titled "Beyond the Tower Board Report," addressed to Don Regan and Frank Carlucci. The theme appears in the second paragraph: "We have a window of opportunity of about thirty days to overcome the danger of a more permanent image of a weakened Presidency. This can not be done incrementally, or by tidying things up a bit. The President and his Administration must act immediately, boldly, and imaginatively. The action must be real, not just show. . . . This thirty-day grace period will be followed by congressional hearings, which will deepen partisanship on the Hill. It truly is now or never."
3. Nancy Reagan, interviews by David Abshire, Jan., 1999.
4. This is the way Lou Cannon put it to me in a letter of May 4, 2000. The good personal relations I had with Don Regan until the eve of the Tower Board are not reflected in his book. By the time he authored his book, I believe he felt I had betrayed him because of the plan for handling the board meeting.

Chapter 13

1. The Tower Board gives the date as Aug. 30; however, the Israeli chronology gives the date of Aug. 20. Since the one hundred TOWs were shipped by Israel, the latter date would appear to be correct. These were originally U.S. TOWs previously transferred to Israel, which the United States had agreed to replace as a part of the deal. See *Report of the Congressional Committees Investigating the Iran-Contra Affair* (Washington, D.C.: GPO, Nov., 1987), p. 172, n. 94. Regardless of the oral authorization controversy, a formal intelligence finding allowing such shipments was not made and signed by the president until Jan. 17, 1986.
2. McFarlane later wrote that Scowcroft was one of his oldest friends. "In many senses, he was almost like a father to me since I first went to work for him and Henry Kissinger" (Robert C. McFarlane with Zofia Smardz, *Special Trust* [New York: Caddell and Davies, 1994], pp. 338–39). The Tower Board interviewed McFarlane at the Bethesda Naval Hospital on Jan. 19 and 21, 1987. Senator Muskie commented

that McFarlane had been the most credible witness to appear before them.

3. Clark McFadden, general counsel of the Tower Board, interview by David Abshire, Sept. 10, 2004.

4. Peter J. Wallison, *Ronald Reagan: The Power of Conviction and the Restoration of the Presidency* (Boulder: Westview Press, 2003), p. 272.

5. The confusion of the president is understandable and deserves an explanation. At an Aug. 6, 1985, meeting consisting of Reagan, Bush, Shultz, Weinberger, McFarlane, and Regan, there were in retrospect differing views on the president's position, and perhaps only McFarlane felt he had the president's backing. (The best piecing together of this meeting is contained in Theodore Draper, *A Very Thin Line: The Iran-Contra Affairs* [New York: Hill and Wang, 1991], pp. 166–69). In his book *Special Trust*, McFarlane asserts that the president did not make a decision at that meeting but that Reagan later called him into the Oval Office and after some discussion gave him the go-ahead. McFarlane states that he reminded the president of the Shultz and Weinberger opposition; Reagan said he realized that but added, "I believe it's the right thing to do," to which McFarlane replied, "Fine, I'll notify the others." McFarlane says that, in a secure conference call later that day with Bush, Shultz, Weinberger, Casey, Regan, and General Vessey, he informed them of the president's decision and that Weinberger's handwritten notes and Shultz's dictated notes that turned up in the Walsh investigation much later confirm his stories (pp. 34–36).

6. Wallison, *Ronald Reagan*, p. 245.

7. Wallison's *Ronald Reagan* gives a detailed and valuable account of the preparations for the two Tower Board meetings and those meetings themselves. His conclusions on the controversial issue were very much in line with Regan's, and he notes the inconsistency in McFarlane's various notes and testimonies.

8. Lou Cannon, *President Reagan: The Role of a Lifetime* (New York: Simon and Schuster, 1991), p. 710. John Tower was later to write the following: "[W]e were left with a major contradiction to deal with, which bore all the earmarks of a deliberate effort to conceal White House Chief of Staff Don Regan's involvement in the Iran-Contra affair. By convincing the president that he, the president, had not authorized the arms shipment, Regan was buttressing his own contention that he had been completely unaware of the transaction despite a reputation for tightly controlling the chain of command within the White

House staff" (Tower, *Consequences: A Personal and Political Memoir* [Boston: Little, Brown, 1991], pp. 283–84). A further discussion of the contradictions is contained in *Final Report of the Independent Counsel for Iran/Contra Matters*, vol. 1 (U.S. Court of Appeals for the District of Columbia Circuit, Aug. 4, 1993), pp. 521–22.

9. Wallison, *Ronald Reagan*, p. 288.

10. In his book titled *Ronald Reagan*, Wallison writes the following: "I realized that I was largely responsible for this disaster, hurting both Regan and the President. . . . I had pressed the president too hard for a recollection. . . . In trying to accommodate me . . . the president had reached too far" (p. 290). Wallison shoulders the blame for all of us involved in this process who share that responsibility.

11. Clark McFadden, interview by David Abshire, Sept. 10, 2004. McFadden said he noted I was away at NATO when the first board meeting took place.

12. In the Iran-contra investigations, these notes opened up a new treasure trove of intimate communications between those principals under investigation. Demands increased for the immediate availability of my office to the Tower Board, the congressional committees, and Judge Walsh's office. Since the PROFS were NSC computer messages, I requested immediate augmentation of the NSC staff to meet this demand, a request that was quickly met. Memorandum for Donald T. Regan and Frank T. Carlucci from Special Counselor David Abshire, "Essential Resources for the Iran Investigations" (Feb. 13, 1987).

13. Feb. 20, 1987, 12:45 P.M.

14. Author's phone log, Feb. 19, 1987.

15. Cannon, *President Reagan*, p. 708.

Chapter 14

1. Author's phone log.

2. Donald T. Regan, *For the Record* (New York: Harcourt Brace Jovanovich, 1998), p. 360.

3. I have drawn on my contemporaneous notes; subsequent conversation with Brent Scowcroft, Rhett Dawson, and Clark McFadden; and Peter J. Wallison's account in *Ronald Reagan: The Power of Conviction and the Restoration of the Presidency* (Boulder: Westview Press, 2003), pp. 276–79.

4. Since different accounts have been written about the president's reaction, I emphasize that this quote is precisely what I recorded on that day in my personal notes.

5. Wallison felt this was double-talk, asking how the board could hold the chief of staff so responsible when they were still not willing to give that position the authority to fulfill that mission (*Ronald Reagan*, p. 279). Of course, the board's position was that the national security advisor had responsibility under the president for the Iran-contra operations, but the chief of staff had to take over once the scandal broke. Theodore Draper argues in *A Very Thin Line: The Iran-Contra Affairs* (New York: Hill and Wang, 1991) that it was Meese, the attorney general, who handled the disclosure and preliminary investigations (p. 596). However, while it is true that the chief of staff had the overall responsibility, it was especially difficult for anyone not involved in the plot to know what really happened, especially since Poindexter and North were fired. Part of Regan's problem with the board was that, before Iran-contra broke, he had played up his all-powerful role as the efficient chief of staff. Thus, he was assumed to be able to meet an almost impossible task during the chaotic days of November, 1986.

6. *Report of the President's Special Review Board: Tower Board Commission Report* (*New York Times* edition), pp. 81–82.

7. Ibid., pp. 82–83.

8. Ibid., p. xviii.

9. The statement about concern for preserving the secrecy of the initiative providing an excuse for abandoning sound process is similar to Admiral Burke's criticism of the Bay of Pigs procedures.

10. Statements of John Tower, Brent Scowcroft, and Edmund Muskie at press conference on Feb. 26, 1987. Author's files.

11. Information on the inner workings of the Tower Board was provided in conversations with Clark McFadden on Sept. 10, 2004; Rhett Dawson on Aug. 20, 2004; and Brent Scowcroft on Oct. 7, 2004.

12. Draper, *A Very Thin Line*, p. 596.

13. Fredrik Logevall, "The Vietnam War," in *Triumphs and Tragedies of the Modern Presidency: Seventy-six Cases Studies in Presidential Leadership*, ed. David M. Abshire (Westport, Conn.: Praeger, 2000), pp. 187–88.

14. On Oct. 28, 1985, Executive Order 12537 reaffirmed the role of the PFIAB. It states the following related to intelligence:

Sec. 2. The Board shall assess the quality, quantity, and adequacy of intelligence collection, of analysis and estimates, of counterintelligence, and other intelligence activities. The Board shall have the authority to continually review the performance of all agencies of the Federal government that are engaged in the collection, evaluation, or production of intelligence or the execution of intelligence policy. The Board shall further be authorized to assess the adequacy of management, personnel, and organization in the intelligence process.

Sec. 3. The Board shall report directly to the President and advise him concerning the objectives, conduct, management, and coordination of the various activities of the agencies of the intelligence community. The Board shall report periodically, but at least semiannually, concerning findings and appraisals and shall make appropriate recommendations for action to improve and enhance the performance of the intelligence efforts of the United States.

It is interesting that the 9/11 Commission Report of 2004 also failed to focus on the role of the PFIAB in the period before the tragic attacks.

Chapter 15

1. Lou Cannon, *President Reagan: The Role of a Lifetime* (New York: Simon and Schuster, 1991), p. 730.

2. Ibid., p. 731.

3. Marlin Fitzwater, *Call the Briefing! Bush and Reagan, Sam and Helen: A Decade with Presidents and the Press* (New York: Times Books, 1995), pp. 168–71.

4. Donald T. Regan, *For the Record* (New York: Harcourt Brace Jovanovich, 1998), p. 369.

5. David Nagy, "Donald Regan Early Loser in Iran-Contra Scandal," *Reuters Library Report* (July 30, 1987).

6. George Hackett with Thomas M. DeFrank, "The First Lady: A Hang-up about Don Regan," *Newsweek* (Mar. 2, 1987), p. 22; Nagy, "Donald Regan Early Loser."

7. Peter J. Wallison, *Ronald Reagan: The Power of Conviction and the Restoration of the Presidency* (Boulder: Westview Press, 2003), p. 171.

8. Regan, *For the Record*, p. 3.

9. Hackett with DeFrank, "The First Lady."

10. When Don Regan's memoir, *For the Record*, was published, I had be-

lieved that there were many unfair judgments of Nancy Reagan and also a misrepresentation of our disagreements. I had recently published an article in the *Washington Post* on May 15, 1988, called "Don Regan's Real 'Record': Looking Out for Number 1."

Chapter 16

1. Lou Cannon, *President Reagan: The Role of a Lifetime* (New York: Simon and Schuster, 1991), p. 650; also from author's several conversations with Howard Baker.
2. Jane Meyer and Doyle McManus, *Landslide* (Boston: Houghton Mifflin, 1988), pp. ix–x.
3. Ironically, they were not even giving Don Regan the credit he was due. The White House under Don Regan may have been politically misguided and overly managed in a way that drowned out differing points of view, but it was never chaotic except just after Iran-contra broke. In general, it was exactly the opposite: overly controlled by one man.
4. J. L. Annis Jr., *Howard Baker: A Conciliator in an Age of Crisis* (Lanham, Md.: Madison Books, 1995), p. 37.
5. That year in Tennessee, Bill Brock of Chattanooga defeated the incumbent, populist Al Gore Sr., and thus Howard Baker became Tennessee's senior senator.
6. Several years later, Judge Walsh asked for our notes taken during the investigation. I gave the review team mine. When the notes were returned in 1988, I asked his reaction of one FBI agent who had been on this case for several years. "We ran into this story, tracked it down; it was not credible." I wished on Feb. 3, in Howard Baker's office, we could have been so sure or had known such a story would not be published.
7. Cannon, *President Reagan*, p. 734.
8. Ibid., p. 656. Also, the author's conversation with Landon Parvin, Aug. 7, 1999. Parvin said that the president was not especially concerned. He had taken Parvin's concern about the insert to Baker and Bush. As the cabinet meeting was breaking up, Baker and Parvin talked to the president, who told them to talk to Weinberger. Shultz was traveling and not at the cabinet meeting.
9. In his radio address of Mar. 14, Reagan appropriately noted that Weinberger and Shultz had strongly advised him against this initiative.
10. *New York Times* (Mar. 5, 1987).

Chapter 17

1. Especially helpful to us was that, on Mar. 14, John Poindexter, during congressional testimony, took the Fifth Amendment four times. The rumors about the drinking captain were wrong. I had been sure they would be, but we were all relieved, nevertheless.
2. Fitzwater later wrote about the heart of our worries: "No one could keep all those dates straight about arms shipments and phone calls from Ollie North to some Middle Eastern con man. But the growing scandal—and probably the Tower Board report—had weakened the president's confidence about himself. He wasn't sure what he knew. This was tragic, because Reagan's great strength as president was that he knew himself and what he believed" (Marlin Fitzwater, *Call the Briefing! Bush and Reagan, Sam and Helen: A Decade with Presidents and the Press* [New York: Times Books, 1995], p. 117).
3. Ibid., p. 121.
4. Ibid., pp. 122–24.
5. David Broder, *Washington Post* (Apr. 1, 1987).
6. However, Senator Nunn, somewhat like Lord Carrington, was concerned that elimination of all intermediate-range missiles might leave us hostage to conventional Soviet military superiority, and thus we needed conventional defense improvements, which had been my pet concern also.

Chapter 18

1. *Congressional Record* (Apr. 6, 1987), S46.11.
2. He redeemed himself in the later publication of his second volume on Theodore Roosevelt.
3. Nancy Reagan, *My Turn* (New York: Random House, 1989). Actually, the choice of a new chief of staff had been mentioned to Republican senate and house leaders, and Don Regan himself started interviews with journalists of the *New York Times* and *Time.* Even though CNN played the Nancy Reagan quote as breaking the story, it is hard to believe that her statement initiated the Baker rumor. See Donald T. Regan's own account in *For the Record* (New York: Harcourt Brace Jovanovich, 1998), pp. 371–73.
4. William Safire, "The First Lady Stages a Coup: She Can't Be Fired or Impeached," *New York Times* (Mar. 2, 1987).

5. *New York Times* (Mar. 5, 1987).

6. George Will, "Tableware, Not the Country," *Washington Post* (Mar. 6, 1987).

7. Instead of opening up the White House to outside advisors, Edith Wilson "isolated Woodrow Wilson from everyone except his doctors, so that even his secretary did not see him for weeks." Betty Boyd Caroli, *First Ladies* (New York: Oxford University Press, 1995), p. 149. This isolation was a severe obstacle to working out any compromise on gaining senate consent to the Treaty of Versailles. According to John Milton Cooper, this failure "stands to this day as perhaps the greatest presidential failure in the politics of foreign policy." David M. Abshire, ed., *Triumphs and Tragedies of the Modern Presidency: Seventy-six Cases Studies in Presidential Leadership* (Westport, Conn.: Praeger, 2001), p. 54.

8. Lou Cannon, *President Reagan: The Role of a Lifetime* (New York: Simon and Schuster, 1991), p. 722.

9. Richard Neustadt, *Presidential Power and the Modern Presidents* (New York: Free Press, 1991), p. 316.

10. Ibid., p. 313.

11. Anthony, *First Ladies*, vol. 2, p. 361.

12. Ibid., p. 352.

Chapter 19

1. On Mar. 4, I also sent him another memorandum titled "White House Cooperation in Due Process" and my *Wall Street Journal* op-ed piece, which can be found in Appendix B. I added, "As compared to those hectic late November-December days at the White House, I think this two-track approach, in which we are not 'investigators' but 'facilitators,' has really built credibility." On Mar. 2, I also sent a memorandum to the entire cabinet with the op-ed piece, as well as the highlights of the Tower Board report. Author's files.

2. This is not to say that, in the two-track arrangement, there was not consideration of the legal defense of the president. If Brower and Abshire had the priority to get it all out, as I had said on *Face the Nation*, Peter Wallison, along with his able associate, legal counsel Jay Stevens, was in charge of any necessary legal defense. Wallison and these deputies were involved in the document review along with the departmental and agency general counsels in the working group chaired by

Judge Brower. Any sensitive documents reflecting adversely on the president were there for the legal counsel to the president to analyze. But the prime thrust of the special-counselor operation was to move the relevant documents to the investigators without any fear or favor.

3. Bob Woodward, *Shadow: Five Presidents and the Legacy of Watergate* (New York: Simon and Schuster, 1999), p. 151.

4. There was such a juicy document dated June 25, 1984, from a foreign-policy staff meeting where Reagan liked the idea of going to other countries, so-called third parties, to solicit contributions to the contras. In typical Reagan hyperbole, the president cautioned against leaks and added, "If such a story gets out, we will be hanging by our thumbs in front of the White House until we find out who did it." I remember Judge Brower showing me this quote in February as it went forward to investigators, embarrassing as it was. But such an item was understandably a shocker to the new team when they saw it for the first time.

5. The president had perhaps confused the diversion issue and the third-party issue, as Vice President Bush and his counsel, Boyden Gray, had to make clear to the new team. The third-party aid may have been poor practice, perhaps initially deceptive of the Congress, but not clearly illegal like the diversion, though ambiguous at best. In a corrective, Reagan almost immediately made known at a press meeting that he knew of those resupply operations and, indeed, they had been his idea (C. Boyden Gray, unpublished manuscript, pp. 51–53).

6. William S. Cohen and George W. Mitchell, *Men of Zeal* (New York: Viking, 1998), p. 67.

7. Ibid., p. 74.

8. Robert C. McFarlane, in his memoir, *Special Trust* (with Zofia Smardz; New York: Caddell and Davies, 1994), notes that "when I made my categorical denials in my letters regarding NSC staff support for the Contras, I was only repeating what Ollie North told me to be true. I had not lied, I had believed I was telling the truth" (p. 356).

9. Arthur Liman, *Lawyer: A Hype of Counsel and Controversy* (New York: Public Affairs, 1998), pp. 336–37.

10. Brendan Sullivan, attorney for Oliver North, conversations with author, Sept., 2001.

11. Ed Kornbleck and Malcolm Byrne, *The Iran-Contra Scandal: The Declassified History* (New York: New York Press, 1993), p. 330; Mitchell and Cohen, *Men of Zeal*, pp. 151–82. I have no doubt that North be-

lieved the president knew.

12. McFarlane, *Special Trust*, pp. 349–50.

13. George P. Shultz, *Turmoil and Triumph: My Years as Secretary of State* (New York: Scribner's, 1993), pp. 910–24. See also Cohen and Mitchell, *Men of Zeal*, p. 112.

14. *Report of the Congressional Committees Investigating the Iran-Contra Affair, with Supplemental, Minority, and Additional Views* (Washington, D.C.: GPO, 1987), pp. 20–22.

15. Ibid., pp. 447–53.

16. Oliver North, with William Novak, *Under Fire: An American Story* (New York: HarperCollins, 1991), p. 413.

17. McFarlane, *Special Trust*, pp. 360–61.

18. Ibid., p. 353.

19. *United States of America v. Caspar Weinberger*, indictment, Oct. 30, 1992, document 99.

20. How do we explain Weinberger's bizarre falsehood about the notes? I learned, as did many others closely involved with Weinberger, that he had a unique and unusual way of operating that he may have developed as an attorney: He would take a position and simply repeat himself over and over again. He was in this respect like the Communist negotiators who would wear down their opponents and drive them to concessions. In the process, I think Cap Weinberger not only developed a tactic but at times built a mental stone wall that led him to avoid rethinking what he was saying and the justifications for it. I am told that in the early days of the Reagan administration, when Secretary of State Haig and Secretary Weinberger would meet, Cap was into this tactic of simple and unflagging repetition. I saw this at NATO in his bilateral meetings, for example, with Weinberger's handling of Defence Minister Michael Haseltine of Great Britain. He was never discourteous, but he was airtight in not rethinking the problem and constantly repeated his original assertion. In his repetition that he had no notes, I believe Cap came to believe the conclusion that he actually had no notes, merely scribbles. I have been told that the notes were "calendarized," so to speak. Maybe that was the way in his own mind he thought he was telling the truth.

However, the Weinberger notes are not the only bizarre occurrence. George Bush began to maintain a diary not much before my arrival at the White House, when the Reagan diary was soon to become a point of contention on Capitol Hill. The oddest thing about withholding the Bush diary is that one can argue that it would have helped him to have it revealed.

21. Charles Krauthammer, "Why No October Surprise?" (*Washington Post*, Oct. 18, 1996), p. A27.

22. Mary McGrory, "Masquerading on Morality" (*Washington Post*, Nov. 3, 1992), p. A2.

23. Krauthammer, "Why No October Surprise?"

24. C. Boyden Gray, unpublished manuscript.

25. George Stephanopoulos, *All Too Human: A Political Education* (Boston: Little, Brown, 1999), pp. 101–102; John Robert Greene, in *The Presidency of George Bush* (Lawrence, Kans.: University Press of Kansas, 2000), does not mention the Walsh indictment as a decisive factor in the campaign.

26. Press release, White House, Dec. 24, 1992.

Chapter 20

1. Stephen E. Ambrose, *Nixon: Ruin and Recovery, 1973–1990* (New York: Simon and Schuster, Touchstone Edition, 1992), p. 135.

2. Joan Hoff, *Nixon Reconsidered* (New York: Basic Books, 1994), p. 2.

3. H. R. McMaster, *Dereliction of Duty* (New York: HarperCollins, 1997), pp. 323–34; Fredrick Logevall, "The Vietnam War," in *Triumphs and Tragedies of the Modern Presidency: Seventy-six Cases Studies in Presidential Leadership*, ed. David M. Abshire (Westport, Conn.: Praeger, 2001), p. 189. At one point in 1967, the Joint Chiefs considered resigning in protest over Secretary of Defense McNamara's misrepresentation of their vows to committees on Capitol Hill. Deborah Shapley, *Promise and Power: The Life and Times of Robert McNamara* (Boston: Little, Brown, 1993), pp. 432–33.

4. James Pfiffner, *The Character Factor: How We Judge America's Presidents* (College Station: Texas A&M University Press, 2004), p. 21.

5. Robert Dallek, quoted in Michael Powell, "The Lost Art of Lying," *Washington Post* (Dec. 8, 1998), p. C1. Dallek's latest book on Johnson is *Flawed Giant: Lyndon Johnson and His Times* (New York: Oxford University Press, 1998). A book by Fredrik Logevall, *Choosing War: The Lost Chance for Peace and the Escalation of War in Vietnam* (Berkeley: University of California Press, 1999), recounts the deceptions involving the Gulf of Tonkin Resolution; see pp. 192–221.

6. Michael R. Beschloss, quoted in Michael Powell, "U.S. History of Great Fibs," *Washington Post* (Dec. 8, 1995).

7. Michael R. Beschloss, *Mayday: Eisenhower, Khrushchev, and the U-2 Affair* (New York: Harper and Row, 1986), p. 252.

8. Powell, "U.S. History of Great Fibs."

9. *New York Times* (Feb. 26, 1999).

10. James Pfiffner, in *Triumphs and Tragedies,* ed Abshire, p. 286. Also see Leonard Garment, *Crazy Rhythms* (New York: Times Books, 1997), p. 297.

11. Carter indeed faced a very different challenge: fifty-two American-government employees seized at the American-embassy compound in Teheran on Nov. 4, 1979, and a fourteen-month crisis, with enormous media coverage in the United States. At that time, I happened to be at the Beverly Hilton Hotel and could see out of my window angry crowds marching at the intersection of Santa Monica and Wilshire Boulevards. This hostage taking became a grassroots political issue and helped elect Reagan.

12. Ben Bradlee Jr., *Guts and Glory: The Rise and Fall of Oliver North* (New York: Donald I. Fine, 1988), p. 551. Ironically, this all occurred under a president whose innate strength and remarkable leadership capabilities were based on being open and direct. And yet, it has been argued that "covert operation" is the wrong term to use with Iran-contra, for it was actually a prolonged covert war and a covert foreign policy.

13. Lanny J. Davis, special counsel to President Clinton from 1996 to 1998, wrote later (July 12, 2001) in a *New York Times* op-ed piece that "President Clinton would have been better off making full public disclosure early in the Lewinsky crisis rather than waiting to acknowledge the relationship eight months later. Many would argue that had he done so he would have avoided impeachment. At least two key House impeachment managers have told me that." See also Susan Schmidt and Michael Weisskopf, *Truth at Any Cost: Ken Starr and the Unmaking of Bill Clinton* (New York: HarperCollins, 2000), pp. 87–89.

14. Writing on Aug. 2, 1998, after saying that Clinton had no one to blame but himself, veteran *Washington Post* columnist David Broder supposed what the president would have said if he had come clean to the court and to the public: "I foolishly let myself become involved with this young woman in a way that is deeply painful to my family and

embarrassing to all of you who have placed your confidence in me. I regret my actions and ask your forgiveness. I take full responsibility for what happened and I hope you will not cast stones at Monica Lewinsky, who is not the one at fault. I also ask out of consideration for the feelings of all the others involved that you accept that these will be my final words on the subject." Broder continued: "I would bet anything that most of the public would have said, 'Make it up to Hillary and Chelsea and get back to work at your job.' And even Kenneth Starr, I think, might have had the good sense to leave the mess alone."

15. In retrospect, it is also quite clear that Republicans in the House made a major mistake in relying too much on the controversial Judge Starr and not calling their own witnesses, as was done in the Watergate case. Ironically, witnesses were avoided because of both the salacious nature of the case as well as the House's self-imposed deadline and the House role vis-à-vis the Senate.

16. Hoff, *Nixon Reconsidered*, p. 339.

17. Ronald Reagan, *An American Life: Ronald Reagan* (New York: Simon and Schuster, 1990), p. 542.

18. *Washington Post* (Dec. 12, 1998).

19. Ibid.

20. *Reuters Library Report* (Mar. 31, 1999).

21. George Stephanopoulos, *All Too Human: A Political Education* (Boston: Little Brown, 1999), p. 443.

Chapter 21

1. Peggy Noonan, *When Character Was King: A Story of Ronald Reagan* (New York: Viking, 2001), p. 317.

2. Haynes B. Johnson, *Sleepwalking through History: America in the Reagan Years* (New York: W. W. Norton, 1991).

3. Frances Fitzgerald, *Way Out There in the Blue: Reagan, Star Wars, and the End of the Cold War* (New York: Simon and Schuster, 2000).

4. There has been a widespread reappraisal of Ronald Reagan by many academic historians, some of whom were his deep critics. A survey of this literature is found in Paul Kengor, "Reagan among the Professors," *Policy Review* 98 (Dec., 1999–Jan., 2000): 15–28. Political scientists have been much slower in any such favorable reevaluation.

5. Richard Neustadt, *Presidential Power and the Modern Presidents* (New York: Free Press, 1991), p. 269.

6. Ibid., p. 270.

7. Stephen Skowronek, The *Politics Presidents Make: Leadership from John Adams to George Bush* (Cambridge: Belknap Press of Harvard University Press, 1993), p. 415.

8. Fred I. Greenstein, *The Presidential Difference: Leadership Style from FDR to Clinton* (New York: Martin Kessler Books, 2000), p. 155.

9. John Lewis Gaddis, in *The United States and the End of the Cold War: Implications, Reconsiderations, Provocations* (New York: Oxford University Press, 1992), not only asserts that Reagan succeeded in bringing about the most significant improvements in Sino-Soviet relations since the end of World War II but also cites SDI as "Reagan's most distinctive personal policy innovation" and a "contributing factor in the rise of Gorbachev" (p. 62).

10. This is the theme of Peter J. Wallison, *Ronald Reagan: The Power of Conviction and the Restoration of the Presidency* (Boulder: Westview Press, 2003).

11. Kenneth S. Davis, *FDR, The War President, 1940–1943: A History* (New York: Random House, 2000), p. 78.

12. Ibid., p. 9. This Reagan-Roosevelt comparison of managerial styles is not to suggest that on political-military matters Reagan had anything like the fount of experience and knowledge that FDR had. Roosevelt read and marked Alfred Thayer Mahan's *The Influence of Sea Power upon History, 1660–1783* when he was a teenager, served as assistant secretary of the navy during World War I, and had as a role model his distant cousin Theodore, a prolific author.

   One of the most interesting personal similarities between the two was the tendency to fantasize about their earlier years. FDR's once-broken nose, he said later in life, came from football at Groton, where, by the way, he did not make the team. See Peter Collier with David Horowitz, *The Roosevelts: An American Saga* (New York: Simon and Schuster, 1994), pp. 106–107.

13. Max Kampelman, conversation with David Abshire, Dec. 13, 1999. Ambassador Kampelman was told of this incident later by Victor Karpov. Reagan also developed a unique relationship with the Japanese prime minister. See Lou Cannon, "Reagan and Nakasone Strategic Partners," in David M. Abshire, ed., *Triumphs and Tragedies of the Modern Presidency: Seventy-six Cases Studies in Presidential Leadership* (Westport, Conn.: Praeger, 2000), pp. 206–207.

14. Ibid., pp. 19–47.

15. Thomas P. O'Neill Jr., *Man of the House* (New York: Random House, 1987), p. 345.

16. Wallison, *Ronald Reagan*, pp. 92–95. Wallison was counsel to Vice President Rockefeller.

17. Kiron K. Skinner, Annelise Anderson, and Martin Anderson, eds., *Reagan, in His Own Hand: The Writings of Ronald Reagan That Reveal His Revolutionary Vision for America* (New York: Free Press, 2001), p. xxiii.

18. Wallison, *Ronald Reagan*, pp. 44–45.

19. We, of course, recognize the interaction between historical contingency and an on-the-scene leader. Following the Goldwater political disaster, a conservative and neoconservative movement bubbled up in conservative think tanks and political campaigns, and this culminated just as Reagan began running for office. And clearly, during the Cold War, Reagan needed an opponent, Gorbachev, deeply worried by his distressed Soviet economy before he could be brought to waltz with Reagan. As a transformational leader, Reagan saw and seized these opportunities.

20. Robert Shogan, *The Double-Edged Sword* (Boulder: Westview, 1999), p. 154.

21. *Washington Post* (Nov. 28, 1999), p. B7.

22. Russell Kirk, *The Conservative Mind* (Chicago: Henry Regnery, 1953), p. 7. It can be argued that Rousseau's *Social Contract* moved to make philosophy into an active ideology.

23. Leo Strauss and Joseph Cropsey, eds., *History of Philosophy*, 3d ed. (Chicago: University of Chicago Press, 1987), pp. 688–96.

24. James David Barber, *The Presidential Character* (Englewood Cliffs, N.J.: Prentice Hall, 1992).

25. In an important article, Beth A. Fischer, a Canadian scholar, challenges the view that East-West relations changed primarily because of Mikhail Gorbachev and that Reagan merely responded. Fischer notes that in the spring of 1982, the administration decoupled arms talks from Soviet international behavior (linkage) and announced a new round of START (Strategic Arms Reduction Treaty) talks as we, however, continued our military buildup and in March, 1983, initiated SDI. Then came Reagan's Jan. 16, 1984, address with the theme of "Reducing the Risk of War—and especially nuclear war—is priority number one." The president worried about "dangerous misunderstandings and miscalculations" and sought "a better working relation-

ship." It was in this same speech that he worried many conservative friends by saying that his dream was "to see the day when nuclear weapons will be banished from the face of the Earth." This speech came while Yuri Andropov was still in power. In September of 1984, during the tenure of Konstantin Chernenko as general secretary, Reagan invited Soviet foreign minister Andrei Gromyko to the White House. Fischer concludes, "Although the Geneva summit is often seen as the beginning of the end of the Cold War, it was actually the culmination of the new policy that Reagan had introduced in early 1984. The Geneva Summit embodied the administration's commitment to dialogue, cooperation and understanding" before Gorbachev had introduced glasnost and perestroika. Within hours of learning of Chernenko's death, Reagan invited Gorbachev to a summit meeting. "Mikhail Gorbachev took the ball and ran with it, but it was Ronald Reagan who put the ball in play." See Beth A. Fischer, "The Reagan Administration and the Ending of the Cold War," *Political Science Quarterly* 112(3) (Fall, 1997): 477–97.

26. David M. Abshire, "Colloquium Honoring the Two Hundredth Year of George Washington's Death," *Vital Speeches of the Day* 66 (12) (Apr., 2000): 375–77.

27. Reagan, in his autobiography, *An American Life: Ronald Reagan* (New York: Simon and Schuster, 1990), writes the following: "These first few months after the Iran-Contra affair hit the front pages were frustrating to me. For the first time in my life, people didn't believe me. . . . While I was unhappy, I never felt depressed about the situation" (Reagan, p. 532). This depends upon the definition of depression, but I believe the fact that the public did not believe him was a very depressing thought, and Nancy Reagan communicated his depression to me.

28. Edmund Morris, *Dutch* (New York: Random House, 1999), p. 615.

29. Wallison, *Ronald Reagan*, p. 168.

30. Noonan, *When Character Was King*, p. 278.

31. Jack F. Matlock Jr., *Reagan and Gorbachev: How the Cold War Ended* (New York: Random House, 2004), p. 320.

32. The most comprehensive book on Reagan's spirituality is Paul Kengor's *God and Ronald Reagan* (New York: HarperCollins, 2004).

33. O'Neill, *Man of the House*, p. 345.

34. Early in his first administration, David Stockman, Reagan's director of the OMB, gave an interview to William Greider of the *Atlantic Monthly* that portrays Reagan as a bumbler who could not bring him-

self to cut his own budget to eliminate a growing deficit. Stockman implied that Reaganomics was a pleasant fraud to woo the rich. The president supposedly "took him out to the woodshed" but promptly forgave the wayward young man. On leaving office, Stockman repaid this leniency and forgiveness by writing *The Triumph of Politics*, an even broader attack on the president's personal foibles and his temperamental inability to make a budget cut that the simplest math showed was necessary.

Index